The Power of Labelling

How People Are Categorized and Why it Matters

Edited by
Joy Moncrieffe
and
Rosalind Eyben

London • Sterling, VA

First published by Earthscan in the UK and USA in 2007

ISBN: 978-1-84407-395-5 (hardback)
ISBN: 978-1-84407-394-8 (paperback)
Typeset by JS Typesetting Ltd, Porthcawl, Mid Glamorgan
Printed and bound in the UK by Cromwell Press, Trowbridge
Cover design by Susanne Harris

For a full list of publications please contact:

Earthscan
8–12 Camden High Street
London, NW1 0JH, UK
Tel: +44 (0)20 7387 8558
Fax: +44 (0)20 7387 8998
Email: earthinfo@earthscan.co.uk
Web: **www.earthscan.co.uk**

22883 Quicksilver Drive, Sterling, VA 20166-2012, USA

Earthscan publishes in association with the International Institute for Environment and
Development.

A catalogue record for this book is available from the British Library.

Library of Congress Cataloging-in-Publication Data

The power of labelling : how people are categorized and why it matters / edited by Joy Moncrieffe
and Rosalind Eyben.
        p. cm.
    Includes index.
    ISBN-13: 978-1-84407-395-5 (hardback)
    ISBN-10: 1-84407-395-5 (hardback)
    ISBN-13: 978-1-84407-394-8 (pbk.)
    ISBN-10: 1-84407-394-7 (pbk.)
  1. Stereotypes (Social psychology) 2. Social perception. 3. Social
interaction. I. Moncrieffe, Joy. II. Eyben, Rosalind.
    HM1096.P68 2007
    303.3'85–dc22

                                            2007004108

This publication is printed on FSC-certified and totally chlorine-free paper.
FSC (the Forest Stewardship Council) is an international network
to promote responsible management of the world's forests.

Mixed Sources
Product group from well-managed
forests and other controlled sources
www.fsc.org Cert no. TT-COC-2082
© 1996 Forest Stewardship Council

Contents

About the Contributors

Cassandra Balchin has been linked with the solidarity network Women Living Under Muslim Laws (WLUML) since the early 1990s, including many years working with Shirkat Gah Women's Resource Centre in Pakistan and the WLUML international coordination office in London. Her research and writing has focused on Muslim family laws and legal reform processes, and she has edited a number of publications arising out of WLUML's action-research Women and Law in the Muslim World Programme. A founding Director of Qanoon-LAWS: legal awareness, women and society, she is currently focusing on networking, advocacy and policy work in the context of Muslim communities in the UK.

Andrea Cornwall is a Fellow at the Institute of Development Studies (IDS) at the University of Sussex, where she directs a research programme on women's empowerment. Her publications include *Beneficiary, Consumer, Citizen: Perspectives on Participation for Poverty Reduction* (Sida Studies, 2000), *Realizing Rights: Transforming Approaches to Sexual and Reproductive Wellbeing* (co-edited with Alice Welbourn, Zed Books, 2002) and *Spaces for Change? The Politics of Citizen Participation in New Democratic Arenas* (co-edited with Vera Schattan Coelho, Zed Books, 2006).

Rosalind Eyben has been a Fellow at IDS at the University of Sussex since 2002 where she is a member of the Participation, Power and Social Change team. A social anthropologist, her prior career was as a social analyst working for various international aid agencies, most recently for the UK Department for International Development (DFID). Her current research interests concern power and relations in the international aid system. She is convenor of the programme of research on global policy processes within a research programme consortium on women's empowerment. In 2006 she published an edited volume *Relationships for Aid* (Earthscan).

Arjan de Haan is currently social development adviser for DFID China, and proud father of two young children. This article was written while he was on special leave from DFID, and was Visiting Professor at the University of Guelph, Ontario, Canada. The material for the article was gathered over a long period of intermittent work in India, starting during a PhD on labour migration in Calcutta (1989–94), subsequent research while at the University of Sussex (1995–98) and, particularly, while working for DFID in India during 2001–2004. His areas of interest have included labour migration in India and elsewhere, social policy and development (resulting in the forthcoming book *Reclaiming Social Policy*), and analysis of poverty trends and policies.

Mamoru Fujita is a former economic and political adviser at the Embassy of Japan in Bolivia, and currently is a PhD candidate at the Department of Latin American Studies, University of Tokyo, Japan. His current interests include indigenous movements challenging internal colonialism in Bolivia, oral history of the urban immigrants, and the Aymara and Quechua languages of the Andean region.

Jaideep Gupte is a doctoral student at the Department of Politics, University of Oxford, and at St Antony's College. His doctoral research focuses on rumours, networks of infra-power and the policing of urban violence in Mumbai, India. He completed his MPhil in Development Studies at IDS, University of Sussex, where he has also been a research assistant on several different projects. He has previously written on refugees, internally displaced persons and related forced migration issues for the Development Research Centre on Migration, Globalisation and Poverty.

Mark Hobart is Director of the Centre for Media and Film Studies, SOAS. Originally trained as an anthropologist, he has conducted over eight years' research in Indonesia. He was co-founder of EIDOS, a European organization of anthropologists interested in the broader implications of development. His publications are wide-ranging, but often address his long-standing interest in philosophical issues in the human sciences. His research in the 1980s into discourses of development in Bali led him into the study of television as the site where development was publicly represented to the Indonesian populace, and so to issues of the media practices surrounding audience reception and their engagement with television. Since then he has broadened his research to a critique of approaches to Asian media and their articulation of alternative visions of modernity.

Tony Klouda is a medical doctor with 30 years of international development experience, mainly in Africa, Asia and the Caribbean. He is proficient in the strategic development of health programmes and services (especially relating to sexual and reproductive health) in the context of development programming at international, national and community levels, with an emphasis on balancing technical service-based approaches with a parallel but independent social development approach. His particular skills are in establishment of integrated programmes for primary health care, sexually transmitted diseases and HIV/AIDS; evaluation of community-based work; training of service personnel and others in interactive communication and challenging (including challenging of the relevance of their own programmes); and civil society strengthening for the inclusion of people outside mainstream social and service support mechanisms. Dr Klouda currently is a consultant in international health and development, based in the UK.

Lyla Mehta is a Research Fellow at IDS, University of Sussex. She is a sociologist and her work has focused on the gendered dimensions of forced displacement and resistance, water scarcity as well as the politics of water. Since 1991, she has conducted research on displacement and resistance in India's Narmada Valley and has also been involved in advocacy work on water, dams and development issues with non-governmental organizations (NGOs) and social movements in India and Europe. She has recently co-convened a programme of research on the rights of forced migrants and their interface with policy frameworks for the Development Research Centre on Migration, Globalisation and Poverty at Sussex University. She is the author of *The Politics and Poetics of Water: Naturalising Scarcity in Western India* (2006, Orient-Longman), editor of *Displaced by Development: Gender, Rights and Risks of Impoverishment* (2007, IDS) and the co-editor of *Problematizing Rights and Policies in Forced Migration: Whose Needs are Right?* (2007, Palgrave)

Joy Moncrieffe is a political sociologist and Fellow at IDS, University of Sussex. She read for her PhD at the University of Cambridge, where she explored the politics of accountability with reference to health administration and provision across a selection of politically polarized communities in Jamaica. Currently, her research interests include power relationships, citizenship and accountability; politics and inequalities; and history, race and ethnicity. She is applying some of these themes to action-oriented research with children who are growing up in violent contexts in the Caribbean, and selected race and ethnic groups in Uganda.

Linda Waldman is a social anthropologist with experience in African poverty and the related issues of gender, racial classification, ethnicity and identity. She obtained her PhD at the University of the Witwatersrand, South Africa, where her research focused on indigenous identity and nationalism amongst the Griqua of South Africa. She joined IDS as a Fellow in 2004 and is a member of the Knowledge, Technology and Society Team. Her recent research activities include an examination of how environmental issues are integrated into Poverty Reduction Strategy Papers (PRSP)s and a study of the socio-cultural ramifications of asbestos-related disease in both South Africa and the UK.

Geof Wood is Professor of International Development, and Dean of Faculty of Humanities and Social Sciences, University of Bath. After early fieldwork in Africa, he conducted extensive research in North India, Bangladesh and Pakistan over three decades, with additional work in Nepal, Afghanistan, Thailand, Venezuela and Peru. He has undertaken policy analysis and action-research with governments, NGOs and international agencies. His previous research themes have been: rural development and class formation, irrigation, social development and empowerment, microfinance, urban livelihoods and public institutional performance. He is currently focused upon insecurity, welfare regimes, well-being and strategies of de-clientelization.

Preface and Acknowledgements

The idea for this book stemmed from an encounter between the editors in 2004, when they discovered a common interest in how inequality is defined and classified within development practice. A joint seminar at the UK Department for International Development (DFID) led to the proposal that a group of interested authors be brought together to explore the power of labelling, 20 years after the seminal publication by Geof Wood and others – *Labelling in Development Policy*. A writers' workshop was held in April 2005 at IDS and this was followed later that year by a conference in London for practitioners and policy makers. Participants included staff from DFID, the World Bank, the International Fund for Agricultural Development (IFAD), the Ministry of Foreign Affairs in the Netherlands, Oxfam, the Overseas Development Institute (ODI), the School of Oriental and African Studies (SOAS) and the Open University. Subsequently, a second writers' workshop was convened to reflect on feedback from the conference. In early 2006, the editors published an IDS Policy Brief on the Power of Labelling in Development. This present book thus marks the end of a fairly lengthy process of collaborative work, in which the editors sought to remain in regular contact with those in the world of policy and practice who were interested in reflecting on the politics of classifying and labelling people.

The editors are grateful to the Central Research Department of DFID for a grant that enabled the two writers' workshops and the conference to take place, as well as for support in publishing the Policy Brief and funding Joy Moncrieffe's fieldwork in Haiti in 2005. They also gratefully acknowledge support for the preparation and publication of the book itself from the IDS Participation and Development Relations Programme, funded by the Swedish International Development Agency (Sida) and the Swiss Agency for Development and Cooporation (SDC).

We would also like to thank all the book's contributors for their interest and enthusiasm in this subject, and particularly Geof Wood for telling us about his original work and his readiness to re-engage and Arjan de Haan for encouraging us to approach DFID.

List of Acronyms and Abbreviations

ABU	Centre for Islamic Studies, Ahmadu Bello University
ANC	African National Congress
ANSR	Argentina National Synthesis Report
CARE	Christian Action Research and Education
CHT	Chittagong Hill Tracts
DCD	Department of Institutional Development
DDA	Department for Disarmament Affairs (UN)
DFID	Department for International Development (UK)
DNGO	domestic non-governmental organization
DRC	Development Research Centre
FCO	Foreign and Commonwealth Office
GEAR	Growth, Employment and Redistribution
HO	Home Office
IDP	internally displaced people
IDS	Institute of Development Studies
IFAD	International Fund for Agricultural Development
ILO	International Labour Organization
IMF	International Monetary Fund
INGO	international non-governmental organization
IRM	institutional responsibility matrix
IRR	Impoverishment Risk and Reconstruction (model)
MCB	Muslim Council of Britain
MG	Methodology Guide
MINAB	Mosques & Imams National Advisory Board
MWN	Muslim Women's Network
NGO	non-governmental organization
NMDC	National Mineral Development Corporation
OBC	other backward castes
ODI	Overseas Development Institute
OECD	Organisation for Economic Co-operation and Development
PPA	participatory poverty appraisal
PRA	participatory rural appraisal
PRSP	Poverty Reduction Strategy Paper
RDP	Reconstruction and Development

SAHRC	South African Human Rights Commission
SC	scheduled caste
SCP	Special Component Plan
SDC	Swiss Agency for Development and Cooporation
Sida	Swedish International Development Agency
SLSA	Sustainable Livelihoods in Southern Africa
SOAS	School of Oriental and African Studies
SR	site report
SSA	Sarva Shikhsa Abhiyan
ST	scheduled tribe
UNCHR	United Nations Commission on Human Rights
UNDP	United Nations Development Programme
UNHCR	United Nations High Commission for Refugees
UNICEF	United Nations Children's Fund
VDH	Volontariat pour le Développement d'Haïti
WCD	World Commission on Dams
WDR	World Development Report
WLUML	Women Living Under Muslim Laws

Introduction

Labelling, Power and Accountability: How and Why 'Our' Categories Matter

Joy Moncrieffe[1]

This book explores the processes and outcomes of labelling people. Though it focuses on international development practice, the issues the authors identify have much wider relevance.

Invariably, we all label ourselves and others to signal different aspects of our identities. We may accept some of the labels society assigned to us in childhood (black, white; Christian, Muslim; Hutu, Tutsi; poor, non-poor) and reject some or add to them. Labels impose boundaries and define categories. They are a means to construct our social world; to define norms in relation to others who bear similar or different labels. Arguably, without labels, social interaction would be costly and cumbersome. Labelling is also commonplace within international development, where it has classificatory and regulatory functions. Policy makers, practitioners and researchers use 'frames' and 'labels' to support their analyses and to describe to others what they do. They quantify and measure categories of people to define needs, justify interventions and to formulate solutions to perceived problems. Such labelling is usually considered objective, efficient, routine and indispensable and, perhaps as a consequence, it continues wantonly, without contemplation of the politics involved and the potential adverse outcomes. Yet, labelling can shift – or sustain – power relations in ways that trigger social dislocation and prejudice efforts to achieve greater equity. Indeed, labelling of the sort that pervades much of development has seriously compromised effective aid relationships and ignores the core principles of accountability that agents claim to endorse. Consequently, the principal purpose of this publication is to expose 'the political in the apparently non-political' (Wood, 1985c, p348) processes of labelling and, therewith, persuade development actors that the power of labelling should 'occupy a more central position in ... policy analyses'.

The politics of labelling is not a new subject. Twenty years ago, Wood, Schaffer and others published 'Labelling in Development Policy', first as a special issue of *Development and Change* in July 1985 and subsequently as a book. Though many of the themes outlined in that publication have become well integrated into the academic literature, the 'power of labelling' appears to have had remarkably little impact on policy actors. Indeed, there are arguments that policy-based labelling has intensified since that time, with the World Development Report (2006), 'Growth and equity', being one of the latest examples of the extent to which processes of labelling have become ingrained in policy and practice.

This book expands on the themes raised in the 1985 publication. It reviews practical experience and theoretical developments over the past two decades and, accordingly, integrates ideas that have since entered mainstream development thinking, including participatory approaches and 'whose voice counts', actor-oriented epistemology, and ideas of 'everyday practice' and the 'weapons of the weak'. All these add new caveats to the original arguments: they allow us to move beyond the preoccupation with the role of the state and to emphasize that labelling from a variety of 'non-state' sources can be just as 'authoritative' and is highly consequential for development and social policy; they highlight the conflicts, struggles, negotiation, dialogue – indeed, the actual and active relations of power – that can counter the negative effects of labelling; they allow us to explore implications for changes in the practice of policy, while recognizing that for such changes to have influence, they must be well grounded and not utopian.

The book presents three overarching arguments:

First, *labelling processes involve relationships of power*, in which more powerful actors – within state bureaucracies, among political leaders, in non-governmental and community-based organizations, in the major financial corporations, across development agencies, within communities and families – use frames and labels to influence how particular issues and categories of people are regarded and treated. Framing refers to how we understand something to be a problem, which may reflect how issues are represented (or not represented) in policy debates and discourse. Labelling refers to how people are named/categorized (by themselves and others) to reflect these frames. It reveals subjective perceptions of how people fit into different spaces in the social order and of the terms on which society should engage with them in varying contexts and at different points in time.

Though labelling and framing are distinct, there is a correlation between them. For example, one of the byproducts of quantifying and measuring, and using these to define needs and justify interventions, is that people (not merely problems) are 'framed' as 'cases'. Thus, persons without access to land are summarily categorized as the 'landless' and a range of behaviours, prospects, capabilities (and so on) are assumed to attend this position. Often, partial stories support these frames and the contending stories – those that make the complete person and that put the problem into its wider historical and social context – become hidden. In the process, the substantive and dynamic power relationships that underpin peoples' conditions are normally diluted or flatly overlooked.

Notably, as framing and labelling processes are linked to the distribution of social, political and economic power, they are critical for securing hegemonic meanings and values.[2] This does not mean they are incontrovertible but that they are often unquestioned, such that the intensely political relations that underpin them can remain unexposed for considerable periods of time. However, challenges are possible and human agency 'causes some issues and their framing to move from the uncontested realm to the contested realm' (Carraggee and Roefs, 2004, p223). Because power is multifaceted and not uni-directional,[3] contestation and resistance are not only possible but common.[4]

Second, *there are diverse motivations for labelling* and *labelling processes produce varied, including unanticipated, outcomes*. Even where there is altruistic intent, labelling can misrepresent whole categories of people; it can stigmatize and incite and/or sustain social and political discord. Conversely, malevolent labelling can lead, unexpectedly, to productive outcomes where, over time, people use these adverse labels as a basis for making claims and gaining political space.

Non-labelling and non-framing are especially significant, for it means that certain issues and peoples can be omitted from policy and programme agendas. They remain unseen and unheard for a variety of reasons; including lack of knowledge of their existence and people's own inability to mobilize, gain access to the right networks and to position their issues in sufficiently commanding and persuasive ways. Furthermore, prejudices on the part of authoritative actors about who is more and less deserving of assistance can relegate some issues and categories of people to very low or no priority, particularly where resources are scarce – at least this is often the pretext.

Third, *labelling and framing processes involve complex relations of accountability and diverse obligatory relationships, complementary and conflicting*. These have significant implications for what frames and labels are recognized and employed in differing contexts, and how; for the types of struggles that ensue over framing and labelling; the spaces allowed for claiming and contesting labels; and the willingness and capability to address problems associated with framing and labelling. Fundamental changes in accountability relationships are critical for recognizing the power of labelling in development, preventing and addressing its worst consequences and, to the extent that it is feasible to reasonably predict, encouraging processes that seem likely to produce social and political gains. Following the chapter overview below, the remainder of this introduction will discuss how the above arguments are developed in the case studies.

Chapter overview

The book's contributors comprise civil society activists, development agency staff and academics from a range of disciplinary backgrounds. Reflecting this diversity, the case studies focus on an array of development actors: the state (Wood, De Haan, Waldman); the media (Hobart); major development and donor agencies, such as the World Bank and the UK Department for International Development (DFID) (Wood, Cornwall and Fujita; Eyben); and charity organizations (Klouda). Some case studies consider the consequences of labelling from multiple sources, including authoritative state and organized non-state actors; local/community levels and self-labelling (Moncrieffe; Gupte and Mehta; Balchin). The product is engaging, wide-ranging and timely.

In Chapter 1, Geof Wood revisits the 1985 publication and provides an overview of its theoretical and practical contributions. He then outlines developments in the theory and indicates how these have influenced his current views on power, labelling and the role of the state. Essentially, Wood modifies his earlier views on the state's hegemonic role in labelling and concedes that the model of bureaucratic rationality characterized by authoritative state labelling only applies to successful societies where the state is sufficiently legitimate to classify people according to needs and can target resources to those needs. However, in many situations, this is not the case. In some contexts, the state struggles and fails to establish the authority of its labelling over the rest of society, leading to various forms of contestation and subversion. In others, the state is obliged to compromise with a hierarchy of intermediary actors who, through patronage relationships, informally manage the prioritization of needs.

While Wood retains his original preoccupation with the state, other authors are keen to show that authoritative labelling pertains equally, and sometimes more so, to powerful non-state actors. Correspondingly, Chapter 2 is the first of a series of contributions on how authoritative non-state labelling pervades development. Eyben provides a personal account of her role in 'labelling for aid'. As a newly hired and eager 'expert', Eyben was sensitive to and even critical of the dominant principles of targeting within her agency but recognized that for pragmatic purposes, bureaucratic labelling – including her own strong control, regulation and management – was the most efficient option for achieving the social justice that she was committed to. She demonstrates the ease with which framing and labelling commonly used for seemingly noble purposes – such as 'empowering the poorest' – can involve questionable methods and strategies and lead to negative outcomes, which development actors do not intend or anticipate.

In Chapter 3, The Politics of Representing "the Poor", Cornwall and Fujita analyse the methods used in the World Bank's 'Voices of the poor' project, which was designed to inform the preparation of the World Development Report 2000/01, *Attacking Poverty*. They discover that despite its claims, the research was designed and managed in ways that elicited particular types of responses. The consultations did not produce knowledge – the authors suggest that was never the intent – rather, they provided the 'evidence' for what the Bank already 'knew' about poverty; consequently, conflicting messages were filtered out.[5] Thus, like Eyben, the authors raise important questions about the strategic motivations for labelling in development and the mechanisms used to achieve desired, and sometimes pre-defined, results.

Gupte and Mehta's research on forced migration (Chapter 4) shows that the almost arbitrary categorization of who constitutes a refugee or 'oustee' can lead to systematic exclusion of large groups of people who may be in an equally precarious situation. Such categories have often proved inadequate for informing the precise strategy or method of intervention. There is also a danger that this labelling presupposes conditions of vulnerability that justify top-down needs-assessment interventions. In this case, it blinds the aid administrator to the resilience and resourcefulness of the forced migrants and, therefore, limits livelihood and reconstruction options.

In Chapter 5, I use my case study of Haiti to reflect on how labelling processes can stigmatize and the power of this stigma, particularly on children. Children on the whole have low priority on the government's agenda and some are labelled in ways that prejudice their life chances. However, these labels have emerged out of particular social conditions and there are deep causal factors that sustain them. I highlight some of these factors and comment on how negative labelling is reproduced through actions and inaction from development experts, societies and families, including how some of those who are stigmatized come to accept and even uphold the meanings of the labels.

Klouda (in Chapter 6) argues that there are multiple, not all salutary, 'purposes' of development and exposes what he believes to be 'pure cant and hypocrisy' among many who claim to be 'eradicating poverty', or helping the most marginalized, least powerful, least healthy or weakest. He studies the mechanics of donating to 'the poor' through charity agencies and shows how differing motivations define perceptions of these abject 'others', their categorization and their labelling. Within the charity industry, the politics of labelling integrally involves the public. Certain, particularly pitiful, representations of poverty and the poor fuel people's sense of compassion and are important for sustaining charitable donations; thus, poverty becomes a 'theatrical event in the sense that a series of artfully contrived pictures or presentations are provided to a public that demands a certain type of show'.

Balchin's (Chapter 7) case study underscores the point that people are often labelled in ways that convey particular interpretations of the underlying problem. Such external definitions and labels can entirely misrepresent the problem or present a partial view of the issues. For example, the current donor emphasis on framing religion as a central development issue may help to narrow the spaces for secular alternatives that are preferred, even by many believers. While religion is undoubtedly important for many women and is certainly part of public political discourse in Muslim countries and communities, it may not be the most significant factor determining the parameters of women's everyday existence. Balchin argues that development initiatives and donor support need to recognize this point if they wish to avoid harming local struggles for gender equality. Privileging financial and other support on the basis of the religious label can create a breach between women's organizations that, until then, were sharing a common platform on many issues.

In his provocative chapter 'Black Umbrellas' (8), Hobart considers the role of the media in labelling and framing development, and concludes that certain representations tend to dominate and even become hegemonic, thereby excluding a range of other possible and valid representations. Politicians, developers and scholars attempt to fix meanings at the point of production, assuming lack of knowledge on the part of the public. The public, in turn, responds to the media in very diverse ways; however, these responses, which include contestations, largely remain unnoticed, entrenching existing hegemonies and intensifying the disarticulation of the vast majority.

Chapters 9 and 10 return to the state's role in labelling. They provide comparable historical analyses of labelling processes in India and South Africa. de Haan's case study (Chapter 9) outlines the role of the state in articulating and upholding deep social stratifications. The labels, which are used to demarcate categories of people, hide wide social and economic variations. However, state labelling can be progressive and even labels that stigmatize, such as 'untouchables' in India, can have unintended consequences: they can become important instruments in the struggles for power.

Waldman's historical account of labelling processes in South Africa (Chapter 10) concentrates, specifically, on naming the Griqua. The chapter traces the ways in which the Griqua attempted to claim new labels in order to reverse the pejorative terms on which they were recognized. There is strong focus on the role of the state in opening and closing the spaces for contestation and negotiation: different ways of framing issues produce different labels, which lead to different policy choices and outcomes. The author emphasizes that negative labels can have long legacies, particularly where authoritative actors do not actively and even aggressively promote the conditions under which those who are misrecognized can transform their circumstances, such that they can be recognized in different, more salutary, ways. Contestation worked – though perhaps only partially – in de Haan's case study of India, in some part because of the direction and quality of leadership and the capacities of the movements for change. In contrast, contestation and counter-labelling were attempted by the Griqua in South Africa but these essentially failed. Together, both chapters are instructive on the real politics of countering negative labelling: what it takes to achieve it; the circumstances under which it fails; the role of varying development actors, including and beyond the state.

Overall, the chapters cover a wide range of issues related to the politics of labelling. The authors acknowledge the significance of framing and labelling for focusing attention on particular areas of need; accordingly, there is no suggestion that we should not frame and label. However, following Wood (1985c), they emphasize the importance of questioning whose labels count, in what circumstances and with what consequences. They hope to inspire self-reflection and policy change; thus, Eyben, in her Afterword, explores how development actors could begin to transform their practice so that the power of labelling becomes more equitable and accountable.

The following sections return to the three overarching arguments outlined above. The first conceptualizes framing and labelling, highlighting distinctions between how the concepts are understood and used in this book, as opposed to the 1985 publication and to earlier labelling theory. It then emphasizes the power of labelling, underscoring the multifaceted nature of the processes. Section 2 reinforces that people have very different motivations for labelling. It then uses evidence from the case studies to pinpoint some of its negative consequences. Section 3 clarifies the relationship between labelling and accountability and poses important questions for self-reflection.

Evolving concepts of labelling and power

In the 1960s, labelling theory was used to explain the unanticipated persistence of criminal and deviant behaviour among those who were categorized in this way, punished and subjected to behaviour modification. Influenced by sociology's symbolic interactionism theory, proponents of labelling theory advanced the basic, and still valid, proposition that people 'form and re-form' their identities/self-concept through ongoing interactions within society; meaning that 'the identity a person takes on will be profoundly shaped by the ways in which others identify and react to him or her' (Akers, 1997, p101). Consequently, 'individuals who are labelled or dramatically stigmatized as deviant are likely to take on a deviant self-identity and become more, rather than less, deviant than if they had not been so labelled' (Akers, 1997, p101). The intent behind the label is to reduce 'deviance'; the unintended consequence is to foment it since 'the disgrace suffered by people who are labelled as delinquent or criminal more often encourages than discourages future deviant behaviour'. According to the debates at that time, labelling of this sort is more powerful and consequential when it is promulgated and enforced by authoritative state agents, such as the police, courts, prisons and government officials (Akers, 1997, pp101, 103).

Critics have rejected what they see as the theory's inherent determinism. Among the more serious points of contention are the views that this older variant of labelling theory does not take due consideration of the actual behaviour of those considered deviant or criminal. Furthermore, it assumes, erroneously, that people simply accept the labels assigned to them whereas people, including those who are less powerful, do refute and contest their identities. Finally, the label does not create the behaviour; there are other causal factors that may remain and continue to incite deviance, in spite of the labels. Given these inadequacies, labelling theory appeared to offer limited analytical value, though it still influenced policy and practice and has made some imprint on other disciplines.

In their 1985 publication, Wood, Schaffer and others brought labelling theory into development policy. They expanded the concept beyond its original exclusive correlation with stigmatization but retained the central thesis on the power relations of dominance versus dominated that underpin labelling; the prime role of authoritative state actors in labelling; and the symbolic interaction position that peoples' identities are shaped by the reactions of others. The book, *Labelling in Development Policy,* was a compelling critique of the common practices of targeting resources to 'the most needy'. Labelling, they argued, is in part a scientific/taxonomic act but to the extent that it requires valuation and judgement, which are then used to designate –'define parameters for thought and behaviour', particularly of the labelled – is deeply political. Furthermore, labelling is pervasive and inevitable: we all label and are, in turn, all labelled. Labelling regulates social interactions: it helps us to define the terms on which we relate to 'others'; without it interaction would be chaotic and inefficient. Similarly, labelling is instrumental for policy, including managing the allocation and distribution of scarce resources, without which resource management would become inefficient and unwieldy. Yet, this seemingly apolitical bureaucratic labelling actually depends on relationships of power (with power understood as domination) that, following Foucault (1977), enforces 'control, regulation and management', thereby allowing authoritative state actors to serve the interests of some to the exclusion of others.[6] Labelling 'defines parameters for thought and behaviour, which render environments stable, and which establish spheres of competence and areas of responsibility' (Wood, 1985c, p349).

Labelling in Development Policy was part of a body of critical studies of state activity, though the analysis was of a particular sort: as Wood explains, this was not the type of state analysis that used observed policy outcomes to explain the relationships between class interests and institutional processes that underpinned them; rather, this was a study of the 'methods and policy discourse by which such relationships are constructed and sustained' (Wood, 1985, p348).

The power of labelling processes: Outlining the current position

Our book advances the application of labelling theory to development in five important respects:

1 Like Wood and Schaffer, it expands the concept of labelling to consider its wider, putatively scientific/taxonomic functions within development and unravels the politics of these seemingly apolitical and asocial processes. It also considers other social and political uses of labelling, including social stratification in India and South Africa; deliberate political manipulation, for example, through strategic (mis)use of the label 'Muslim women'; the use of labelling to stigmatize groups and individuals, as the original theory

describes; and non-labelling, through which some issues and peoples are left off policy agendas.[7] All these can politicize ostensibly apolitical functions, such as targeting, for they convey perceptions and preferences – certainly from those who have the power to shape them – about who deserves assistance and on what basis.[8]

2 The authors accept the pervasiveness of labelling – we all label and are, in turn, all labelled – and emphasize the view that while classificatory framing and labelling are often presented as distinct from the everyday forms of labelling that govern social relations, they are not unrelated. Rather, *frames and labels are socially not naturally derived*. Yet, people experience their social worlds in unique ways and, accordingly, have individual interpretations of reality. 'The world exists only in so far as it is represented to us.' 'Reality is as variable as the knowledge people have about it' (Durkheim, 1909, p238, quoted in McCarthy, 1996, p2).

Rein and Schön (1993, p146) explain how socially derived knowledge shapes framing and labelling. Policy framing, they suggest, 'is a way of selecting, organizing, interpreting, and making sense of a complex reality to provide guideposts for knowing, analyzing, persuading and acting. A frame is a perspective from which an amorphous, ill-defined, problematic situation can be made sense of and acted upon'. However, what is questioned and what is taken for granted are likely to differ depending on individuals' socially acquired knowledge, and perceptions of reality and of the possible:

> *Framing is problematic because it leads to different views of the world and creates multiple social realities. Interest groups and policy constituencies, scholars working in different disciplines, and individuals in different contexts of everyday life have different frames that lead them to see different things, make different interpretations of the way things are, and support different courses of action concerning what is to be done, by whom and how to do it.* (Rein and Schön, 1993, p147)

By implication, what one perceives as 'the whole truth' may reflect only a circumscribed view or even a profoundly misguided and incorrect position. Rein and Schön are careful to emphasize that 'not all frames and not all stories in which they are expressed are equally acceptable or compelling'. Thus, they seek an empirical epistemology, a frame-critical policy analysis, which opens space for frame-reflective policy discourse – a method of identifying the hidden assumptions that underlie people's policy understandings and positions.

As with frames, labels or names are not equally valid. Labels/names can emerge from frames and from the (often partial) stories that support them; labels also influence/give shape and form to frames since the name given to a particular 'problematic terrain' focuses attention on certain elements and deprioritizes or excludes others (Rein and Schön, 1993). Thus, a liberated 'sex worker' in one social context may be presented as an exploited 'prostitute' in the next: different frames produce different labels and different policy responses.

3 Significantly, *what is not framed – that is, what is beyond the discursive horizon – can result in costly under-representation of critical issues, with serious consequences for the non-labelled.* Moncrieffe's paper on street children and restavecs in Haiti shows that when issues are not framed and positioned in debates in persuasive ways, there can be disastrous consequences for the persons affected. Bird and Pratt (2004) have written about the

chronic poverty that exists among alcoholics and persons designated mentally ill and the minute space their situations occupy in many policy circles; those bearing these labels normally fall within the category of the undeserving and are, accordingly, underrepresented and underserved. Barbara Harris-White (2002) explains that 'the destitute' in the slums of Bangladesh lack visibility in the policy arenas, where presence is crucial; in contrast, gender issues are packaged and presented in ways that ensure that concerns are considered. Similarly, White (2002) argues that gender issues are politicized and represented in ways that obscure critical issues of race and racism in development. Within academia and among development consultants, certain issues and areas are prioritized because they attract funding or fit within donors' current agenda. This targeting excludes other issues and areas that may be equally significant. This type of selective framing and labelling has varied causes, including 'pragmatic decision-making', lack of information and even blatant prejudice.

4 In contrast with contemporary theories on framing that understate the role of power, this publication strongly agrees with Carragee and Roefs (2004) that 'asymmetries in power influence the framing [and, by extension, labelling] process' (p226); that 'frames [and labels] as imprints of power are central to the production of hegemonic meanings', (p222) and that the 'challenge of framing [and labelling] research is to study the complex ways power informs frame sponsorship' (p228).

The power of labels becomes salient when labelling is put into action and influences relationships: Power exists in and through relations; power is not an abstract 'thing' (Foucault, various publications). Inevitably, the meanings one assigns to labels influence relationships each time there is an encounter. It is in this sense that Wood suggests that labelling moderates and is, indeed, intrinsic to social interaction: labels help to define the terms on which we engage. Without them, interaction would be chaotic and inefficient. Social interactions serve critical functions. While they may provide occasions for the imposition of labels and for substantial conflicts and contestations, even from these conflicts opportunities may emerge for confronting and tackling labels and their attendant subjective meanings (Goffman 1963; Carraggee and Roefs, 2004). The crucial point here is that the frames of reference and the labels we employ and those that are assigned to us can evolve as our experiences change.

It is worth underscoring two critical points. First, it is, arguably, more problematic when processes of labelling persist at a distance (social, political, economic, spatial), with little possibility of encounter between the labeller and the labelled. It is this labelling at a distance that characterizes much development practice. Second, counter-labelling, as understood by a number of authors in this book, is a radical concept that is much less concerned with the superficial practice of changing names than it is with surmounting and/or transforming the causal factors that may give rise to certain negative labels, particularly those that stigmatize. In this sense, various authors accept and respond to critiques of earlier labelling theory, acknowledging that changed realities are important for countering and transforming the meanings assigned to labels; name changes may help to recast the ways in which people are regarded and prompt attention to their circumstances but, often, they have very little impact on the conditions that generated the labels in the first place.

5 *At all levels, labelling processes can be intensely political, as people's knowledge, realities and the meanings they assign to categories conflict.* For example, there is ample evidence from

many practitioners in development that external, hegemonic labelling of who comprises the poor conflicts with people's perceptions on the ground and results in rejection of the label and outright refusal to participate in the programmes designed for their benefit: 'the poor are definitely not us'. Therefore, hegemonic labels such as these can have very little substance in certain places and spaces and can undercut policy intentions.

Labelling: Motivations and outcomes

As discussed above, the real politics and powers of framing and labelling get disguised, in large part because they are viewed as natural and indispensable for policy. Furthermore, there is a popular sentiment that the costs of labelling may well be outweighed by its benefits, particularly when the objective is development. The book challenges these understandings.

First, there is no consensus on what 'development' is and what has to be done to secure it. What exists are competing moral stories on the meanings and objectives of development and, perhaps, a prevailing discourse on 'how to do' development; that is, promoting growth and equity. Hobart (this volume) is the most audacious of our contributors, for he contends that in a certain sense there is no such thing as development. Like the mass media, development substitutes 'hyper-reality' for reality, since the labelling processes we wittingly or unwittingly support create manageable masses of target populations, who are – contrary to our stated aims – misrepresented, decivilized and disempowered.[9]

Second, there are diverse motivations for framing and labelling and diverse and unpredictable outcomes. As the case studies show, framing and labelling can have calculated and manipulative, political intent. However, they are also commonly used for seemingly noble purposes but lead to negative outcomes, which are neither intended nor anticipated. Eyben's account is not unfamiliar to experts who, despite their best intentions, are forced to append their personal objectives to the dominant frame and, in the process, unwittingly perform in ways that compromise their own objectives and, worse, sustain and even exacerbate the very conditions they intend to transform. *Yet, the outcomes of these innocent actions may be no less significant than those that result from more strategic motivations. Similarly, the outcomes of seemingly innocent and personally generous actions may be no different from those motivated by veiled desires for self-aggrandizement.* As Goffman (1963) argues, framing and labelling serve the interests of the 'normal', 'better off', 'us' as much as – and perhaps more than – they do those classified as needing assistance.

Labelling, then, has multiple and interrelated dimensions and is shaped by diverse frames of reference, motivations and objectives. What are some of the potential *negative* outcomes of labelling? The case studies underscore the following:

- Framing and labelling, particularly that conducted at a distance, can overlook whole sub-categories of people and a range of substantial issues (see Eyben, de Haan, Gupte and Mehta, Cornwall and Fujita).
- Frames and labels can obscure the diversity of interpretations that may be critical for addressing the very problems/cases that the label highlights (Hobart, Moncrieffe, Balchin, Gupte and Mehta, Eyben).

- Hegemonic framing and labelling can focus on particular problems and solutions to the exclusion of other salient ones, also with negative consequences (Gupte and Mehta, Klouda, Balchin).
- Bureaucratic frames and labels can easily conflate the observed problems with the people involved, generating social dislocation, fostering new forms of inequality and sustaining pre-existing unequal power relations (Eyben, Wood, Gupte and Mehta).
- Frames and labels can discriminate, stigmatize and underpin persistent human rights abuses (Moncrieffe, Waldman, de Haan). There is ample anthropological evidence to prove that substantial negative labelling can abound even where there are purportedly close social relations, such as within families, kinship systems, communities. State actors, as products of the society, can pick up on these labels and use them with the intended prejudicial intent. Policy makers may adopt societal labels and overlook what they signify on the ground, the implications for relations of power and for the policies they implement. As Moncrieffe's case study shows, the same label can have very different meanings at varying points and spaces within the policy making and implementation process and produce different consequences.

Labelling, framing and relations of accountability

The outcomes noted above are commonplace; yet, there is a long-standing failure and even reluctance to acknowledge and address them. This book elucidates four principal shortcomings in existing relations of accountability, which exacerbate the negative consequences of labelling:

1 One common characteristic of bureaucratic labelling is that it ensues at a distance with minimal and, often, no contact between the labeller and the labelled. This distance facilitates a lack of accountability to the labelled not only for how they are categorized but also for the outcomes of this categorization.
2 In many places the accountability mechanisms for curbing the worst forms of labelling (including those that persist at close societal levels) are weak and ineffectual, if they exist at all. de Haan is clear: 'The point is not that power has not been challenged in India – it has – but … in the absence of systems of accountability or challenges the administrative system can continue to contain discriminatory attitudes, while the official categories – arguably – function to fixate the groups in an official hierarchy' this volume, p151. Certainly, one of the main drawbacks of the many mechanistic approaches to understanding accountability is that they seem to assume that the institutions can operate acceptably in spite of the people and power relationships that give shape to them. Yet, as Moncrieffe shows, our socially acquired dispositions, including ingrained prejudices inform our actions, such that the deepest prejudices can be defended in the highest circles, despite public affirmations of commitment to rights, equality and justice. Development is often framed in such apolitical and asocial ways that it masks the diversities among the actors; such can be the hypocrisy of framing and labelling.
3 Accountability systems do not allow sufficient space and opportunities for contestation and for effective counter-labelling. Accountability, as it is conventionally framed,

denotes answering for the use of authority *ex post facto*. It features checks and balances, monitoring and sanctioning mechanisms. *Ex-ante accountability* (Moncrieffe, 2001), by contrast, encourages deliberative and consultative relationships such that those who claim to act in the interest of others will have a sufficiently broad and deep grasp of the interests, needs, motivations, capacities involved and mechanisms, including through use of dialogue, in which people will be able to assess the quality of the intervention. It is this sort of deliberation that is considered important for facilitating the contestation of labels.

Ex-ante accountability presupposes that development actors have substantial responsibilities to the persons and groups they purport to serve. Intuitively, we know that development actors ought to be better held to account for the work they claim to do. However, accountability is hardly straightforward. Many development actors have some form of obligatory relations with the people they represent but are actually answerable, meaning accountable, to very different interests. These formalized relations of accountability can compromise the quality of their response to those they designate as 'target populations', particularly where there is divergence between how problems and their solutions are framed by those they are answerable to and those they purpose to serve. This is the standard explanation but it is not complete. It assumes and hopes that formalized relationships of accountability necessarily translate to anticipated performance. This, of course, is not necessarily the case. Eyben's project in Sudan was specifically designed to provide employment training to 'school drop-outs', with the expectation that the beneficiaries would become successfully employed. Until her arrival, officers on the ground funnelled resources to their own neighbourhoods and were blatantly unaccountable both to funders and to those who appeared to need resources the most. As Eyben shows, development actors, working within their own socially derived frame of reference, can act in ways that profoundly breach their terms of accountability, particularly when these relations of accountability are sustained over a distance.

This raises a critical, and still under-analysed, question about how power performs where there are multiple levels of accountability and diverse and conflicting obligatory relationships. In short, because power is polyvalent, diverse and not monolithic, people have the capacity to impute their own frames and labels in the spaces where they have some degree of control.

4   Without strong relations of accountability, policy makers can easily de-prioritize the needs of many who bear the most limiting labels, such as Haiti's street children and restavecs; Bird and Pratt's alcoholics and mentally ill; Harris-White's destitute in Bangladesh. These are the groups that are easily forgotten, non-labelled, often under the guise of limited resources. Accountability does not suggest an equal regard for all needs at all moments in time; balance is important. However, accountability does suggest that particularly categories of need should not be persistently excluded from policy agendas; for this, there is no justification.

Is change practicable?

There is a strand of argument that maintains that since labelling is inevitable and critical to bureaucratic management, reform attempts are futile. Klouda is sceptical that the deliberative reforms that Eyben and others suggest (see Afterword) are practicable; he contends that since differing motivations give rise to different labels, deliberation over labels would only make sense if persons could agree on the purpose of development. Wood, too, is doubtful about the extent to which labelling can be addressed; he warns against utopian solutions that overemphasize the benefits of participation. Hobart suggests that practices of labelling are likely to continue as they do for some time, given the role of labelling in development, but notes that more dialogue would be necessary if labelling either of the deliberately or unintentionally negative sort discussed is to be addressed. However, there are examples that the proposed change is feasible and that reactions to labelling are likely even where authoritative state and non-state actors are recalcitrant. Thus, de Haan depicts the beginnings of transformation in India and the factors that facilitate and limit it. (See also Wood, this volume; Appadurai, 2004; Waldman, this volume.)

The Afterword to this volume outlines Eyben's vision for changes in policy and practice. She is clear that as we all label, even authoritatively, self-reflection is critical and indispensable. (Her own case study demonstrates this.) Pertinent questions may include:

- How do our own reference frames influence the ways in which we label and our choice of labels themselves?
- Do the labels we use put undue constraints on people's ability to shift their identities?
- What are the socio-psychological effects of labels such as 'the poor'?
- To what extent do the methods of labelling we employ reflect and respond to conditions on the ground? For example, what are the consequences of adopting, and ignoring the meanings of, society's labels?
- Do the mechanisms we use allow people the right to contest the labels we impute?
- To what extent can development agencies insist on implementing mechanisms that will restrict labelling in its worst form, particularly labels that stigmatize?

Labelling is indeed inevitable and is important for policy but the languid, uncritical approach to such hegemonic practices has harmful consequences that undermine many of the stated moral goals of development.

Notes

1 I thank Rosalind Eyben and Mamoru Fujita for their invaluable comments on earlier drafts and the team of authors in this volume for the ideas they inspired. Of course, any shortcomings are this author's sole responsibility.
2 See Gramsci, 1971; Laclau and Mouffe, 1985; Carraggee and Roefs, 2004.
3 Haugaard, 1997, 2002; Foucault, 1977; Carraggee and Roefs, 2004; Gaventa, 2006.
4 'Discourse' as Dryzek, drawing on Foucault, defines it, is a 'framework for apprehending the world [that is] embedded in language, enabling its adherents to put together diverse bits of sensory information into coherent wholes'. It is distinct from the formal rules, procedures and customs that define institutions; instead, discourses are the informal, often 'taken for granted', frames of reference that support institutions and that, conversely, can destroy them – specifically, where there is discrepancy between the popular discourse and the existing institutions. Therefore, discourses are 'rarely hegemonic; more than one discourse is normally available in any particular setting; discourses are only partially incommensurable; they are open to informed scrutiny and reconstruction at the margins' (Dryzek, 1996, p103).

5   There is a larger point here about how authoritative actors frame knowledge, determining what is valid and what is not, depending on what suits their interests or not. For example, like Hobart and Cornwall and Fujita (this volume), Lewis et al's 'Fiction of development: Knowledge, authority and representation' (LSE, 2005) presents an interesting critique of how knowledge is constructed in development. They argue that formal, academic presentations are considered the authentic voice of development issues (in this sense, they are hegemonic), though much can be gained from fictional literature that focuses on development issues with academic and policy-related representations. The authors demonstrate their claims, using a selection of fictional writings. Likewise, we know from various, including postcolonial, studies (e.g. Said, 1979; Escobar, 1984; Ashcroft et al, 1989) that people's histories can be framed in similarly selective ways, producing partial accounts and, worse, entirely misrepresenting them. Not much attention is paid to the potential long-term consequences of misrepresented histories and the labels they generate.

6   Up to the 17th and 18th centuries, in feudal type societies, power was conceptualized largely as the right of the sovereign, who had control over the wealth and commodities that his/her subjects produced. Foucault (1977) contends that this theory of sovereign power and the legal codes that were based on it still persists and functions both as 'ideology and organising principle', effectively masking the pervasive disciplinary power that developed subsequently. This disciplinary form of power, which characterizes bureaucratic administration, features more and less subtle procedures of surveillance, classification and registration, measurement and evaluation. Foucault describes disciplinary power as antithetical to the theory of sovereignty.

7   Non-labelling can but need not be intentional; it can result from lack of knowledge. However, the question still remains: Why and through what processes are some people entirely overlooked?

8   For example, used in some western circles, the label Muslim Women immediately conveys images of docile, even tragic women, who are trapped in circumstances from which they must be freed, invariably by the West (Balchin, this volume). This may result, partly, from lack of knowledge and, as Balchin contends, from Orientalist presumptions about what transpires in the 'Muslim world'. However, it is also part of a political project of categorizing the behaviours of the uncivilized. For a number of development organizations, targeting has the political objective of protecting these poor, disempowered women and, perhaps less patently, exposing them to the progressive culture of the civilized West.

9   In one sense, this lack of clarity about the meaning, purpose, capacities and even authenticity of development presents an immediate challenge to our analysis of labelling and to the position that many authors adopt in this volume: that something must be done about it. As Klouda points out, how can we seek to address labelling in development when we cannot agree on what the purpose of development is? However, in another sense, this lack of agreement justifies and reinforces the urgency of understanding the dynamics of framing and labelling and curbing their worst effects: If there is no agreement on what constitutes development, how and why are some frames and labels so dominant and what are their effects? Would greater accountability to the populations we claim to serve not require genuine opportunities to present other realities and to effectively counter-label?

References

Akers, R. (1997) *Criminological Theories: Introduction and Evaluation*, Los Angeles, CA, Roxbury Publishing

Appadurai, A. (2004) 'The capacity to aspire: Culture and the terms of recognition', in V. Rao and M. Walton (eds) *Culture and Public Action*, Palo Alto, CA, Stanford University Press

Ashcroft, B., Griffiths, G., Tiffin, H. (1989) *The Empire Writes Back: Theory and Practice in Post-Colonial Literatures*, London, Routledge

Becker, H. (1963) *Outsiders: Studies in the Sociology of Deviance*, New York, The Free Press.

Bhatia, M. (2005) 'Fighting words: Naming terrorists, bandits, rebels and other violent actors', *Third World Quarterly*, vol 26, no 1, pp5–22

Bird, K. and Pratt, N. (2004) 'Fracture points in social policies for chronic poverty reduction', CPRC Working Paper 47, Manchester, CPRC

Bourdieu, P (1980) *The Logic of Practice*, Palo Alto, CA, Stanford University Press

Carragee, M. and Roefs, W. (2004) 'The neglect of power in recent framing research', *Journal of Communication*, vol 54, no 2, pp214–233

Cornwall, A. and Brock, K. (2005) 'What do buzzwords do for development policy? A critical look at "participation", "empowerment" and "poverty reduction"', *Third World Quarterly*, vol 26, no 7, pp1043–1060

Crewe, E. and Fernando, P. (2006) 'The elephant in the room: Racism in representations, relationships and representations', *Progress in Development Studies*, vol 6, no 1, pp40–54

Dryzek, J. S. (1996) 'The informal logic of institutional design', in R. E. Goodin (ed) *The Theory of Institutional Design*, Cambridge, Cambridge University Press

Escobar, A. (1984) 'Discourse and power in development: Michel Foucault and the relevance of his work to the Third World', *Alternatives*, vol 10, pp377–400

Eyben, R. (2006) *Relationships for Aid*, London, Earthscan

Foucault, M. (1977) *Power/Knowledge: Selected Interviews and Other Writings, 1972–1977*, New York, Pantheon Books

Foucault, M. (1991) *Discipline and Punish: The Birth of the Prison*, London, Penguin Books

Gaventa, J. (2003) 'Power after Lukes: An overview of theories of power since Lukes and their application to development' (Draft)

Gaventa, J. (2006) 'Finding the spaces for change: A power analysis', *IDS Bulletin*, vol 37, no 6, pp23–33

Goffman, E. (1963) *Stigma: Notes on the Management of Spoiled Identity*, Englewood Cliffs, New Jersey, Prentice-Hall (reprinted 1968, Harmondsworth, Penguin)

Gramsci, A. (1971) *Selections from the Prison Notebooks*, London, Lawrence and Wishart

Harris-White, B. (2002) 'A note on destitution', QEH Working Paper Series 86, University of Oxford

Haugaard, M. (ed) (1997) *The Constitution of Power*, Manchester, Manchester University Press

Haugaard, M. (ed) (2002) *Power: a Reader*, Manchester, Manchester University Press

Jenkins, R. (2004) *Social Identity*, London, Routledge

Kothari, U. (2006) 'Critiquing race and racism in development discourse and practice', *Progress in Development Studies*, vol 6, no 1, pp1-7

Laclau, E. and Mouffe, C. (1985) *Hegemony and Socialist Strategy*, London, Verso

Lewis, D., Rodgers, D. and Woolcock, M. (2005) 'The fiction of development: Knowledge, authority and representation', LSE Working Paper Series, no 05-61

McCarthy, Doyle E. (1996) *Knowledge as Culture*, London, Routledge

Moncrieffe, J. (2004) 'Beyond categories: Power, recognition and the conditions for equity', Background Paper for *World Development Report 2006*, www.worldbank.org/wdr/

Moncrieffe, J. (2001) 'Accountability: Idea, ideals, constraints', *Democratization*, vol 8, no 3, pp26–50

Rein, M. and Schön, D. (1993) 'Reframing policy discourse', in F. Fischer and J. Forester (eds) *The Argumentative Turn in Policy Analysis and Planning*, Durham, NC, Duke University

Said, E. (1979) *Orientalism*, New York, Vintage

Scott, J. (1985) *Weapons of the Weak: Everyday Forms of Peasant Resistance*, Philadelphia, Temple University Press

Utting, P. (2006) 'Introduction' in P. Utting (ed) *Reclaiming Development Agendas: Knowledge, Power and International Policy Making*, Basingstoke, UNRISD Palgrave

Wacquant, L. (2005) 'Habitus', in J. Becket and M. Zafiovski (eds) *International Encyclopedia of Economic Sociology*, London, Routledge

White, S. (1996) 'Depoliticising development: The uses and abuses of participation', *Development in Practice*, vol 6, no 1, pp6–15

White, S. (2002) 'Thinking race, thinking development', *Third World Quarterly*, vol 23, pp407–419

Wood, G. (ed) (1985a) *Labelling in Development Policy: Essays in Honour of Bernard Schaffer*, London, Sage Publications

Wood, G. (1985b) 'Targets strike back: Rural works claimants in Bangladesh', in G. Wood (ed) *Labelling in Development Policy*, London, Sage Publications

Wood, G. (1985c) 'The politics of development policy labelling', *Development and Change*, vol 16, no 3, pp347–373

World Development Report (2006) *Equity and Development*, Washington DC, World Bank

Young, I. M. (2000) *Inclusion and Democracy*, Oxford, Oxford University Press

1

Labels, Welfare Regimes and Intermediation: Contesting Formal Power

Geof Wood[1]

Introduction

In revisiting my earlier arguments about the 'politics of development policy labelling' (Wood, 1985b) for this volume, this chapter focuses upon the general relationship between processes of categorization and forms of intermediation. The argument starts with a review of the context for the original labelling thesis, and a summary of the 'labelling as political manipulation' argument that dominated that original paper. This leads into a brief overview of the relevant development and sociological discourses that followed those earlier arguments and thus an autocritique built around the limitations of the hegemonic, statist assumptions of authoritative labelling. This reflection sets up the basis for a revised argument which recognizes the greater significance of plurality and contestation in the labelling process as a way of understanding how formal power is either directly challenged or by-passed in societies where the exercise of informal, less bureaucratically configured power prevails.

This is the basis of deploying a comparative welfare regimes approach (Gough et al, 2004; Wood and Gough, 2006) to capture more systematically the variation in forms of intermediation, as informed by labelling, through which power is exercised and through which people have to pursue their livelihoods and well-being. The central feature of this welfare regimes framework is the relationship between rights, claims and correlative duties, and how these vary between different welfare regimes. It observes that scarcity is managed in different ways in different regimes through variations in the process of intermediation between rights and claims on the one hand, and correlative duties on the other. It also observes that the model of bureaucratic rationality characterized by authoritative labelling only applies successfully to societies where the state is sufficiently legitimate to perform both de-commodification and regulatory functions over the market, as well as community and household institutions. Within that notion of legitimacy is the widespread acceptance of the practices of bureaucratic rationality in classifying need and targeting resources to those needs.

However, in societies where these principles of the welfare and developmental state do not obtain, then the relationship between rights, claims and correlative duties is not governed by bureaucratic and authoritative labelling. Thus we enter a range of situations that will be schematically outlined. A contrast is used between simple and dynamic reproduction in order to distinguish between situations of strong path dependency and thus simple reproduction through the domination of uncontested state categories of rights, and situations of weaker path dependency, characterized by plurality and/or contestation, entailing prospects for dynamic reproduction – positively or negatively in terms of the well-being of the powerless. The plurality of authoritative labelling refers to what elsewhere is termed 'informal security regimes', where the domain of policy and state implementation is more obviously obliged to compromise with the hierarchy of intermediary actors who *de facto* but not *de jure* command the relationship between rights, claims and correlative duties through forms of patronage and other informal practices that nevertheless entail the management of scarcity through the informal prioritization of needs. The 'contestation' end of that range is where the state is struggling but failing to establish the authoritativeness of its labelling over the rest of society – leading to various forms of contestation and subversion.

The context for earlier labelling theses

What was the point of departure for the original arguments?[2] They were several. *Empirically*, they were an instinctive counter-reaction to the practices of targeting, or even extreme targeting, which also required the convincing of other needy people outside the target that those so targeted were legitimately within it. Interestingly, in the late 1970s/early 1980s (partly as a continuation of Basic Needs discourses) it was the 'progressive', poverty-oriented like-minded Scandinavian, Dutch and Canadian donors along with international non-governmental organizations (INGOs) and domestic NGOs (DNGOs) who pursued targeting in mass poverty societies like Bangladesh. The Overseas Development Administration (known since 1997 as the UK Department for International Development (DFID)) was, at that time, out of the loop, still committed to non-targeted programme aid. While targeting the poorest appeared to be progressive (e.g. in rich, but unequal, western societies), in the context of mass poverty it could be understood as regressive in the sense of actually excluding the needy. That problem remains located in the contemporary micro-classifications of poverty (chronic, extreme, hard-core etc.) for policy focus, as illustrated in DFID's current poverty-focused programmes in Bangladesh. *Ideologically and politically*, although Schaffer was my guru, we approached these issues via a tension between Schaffer's critical Weberianism and my Marxism in the way the state should be analysed. However, both of us had written about 'access' (i.e. state–society relations at the interface of service provision and resource allocation) in the late 1970s, from our respective positions (i.e. for Schaffer, the mechanics of bureaucratic rationing via queues, interface and encounters; and for Wood in terms of the exercise of inequality, rooted in political economy, together with the social incompatibility of bureaucratic and peasant rationalities). Meanwhile I had been reading Althusser, Foucault and post-structuralists, as well as remembering Gramsci, Dahl and Lukes. So the *theoretical convergence* between Schaffer and Wood focused upon a frustration with the contemporary form of Marxian discourse about the state, which was silent on the actual processes of power amid the formal assertions that the 'state acted' in either fully captured or relatively autonomous ways that were necessarily consistent with the interests of prevailing dominant classes. So we were interested in the unasked questions about 'how' the state might serve the interests of some to the exclusion of others. Our entry point into this 'how' question was therefore the process of labelling, as a fundamental activity of exercising power. Althusser wrote about ideological apparatuses of the state. Foucault about hidden, unobserved power expressed through repeated, normalized technique. The post-structuralists nevertheless remained gloomy about agency, seeing it as always overridden. So our work was intended to reveal these hidden, insidious dimensions of power, where authoritative, 'scientific' technique is used to de-politicize an essentially political process of resource allocation and management of scarcity through the realization of conformity to labels that indicated the distribution of rights to entitlements. We settled upon this entry point as, in effect, the next step in our joint earlier interest in access. But in pursuit of this dimension of power, we thus entered a world of shadows, illusions and disguises. And arguably, all large organizations operate with these characteristics, which reflect internal power configurations as well as organizational power over others.

Labelling as a fundamental social process

The acts of classification and taxonomy are rather fundamental to human behaviour and interaction. If we consider the world around us as constructed by concentric circles of increasing moral distance, then we increasingly rely upon our skills and memories of classification as our relationships move from inner to outer circles – that is from intimate kin and friends to strangers, from multi-dimensional to single-dimensional transactions, from *gemeinschaft* to *gesellschaft*. Of course, many things intrude into these processes of classification for personal survival: values, interests, preferences and learning from repeated interactions. Continuous adjustments to our taxonomies are made through symbolic processes of interaction. In this way, relationships can settle down to a pattern, and do not have to be derived from first principles each time, which would be too costly and insecure for functional interaction. To this social convenience of labelling as a proxy for unique and primary assessments must be added 'power'. It is of course everywhere, when two or more persons interact. For interactions towards the outer circles, power is more institutionalized rather than the idiosyncratic outcome of personalities in interaction. But of course, even within the immediate family, age and gender provide non-idiosyncratic accounts of power. From this we can understand that the interesting question is not whether we label and categorize. We all do that, as asserted above. Rather, the interesting questions are which and whose labels prevail, and under what contextual conditions? These 'which', 'whose' and 'what' questions become more significant as we move to the outer circles, because these are the transactions more in the public than private domain. The public domain is one of institutionalized power within a wider framework of political economy, within which policies (through deliberation or default) are constructed to allocate resources and opportunities under conditions of overall scarcity. Such policies and their outcomes are an inextricable aspect of the power of labelling – the process of classifying needs and entitlements. And the interesting question here is whether that labelling is transparent and the result of open political competition, or whether it is hidden and arbitrarily imposed upon an unconvinced population. However, this is an extremely complex question to answer. *Labelling in Development Policy* (1985a) sought to answer this question both theoretically and ontologically as well as through case study application.

Labelling as political manipulation: Arguments from the 1980s

While, as argued above, labelling, categorization and classification is an intrinsic component of human agency, this is not the place to survey the entire breadth of labelling in all human interaction. Thus the interest here lies in a sub-set of the labelling process that pertains to prioritizing claims to welfare. Sometimes these claims will be understood as rights, and sometimes as effective demand. When understood as rights, the discourse of labelling will concern universal and moral concepts of need, deserving, targeting, inclusion/exclusion, prioritizing and queuing for access. When understood as effective demand, although an implicit list of similar qualifications may be deployed, there will also be the dimension of effectiveness of voice, meaningful threats of disloyalty, and realistic exit options that might harm resource controllers and service providers. There is, therefore, a tension between labelling as a hidden political process of technique, having recourse to 'science' for legitimacy and authoritativeness, and labelling as a negotiated, more obviously political process, reliant upon contingent settlement, always vulnerable to change. The central proposition is that the process of labelling is a relationship of power, in that the labels used by some sets of actors are more easily imposed upon a policy area, upon a situation, upon people as classification than those labels created and offered by others.

Labelling is a pervasive process, occurring at different levels and within different arenas of interaction. So, not just between the state and people in the society, but between people through constructions of social othering and identity creation. We are all labellers, and therefore we are all in turn labelled. Thus we abstract from the individual, the actuality, and then stereotype via the use of metaphor. All interaction requires labelling in the form of images, badges, stereotypes and metaphors which as signals guide perceptions and thus interactional behaviour. The power issue is expressed in terms of whether the individual controls the presentation of self-image, or receives and lives within the images imposed by others.

The original paper concluded, therefore, that the issue is not *whether* we label, but *which* labels are created, and *whose* labels prevail to define a whole situation or policy area, under what conditions and with what effects? Applied to the analysis of the state, and more particularly for this chapter an analysis of welfare state regimes, we have to ask how specific sets of labels become universalized and legitimized instead of some other set. How does one set become authoritative at the expense of other options and choices? This is the crucial insight into political process. Accepted or authoritative labelling is the entry point into understanding the political settlement that underpins stable social policy. This is to be contrasted to unsettled political circumstances when labelling is far more contested. Thus, authoritative labelling represents the conclusion or outcome of political settlement, when historic agreements have been reached between contending classes, ethnic and linguistic groups, genders and generations. While such agreements are not set in stone, their basic premises and assumptions are difficult to shift radically. *Simple* reproduction is more likely than *dynamic*, or *extended* reproduction. Thus the notion of political settlement reflects a situation of induced consensus where each potentially contending party and advocate of change also calculates the odds of achieving any significant improvement as remote and likely to put present, albeit inadequate, entitlements at risk. Thus were revolutions always contained. This is how political settlements can reflect highly unequal social and economic conditions, as in the UK.

The process whereby acceptance is gained is assisted by 'politics appearing as technique'. This has been the contribution of Foucault. The authoritative labels of the state, and thus political settlements, are buttressed by the activities of science and the rationality assumed therein. Social sciences, especially in the forms of social policy and development studies, are essentially in the business of arranging people in different classifications and taxonomies for the purposes of data comparison to explain key variables in behaviour. Thus science, rationality and expertise appear as apolitical technique making the underlying assumptions about classification, arranging, grouping for the purposes of data comparison and policy justification unassailable in political debate. Grouping and classification is all about boundaries and thresholds, and where they are to be set for the purposes of attributing significance. While regression analysis offers more flexibility in terms of attributing significance to linear options, and thus more independence from the terms of the original question, it does not remove the arbitrariness of original category selection. A good example of politicized category selection has been Sida in Bangladesh when, in the late 1980s, it attempted to target the extreme poor (a different concept and label from chronic) by using <0.5 acres as the divider between included and excluded families for targeted benefits in a village 'para'.[3] But such an arbitrary snapshot approach bore little or no relation to the experience of being poor in those paras.

This point sets up a key issue – the extent to which the authoritativeness of a label is undermined by lack of self-evident fit to the condition of the labelled. If we take the Sida case again: let us assume that 30 families live in a para of a Bangladeshi village. As nuclear entities, these families are 'paribars'. But these nuclear entities are frequently grouped into immediate, perhaps extended, kinship groups as 'baris' – perhaps with dwellings surrounding and facing into a common courtyard where some activities are done together. While all these paribars may share poverty, for various reasons of multiple inheritance and debt circumstances they have variations in control over land at any one snapshot in time. But they know that the poorest family today was better off yesterday, and those who are coping today could be in a rapid downward trajectory tomorrow. In other words they are all in a livelihoods process, improving, coping or declining at any one point in time but always highly vulnerable to crisis round the corner. And each family knows this of each other. What sense then in trying to differentiate between them for targeting purposes on the basis of only one variable – land control? That control is so precarious for all. Can the label be imposed? Yes. But was it authoritative in the sense of being a self-evident and valid discriminator locally? No.

What has happened in this example? The agrarian economy has been understood too strongly in terms of land access and ownership as the prime determinant of livelihoods success. Thus landlessness becomes a key policy concept, as indeed it has been for three decades in the Bangladeshi discourse. From among the many roles, and thus including the many ways of earning a living, the land-owning variable has been plucked as indicating everything else about a family's livelihoods prospects. Behavioural assumptions flow from this indicator. No account is taken of how a family may have entered or will exit from this condition. No attention to routes, in other words. Instead, the individual has been transformed into a client (i.e. the policy target) by being differentiated and disaggregated into components, and then identified with one component, with one principal label as the insight into the whole condition. The individual has thereby been transformed into an object, into a 'case' and de-linked from his/her own story. The greater the separation of the case from the story, the more the tendency away from self-evidence in terms of label applicability, and thus this separation is an index of power for the possessor of the case. Taking the Sida example of targeting in Bangladesh, the political significance of de-linking lies in severing the target families from their social context, breaking identities to kin, clan and neighbourhood, and re-establishing identity on the basis of the family's relationship to or dependency upon an actual or potential category of state activity.

To those in power in unequal political economies, poverty is best conceptualized as behavioural rather than structural in order to separate the rich and powerful from responsibility for poverty through exploitative relations of production and exchange. This translates into behavioural rather than structural labels to designate the poverty problem and politically disorganize the poor through atomizing the causes of their condition. Such conceptualization underpins policy and strategy, directing it towards activity which is weakly linked or de-linked by this ideological representation to historical systems of unequal exchange. Thus the poor become labelled through other self-incriminating badges: beggars, street urchins, itinerants, refugees, slum-dwellers, lazy, incompetent and so on. In this way, we see the de-linking of individuals from their histories, enabling the de-linked explanations of poverty and deprivation to appear ideologically as the 'culture of poverty' in which the victims are blamed for their own condition. By de-linking explanations structurally from the non-poor, poverty is therefore easily explained as deriving from characteristics internal to the poor. People are labelled with badges independent of the capitalist relations of production through which their poverty, their vulnerability, their insecurity, their underemployment, their alienation is reproduced.

Within the terms of the global neo-liberal discourse, the main policy response to poverty alleviation from these de-linking labelling processes has been to increase the capacity of the poor to enter and operate successfully within the domain of markets. The central principle has been small-scale entrepreneurialism and the spread of enterprise capacity. This has incorporated some strange bedfellows: capability thinkers; human development, rights and education advocates; even the most socially radical NGOs; the micro-finance industry; the small-scale enterprise lobby; alongside international finance organizations. In welfare regime terms, the entrepreneurial panacea implies a weak political settlement, avoiding the harder structural questions about redistribution through, for example, wider and deeper taxes upon the rich.

Thus the original arguments about authoritative labelling in the poverty arena concluded, in effect, that social science, policy makers and the rich and powerful all conspired in the process of de-linking poor individuals from their stories, representing them through a series of degraded labels involving behavioural incompetence, pathologies and deviance. If the process fails to convince, it is difficult to maintain targeted, well-defined, case-oriented labels. In other words the problem is no longer successfully contained because the separation of case and story collapses. People re-assert their stories – in other words, they exercise voice, they struggle, they critically participate. The citizenship side of capabilities overrides the market entry side. This opposition sets up the main challenge to the idea of neo-liberal, welfare state regimes addressing mass poverty in poor countries – which is the general thrust of global development discourses, especially those emanating from richer countries. It is self-evidently very difficult to label, de-link and therefore target the poor in conditions of widespread, mass poverty. This was Sida's problem in Bangladesh in the 1980s, and remains the problem for all those contemporary programmes focusing upon the chronic and/or extreme poor. It is difficult to positively discriminate in favour of the majority! They cannot all be blamed as incompetent and thus responsible for their own predicament.

Autocritique: Hegemony, authoritativeness and simple reproduction

Subsequent to publishing the original work, I was influenced by several intellectual contributions in the second half of the 1980s which further moderated my earlier attempts at Marxian institutional ethnography via labelling. In 1985, Booth critiqued the over-reductionist, over-determinist dependency arguments as a failing paradigm within development sociology. I caught up with the Giddens (1984) reconciliation of structural determinism and free agency via his structuration thesis. For development anthropologists and later sociologists, the adaptation of dependency critiques and structuration as actor-oriented epistemology by Norman Long (1990), and his colleague in Wageningen, van der Ploeg (Long and van der Ploeg, 1994), liberated the analysis of dynamic change in the interface between individuals/local communities and large-scale bureaucratic agencies from its erstwhile hegemonic grip.[4] Latour's (1987) actor-network theory in the formation of knowledge stimulated the breakdown of expert-local dyads by Stephen Biggs and others (1997, 1998), thus opening up the labelling approach to the idea of more negotiation and contestation.

These post-publication insights have modified my earlier thesis, requiring autocritique. We assumed too much for the state, and were too universalist in our normative expectations of the state as the key authoritative entity in any society. Furthermore, where our empirical knowledge informed us of the problematic state (conceived in both Weberian and Marxian terms), we nevertheless operated within the assumption that the authoritativeness of the state was only a matter of time in societies where it had yet to be reached. These assumptions led us to concentrate, therefore, upon a quintessential 'western' problematic: the inner, hidden workings of the advanced state which purported to operate within a liberal–democratic, pluralist political system underpinning a neo-liberal, welfare state regime. We were overly preoccupied with the Foucauldian perspective (Foucault, 1979) on the de-politicization of legitimate political choice in resource allocation via the activity of technique. Our focus was the penetrative capacity of the state to organize and reorganize the basic societal categories and accompanying ideologies through which ordinary people transacted among themselves in the outer circles of their moral universes.

Thus the arguments drew heavily upon Althusser and Poulantzas, as well as Habermas and Marcuse, who offered a precise critique of the simplistic Marxist proposition which associated the state solely with the interests of the dominant classes in any epoch, especially a capitalist one. That critique proposed, instead, the relative autonomy of the state as an actor within the mode of production, rather than simply a determined function of it. It was this epistemological breakthrough in Marxian thought, with due acknowledgement to Weber and more obviously, Gramsci, which enabled us to ask the 'how' question about the state's penetrative performance, rather than just the 'what' question. The 'relative autonomy' of the state also presumed that the state was not just a slave of market forces in capitalism, but in some way a moderator of such market forces. In other words, it had the power to introduce countervailing allocative rationalities to those of the market. This brings us, now, closer to Polanyi and the subsequent arguments of Esping-Andersen (1990, 1999). But, by acknowledging diversity in the performance of relative autonomy across different versions of capitalism in industrial and post-industrial societies, the way is opened up to examine a wider range of societal types which include the incomplete presence of capitalism in today's transforming or developing societies. This is the way in which the argument needs to move on from the limitations of the original labelling arguments on two fronts: first, the penetrative extent of the authority of the state under, second, conditions of highly imperfect markets (labour, product and financial).

Welfare regimes as rights, claims and correlative duties

Essentially the *power* of labelling and categorization is a dialogue between those in authority (formal and perhaps informal) and those trying to activate rights or make claims on those with the power and authority to dispose of matching resources and services – that is, the performance of correlative duties. In this dialogue, labelling is a rationing and allocation activity, and thus is essentially political. It is a mode of distribution and redistribution, either *simply* reproducing stratification outcomes or *dynamically* reproducing new forms of mobilization and voice, which thus become new constituencies for changing the classification discourse. There is a necessary circularity between rights and correlative duties. Rights are defined by those willing or obliged to provide the correlative duties via a process of authoritative labelling. However, correlative duties can also be defined by those claiming rights when their mobilization into powerful constituencies can make effective demands on those providing correlative duties by undermining the validity of the original 'rights' classification and compelling revised labelling. This is why we must retain an interactionist (Goffman, 1971, 1972) dimension to the analysis of this process. By introducing claims as well as rights into this argument, attention is also drawn to a contrast between formal, statutory relationships, entailing rights and correlative duties, and the more informal processes by which claims are made upon potential service providers. This contrast effectively distinguishes between welfare state regimes and other non-state-centred welfare regimes (informal security and in/security regimes), with 'rights' associated with the former and 'claims' more associated with the latter. Thus 'claims' are not statutory, correlative duties but a range of service responses within a more arbitrary, patron–clientelist structure: voluntarism; reciprocity; patronage; arbitrary discretion.

From this, we can conclude that a 'rights' context features authoritative labelling, operated by bureaucratic rationality and a principle of universalism; whereas although a 'claims' context also entails processes of labelling, the authority of that labelling is exercised more coercively and more particularistically. This is an important adjustment to our original, sole focus upon authoritative labelling and bureaucratic rationality, since it acknowledges that outer circles, while outside of immediate moral intimacy, can nevertheless continue to be managed outside of moral *universals*, and therefore beyond the reach of the state.

A comparative intermediation framework

In this paper, the labelling process is being used as a variable to distinguish between different forms of intermediation between resource controllers and resource/service users. The concept of intermediation is almost a proxy for the notion of welfare regime since it represents the process by which rights or claims are met by correlative duties, or the extent to which they are not met but manipulated and avoided. Intermediation comprises many activities and practices:

- creation of resources and their allocation to different purposes;
- translation of resources into services;
- analysis of need in respect of services;
- elaboration of criteria to differentiate between types and degrees of entitlement to service;
- creation and operation of appellate processes to handle disputes and challenges to the application of such criteria to distinguish between the included and excluded;
- actual disposal of resources via these services;
- monitoring of the effectiveness and impact of such services;
- adjustments to practice in response to feedback from monitoring;
- overall evaluation against wider objectives for generating and operationalizing this aspect of social policy.

Now, while this list of intermediation practices has been presented in rather formal terms, it is important for our overall analysis that we recognize a formal–informal continuum along each of these practice dimensions, and they have to be deconstructed accordingly.

This process of intermediation is central to any understanding of sustained livelihoods involving people negotiating resources within the society's institutional responsibility landscape or matrix (IRM). This concept of the IRM has been elaborated elsewhere (Wood and Newton, 2005; Wood and Gough, 2006), but a summary is required to advance our argument here. The comparative analysis of welfare regimes extends beyond Esping-Andersen's contrast between three different welfare state regimes for rich, advanced countries: social-democratic, conservative and liberal (Esping-Andersen, 1990). Each of these variants reflected differences in the way the state intervenes formally in the society to reduce the impact of unregulated markets on people's livelihoods, through the principle of decommodification. In adapting this approach into a broader comparative understanding of welfare regimes globally (see also Gough and Wood et al, 2004), both the state and market arenas are more problematized, requiring people to rely more upon community and informal clientelism, as well as kinship and households. These arenas comprise the IRM. And, as we know, once we move outside the long established, richer democracies, the state is less respected and legitimate, and therefore less authoritative for ideological purposes and labelling functions. And markets are highly imperfect and socially embedded in arbitrary behaviour rather than commodified: thus, fragmented, segmented, preferential, unstable and insecure. They are less amenable, therefore, to regulation. Under these conditions, a rights-based intermediation process involving consensus about labels triggering social protection and other services is much weaker. Instead a more informal, discretionary claims-based, clientelist intermediation prevails, where the labelling game is less secure for the supplicant players.

This critical perspective about the state in terms of comparative welfare regimes, in which distinctions are made between welfare state regimes, informal security regimes and in/security regimes (Wood and Gough, 2006) thus modifies the assumptions about authoritative labelling in the original labelling arguments. In other words, the intermediation between resource controllers and users has to be understood across the IRM in the contrasting domains of formality/informality, rights/claims and security/ insecurity. Labelling, as a precondition of resource allocation, becomes less authoritative and more contested on the right-hand side of these dyads. The state is less penetrative ideologically, resulting either in more substitute coercion, or less control. And political settlements around the key principles of social policy (e.g. tax funded universal protection with tax clawbacks, or lower tax participation and highly targeted protection) harder to reach and less stable, with rights consequently more fragile. Under these conditions, labelling itself changes from the disguising functions of Foucauldian technique into more politically obvious but less universal classification.

Labelling and social reproduction

The translation of resources into services is a fundamental act of societal construction. How is the basic social contract to be broken down into its constituent elements in a manner that will reproduce what is valued overall in the society? Like the writing of history, what is valued primarily reflects the interests of power holders, and secondarily the compromises they have to make to remain in power. Basic choices exist between forms of social investment in human capital to generate greater resources for the future (education, health, communications infrastructure and so on) and forms of social protection to offset the present destabilizing threats of inequality, poverty and exclusion (social insurance, pensions, employment protection and so on). Even informal security regimes (quasi-democratic, dictatorial and hybrids of state and clientelism) have to have some sense of a social contract, but are likely to be more exposed to the pressures of preferred constituencies in applying particularistic rather than universal criteria, and to be far more constrained in terms of a universal tax base. Such national state weakness opens up the political space for other processes to occur, either in the form of NGOs and other forms of voluntarism, or in the forms of local patronage.[5] At the local level, under such conditions, the blurring of boundaries between a universal service and its particularistic mode of delivery is prevalent. Consider the way access is managed via 'mafia' type intermediation[6] in poor country urban slums to essential public goods like sanitation, electricity, clean water, secure pathways, as well as to educational or employment opportunities.

In formal, open democratic systems, the public creation of resources for designated purposes is the essence of the policy process – a transparent manifestation of a stable, path-dependent political settlement and simple reproduction of the political economy. Resources are generated through various forms of taxation, and thus reflect an element of consent. Purposes are defined through processes of political debate in which some consensus is reached on how much to tax, and who has what entitlements. The labelling of both taxpayers and entitlement recipients is indispensable to these regime functions of market decommodification. However, under other institutional conditions (problematic state, imperfect markets and clientelist political cultures), resources are gathered up more privately and arbitrarily through rents and tributes as well as indirect taxation, and redistributed to meet political objectives, including the reproduction of patron–client forms of power and control. Because of the informality of these processes, they may occur at very local levels of resource generation and redistribution as well as at more regional and national widespread levels. In a strong and unchallenged clientelist system, the inequalities of livelihoods and power are also simply reproduced.

The analysis of need is another element in the social construction of society, and in a welfare state regime comprises a merging of ideology and technique. But in other informal security (or clientelist) welfare regimes, the identification of need and correlative responses to it is more preferential and partial. Any analysis of need (formal or informal) evolves seamlessly into the next stage: elaboration of corresponding qualifying criteria for entitlements and services, either as rights or, less securely, as claims. Any analysis of need is a rationing activity and thus constitutes also the management of scarcity, whether bureaucratic or clientelist. So the concept of 'need' is rarely an untainted, objective view of necessary well-being items for would-be recipients. There is an iterative process between a sense of recipients' potential needs and what is actually available for distribution.

In a welfare state regime characterized by open democracy, that iteration has to be ideologically justified in order to be palatable to both the generators of revenue as well as the recipients of it. If science and technique can support such rationing decisions, then other bases for rationing can be disguised, such as prejudice, ignorance, self-interest, political discrimination and exclusion, gender and ethnic blindness, ageism and so on. Effective disguises increase the universal validity of qualification criteria, and thus reduce the effort required to secure compliance. Appeals, challenges and contestation are reduced, and thus the transaction costs of rationing. Thus, in such systems, science and technique is more available to assist a process of matching qualification criteria to political assumptions and objectives, embedded within basic and usually dominant cultural stances. Most open democratic systems struggle with the boundary between worthy and unworthy, deserving and undeserving. While the rationing rationale may be to sweep as many potential recipients into the unworthy and undeserving categories as possible, this cannot simply be the product or outcome of the prejudices of dominant groups. The Tories under Thatcher tried this with culture of poverty arguments about laziness and circles of deprivation, induced in their minds by over-generous benefits from the state. They, and others on the 'right' of politics, also tried similar formulations with immigrants in different epochs. Such prejudicial behaviour is of course quite generic in different societies and cultures, with constructions of the other being part of self-identity creation. However, for the most part, the Tories could not make the negative labels stick because they could not assemble sufficient supporting science and technique for validation, and attempts to impose such categorization met with increasing contestation and loss of popular political support.

In other political systems, where the authoritativeness and legitimacy of the state is contested, the prospects for science to disguise prejudice are weaker. Almost a tautology. The analysis of need is thus an even more complicated business. Criteria are less explicit, and contestation more likely to be met with force and repression either from the beleaguered state or from power holders outside it. Clearly, constituencies of clients need to be serviced if they are to remain loyal, without being equal in terms of wealth and status, to their patrons who have also captured the state and other organizations in the so-called civil society. Of course, in insecure societies, need is Hegelian as well as Polanyian. It is about secure and orderly conditions for the pursuit of livelihoods and well-being as well as needing protection and/or compensation from the discriminatory practices of imperfect markets. The principle of universalism is more likely to apply to the Hegelian agenda under these circumstances than to the Polanyian one, where the public goods dimension is less evident while the particularistic, individual dependencies are more prominent. This is the basis for favouritism and preferentialism. A sort of mafia model of social policy. Thus, the understanding of need does not occur through formal processes of analysis, but through far more personalized and iterative forms of communicating the relation between dependency and largesse. These societal forms of dependent security, operating through informal relationships outside the state, imitate the welfare state regime in one crucial respect. They are also path-dependent and simply reproducing the political economy, thus earning 'regime' status. Contestation with the state has not translated into contestation with power holders in clientelist structures.

Contestation and dynamic reproduction

Are there more optimistic scenarios in which the authoritative labelling by the state or other power holders outside the state is contested and challenged, or at least deployed in new forms, thus representing new forms of empowerment, heralding prospects for improving the governing conditions for the institutional responsibility landscape? What would indicate such dynamic contestation? Certainly we have to get behind the rhetoric of civil society and trade union or NGO movements which would have us believe in their independence from the state with a corresponding empowerment agenda. There are too many examples across the world where the empowerment claims belie a corporatist or syndicalist process of incorporation of trade union and NGO leaders into elite positions in the society, conspiring in the labelling processes which keep their followers in subservience. At the same time, there is a potential generic contradiction in which the political disorganization of labelling actually produces new forms of organization and solidarities under precisely those imposed labels. This was the purpose of my 'Targets strike back' chapter in the original volume of labelling papers (Wood, 1985c). If the landless were to be organized via that label into rural works labour during the lean agricultural periods of the year in Bangladesh, could they then embrace that label as a vehicle for organizing the promotion and defence of their labour rights to an extent not intended in the original policy instrument which had been about reproducing dependency via state hand-outs – sweat for wheat? Supported as it happens by a combination of Sida and local NGOs, some empowerment progress was made under the new label (Wood, 1994, as well as 1985a). Lest one think this is an old, insignificant example, consider the expansion of the Employment Guarantee Scheme in India as a response to the problem of jobless growth (Luce, 2006; Wood, 2006). This is a major programme of herding disparate, poor rural labour across different parts of India into a single relationship to the state. Can one really imagine that they will stay dispersed and disorganized in such a process? Rather, this has the potential to produce serious levels of contestation and rights claiming (at least until this chapter is read by the nervous in the Indian Planning Commission!). Of course, this potentially mobilized labour solidarity will have to deal with the local-level intermediation processes involving local contractors and preferentialism in recruitment to schemes, alongside the cheating and corruption in the measuring of work and payments therefrom. But the optimistic lesson comes from the proletarianization of labour under the conditions of early industrial capitalism in the West in which the newly formed labour forces eventually organized to resist the exploitative cheating of pre-commodification capitalist employers freshly weaned from slavery in the colonies. It was only much later that they became incorporated.

There are other examples from India. The constitution is replete with labelling, with some progressive intent by the avuncular authors of it. We have seen over the intervening decades how the labels of backward classes, castes and tribes have enabled those belonging to these categories to use the labels imposed upon them as rallying cries to enhance programmes of positive discrimination and affirmative action by the state. The Mandal Commission, reporting in 1990, was a famous example of newly formed solidarities under the inspiration of state labels translating into successful demands for preferential recruitment into the civil service and educational opportunities via reserved places. The 'Backward' caste Yadavs or Goalas in Bihar have successfully deployed their degraded caste label into the basis for entry into public service opportunities across the state, much to the disgust of the 'Forward' castes who have had to surrender their monopoly rents over these positions. Their caste colleague, Laloo Prasad Yadav, has run the state, albeit bizarrely and corruptly, for the last two decades! The 'outcaste' Dalits have shaken off the Harijan label awarded them paternalistically by the high-caste Gandhi, moving from an imposed to a self-asserted label as a vehicle for political mobilization to the point where they cannot be electorally ignored in some Indian states. They can no longer be left out of public social policy, and they are no longer completely trapped into local clientelist domination, although given the continuance of atrocities against them, and especially women, by upper-caste landlords and moneylenders, there is some way to go.

And of course, there are so many further examples of such processes from other parts of the world. Some are highly ironic. Consider the relation between the US government and the Taliban in Afghanistan. A clear association, based on much labelling. Afghan refugees in and around Peshawar, labelled in ways which kept them apart from mainstream entitlements in Pakistan during the 1980s,[7] were constructed into 'freedom fighters' as Mujahuddin embarked upon Jihad and financed to turn them from farmers, traders and teachers into a guerrilla force to fight the US proxy war against Brehznev. Not surprising that their identities and solidarities were consolidated over a decade of intense struggle against the Soviet occupation. And given that 90 per cent of US financial support during that decade went to Gulbuddin Hekmatyar, it is also not surprising[8] that that should translate into the overwhelming Pashtun liberating force which became the Taliban identity – with the accompanying irony of 'Talib' meaning student, but of Madrassas, since mainstream education had been denied them.

In addition to these processes of contestation, where imposed labels are 'turned' against the labellers, we also need to consider the rejection of imposed labels and the assertion of counter-labels. Perhaps the most obvious generic example of this has been the feminist movement worldwide. For many societies, behavioural expectations associated with the category 'women' arising from patriarchal labelling have been successfully challenged and translated into different forms of policy and rights. Of course, most feminists would argue that there is a long way to go, even in those societies that have moved the farthest from the patriarchal image of women. But there can be little doubt of successful counter-labelling to centuries of patriarchal assumptions. The whole policy arena of 'equalities and diversities' in the public sector in the UK, together with anti-discriminatory legislation for compliance by the private sector, is effectively the outcome of extending counter-labelling beyond gender to ethnic minorities, the disabled and sexual orientation. The literature of colonialism and post-colonialism is full of counter-labelling. Today's protest movements over mining, oil extraction, pollution, US domination of IPR, unfair trading practices under the WTO are all examples of misplaced assumptions about ignorant, illiterate, disorganized, acquiescent peasants who were not expected to mobilize against unfair prices, wages and conditions at work.

Such processes of counter-labelling (and other examples are explored in the various chapters of this volume) become the true test of participation. I revert to a conundrum, which I have used in teaching for many years: the good participant is the bad participant, the bad participant is the good participant. The analysis of labelling provides the answer. Thus the measure of true participation is when successful counter-labelling has occurred, so that the less powerful have demonstrated an ability to negotiate the institutional responsibility landscape (state, market, community and household at domestic and global levels) from their own preferred identities and agendas rather than entrapped within the frameworks set by others. Such mobilization thus leads to dynamic rather than simple reproduction of political economy and political culture, since the terms of exchange in the realm of images, ideas and frames of meaning have been changed. Optimistically, this leads to circumstances where formal rights replace informal claims, and thus more security is enjoyed by the vulnerable and poor. But remember, under such conditions, labelling itself has not disappeared. What has been re-arranged is the 'which' and 'whose' labels that prevail in the intermediation between resource controllers and resource users. And under conditions where the state is less legitimate and authoritative and where political settlements around the basic principles of social policy are less stable and secure (non-welfare-state regimes in other words) we can expect less authoritative labelling and greater contestation. The large question that remains is whether such processes of label contestation will eventually lead to stable political settlements about welfare and entitlements in the longer term. Clearly, this has happened strongly in SE Asia and parts of Latin America, though the possibilities of breakdown are always near. Some way to go in South Asia, where much labelling remains outside the state in terms of widespread discriminatory practices and degraded rights. And a long way to go in much of sub-Saharan Africa, where the evidence of state capture by groups and elites is not evidence of stable political settlements for welfare-oriented intermediation (Bevan, 2004; Lockwood, 2005).

Notes

1 Geof Wood, Professor of International Development, Dean of Humanities and Social Sciences, University of Bath, Claverton Down, Bath BA2 7AY, UK. g.d.wood@bath.ac.uk.

2 It is important to acknowledge that these arguments had their origins in debates between myself and Bernard Schaffer. He died in May 1984 before I had drafted the central theoretical chapter of the earlier (1985a) publication. Bernard had supervised my original MPhil thesis on post-colonial administrative training in Zambia, and then I drifted off into Marxism, development anthropology and India/Bangladesh. But we remained very close. He was an intellectual colossus, continuously challenging my dialectical materialism. These labelling debates reconnected our projects – alas not for long enough.

3 A 'para' is an identifiable geographical section of a village, where the families may trace common genealogical descent making some of them intimate to each other, and others more remote by blood but nevertheless acknowledging some bond and identity.

4 Schaffer would have hugely approved of these intellectual developments.

5 And the connection between voluntarism and patronage should not be underestimated.

6 In Bangladesh, the '*mastaan*' are a broker class of intermediaries who operate in the zone between desperate people and their essential livelihoods resources, dominating access to employment, municipal services and so on. They 'run' these slums. Indeed, it is common now to refer to a mastaani system or culture, as being more pervasive across the society, as the dominant form of clientelism.

7 In the original labelling volume, Zetter wrote interestingly about the labelled conditions of the Greek Cypriot refugees who had had to move from the Turkish-held North.

8 Though clearly a surprise to the US military attaché in Pakistan with whom I had an Islamabad dinner in 2002!

References

Bevan, P. (2004) 'The dynamics of Africa's in/security regimes', in I. Gough, G. Wood, with A. Barrientos, P. Bevan, P. Davis and G. Room, *Insecurity and Welfare Regimes in Asia, Africa and Latin America*, Cambridge, Cambridge University Press

Biggs, S. D. and Smith, G. (1997) 'Contending coalitions in agricultural research and development: Challenges for planning and management', *Knowledge and Policy: The International Journal of Knowledge Transfer and Utilization*, vol 10, no 4, pp80–92

Biggs, S. D. and Smith, G. (1998) 'Beyond methodologies: Coalition-building for participatory technology development', *World Development*, vol 26, no 2, pp239–248

Booth, D. (1985) 'Marxism and development sociology: Interpreting the impasse', *World Development*, vol 13, no 7, pp761–787

Esping-Andersen, G. (1990) *The Three Worlds of Welfare Capitalism*, Cambridge, Polity Press

Esping-Andersen, G. (1999) *Social Foundations of Postindustrial Economies*, Oxford, Oxford University Press

Foucault, M. (1979) *History of Sexuality*, London, Allen Lane

Giddens, A. (1984) *The Constitution of Society: An Outline of the Theory of Structuration*, Cambridge, Polity Press

Goffman, E. (1971) *Presentation of Self in Everyday Life*, New York, Pelican

Goffman, E. (1972) *Interation Ritual*, Harmondsworth, Penguin

Gough, I., Wood, G. with Barrientos, A., Bevan, P., Davis, P. and Room, G. (2004) *Insecurity and Welfare Regimes in Asia, Africa and Latin America*, Cambridge, Cambridge University Press

Latour, B. (1987) *Science in Action: How to Follow Scientists and Engineers through Society*, Cambridge, MA, Harvard University Press

Lockwood, M. (2006) *The State They're In*, London, ITDG Publishing

Long, N. (1990) 'From paradigm lost to paradigm regained: The case for an actor-oriented sociology of development', *European Review of Latin American and Caribbean Studies*, vol 49, pp3–24

Long, N. and van der Ploeg, J. D. (1994) 'Heterogeneity, actor and structure: Towards a reconstitution of the concept of structure', in D. Booth (ed) *New Directions in Social Development: Relevance, Realism and Choice*, London, Longmans

Luce, E. (2006) *In Spite of the Gods: The Strange Rise of Modern India*, London, Little Brown

Wood, G. D. (1985a) *Labelling in Development Policy: Essays in Honour of Bernard Schaffer*, London, Sage Publications

Wood, G. D. (1985b) 'The politics of development policy labelling', in G. D. Wood (ed) *Labelling In Development Policy*, London, Sage (and Special Issue of *Development and Change*, vol 16, pp347–373, July 1985)

Wood, G. D. (1985c) 'Targets strike back', in G. D. Wood (ed) *Labelling In Development Policy*, London, Sage (and Special Issue of *Development and Change*, vol 16, pp347–373)

Wood, G. D. (1994) *Bangladesh: Whose Ideas, Whose Interests?* London, IT Publishers

Wood, G. D. (2006) 'The poverty of security: A problem for well-being and work', presented to the UN Expert Group Meeting on Full Employment and Decent Work, New York, 10–12 October

Wood, G. D. and Gough, I. (2006) 'A comparative welfare regime approach to global social policy', *World Development*, vol 34, pp1696–1712

Wood, G. D. and Newton, J. (2005) 'From welfare to well-being regimes: Engaging new agendas', presented to the Global Issues in Social Policy Conference, Arusha, Tanzania, December, World Bank Environment and Social Development Division

2

Labelling People For Aid

Rosalind Eyben

Introduction

Fearing those who bring gifts includes worrying about being the object of another's attention. In this chapter I explore why and how recipients have been objectified in the world of international aid – what Apthorpe calls 'Aidland' (2003)[1] – and look at the history and current status of efforts to change how aid bureaucracies conceptualize their intended beneficiaries.

I consider the efforts made during the last three decades by some Aidlanders (including myself) to first introduce the idea of 'target populations' and then seek to get rid of it. I discuss how and why bureaucracy 'bit back', once again converting subjects into objects furnished through our own efforts with the additional material we had provided by insisting that poor people were not a single homogeneous target. My mistake, at least, had been to focus on categories rather than relations in the world of aid, thus unintentionally strengthening the objectification process.

Drawing on the lessons learnt from the boomerang effect of the previous efforts to shift Aidland's perceptions of intended aid beneficiaries from objects to subjects,[2] I came to the conclusion that social analysis in development programmes will fail to tackle the fundamental issues of power and inequality, typified by such objectification, unless the analyst turns her attention from what aid does to how it works. This means studying and seeking to change the bureaucratic organizations engaged in delivering aid for development. This paper explores the current challenges and opportunities in that respect, identifying some pointers towards the kinds of processes that a concerned change agent might want to support and magnify.

The modern forms of aid bureaucracies both shaped and were shaped by the relations between the colonial powers and the countries they were ruling. Perhaps, this time with a less oppressive agenda, the descendants of the old colonial ministries may take a lead in developing new forms of public sector organizations that carry within them possibilities for achieving international aid's objectives of greater social justice.

The perils and pitfalls of advocating differentiation

Target populations: My Sudanese experience

Although 'targeting' is a very popular concept in aid bureaucracies, 'target population' has become a relatively unfashionable phrase because a generation of practitioners, including myself, objected to the term, pointing out that 'targets' were something you shot at. However, 30 years ago it was an innovative phrase that I learnt from the development literature and introduced into the first aid project on which I was employed. I worked hard for several years to persuade my colleagues that to reach our target population we had to change what the project did and where it worked. Thus labelling was a central concern in my first development experience.

The United Nations Development Programme (UNDP) and United Nations Children's Fund (UNICEF) were funding the International Labour Organization (ILO) to implement in Sudan a government vocational training project for unemployed school dropouts and those who had never been to school. It had been designed at the time when 'meeting basic needs' was the language of poverty reduction and this project's aim was to do something about reducing poverty. At the height of the project, there were training centres in 20 towns throughout Sudan. The hope was that the trainees would subsequently find gainful employment or become successful self-employed entrepreneurs. However, until I was hired as the project's first research officer, no effort had been made to find out whether we were reaching our 'target'. This is what I set out to remedy.

During British rule, Sudanese towns had been developed or redeveloped into four classes of housing. These were distinguished by the range of services provided (electricity, water, paved streets) ranging from first class where were located the spacious bungalows of the colonial civil servants and their Sudanese administrative successors to fourth class with flimsy straw or mud houses occupied by street traders, domestic servants and so forth. On the fringes of the town were squatter areas with even flimsier housing. I discovered that these had transient populations with people coming in from rural areas to look for work in the town during the dry season and going back to their farms when rains were due. At regular intervals, these unclassified areas were subjected to a bulldozer dispatched by the urban administration.

On investigating whom the project was training, I found it was largely young people with a secondary education living in first- and second-class housing areas. This was not surprising bearing in mind that each training centre had been built close to the town's administrative offices that were themselves always in the first-class housing area. On the other hand, our target population (in terms of educational attainments) was living in third- and fourth-class areas and the squatter camps. My medium-term objective was to move the physical location of each training centre to a fourth-class area as well as for the project to offer in temporary sub-centres in the unclassified housing areas courses aimed at the dry-season squatters. However, in the short term I persuaded (or bullied) the centre managers to make strenuous efforts to stop recruiting trainees from among their own neighbours and relatives and recruit from the poorer parts of town. I felt that until the project managed to reach its target population we were failing in accountability to our donors – UNDP and UNICEF – who had funded us on the assumption we would have a poverty focus. Significantly, I was much less concerned about failing the citizens of Sudan – or indeed the Ministry of Youth and Sports that hosted the project.

I developed a complex monitoring and reporting system to check that centre directors were following my instructions. If I could not be present at the moment of enrolment for new courses, one of my research assistants subsequently interviewed each registered trainee as to their level of schooling, their parents' occupation and their place of residence. Training centres with the highest proportion of the target population were commended by the Project Manager, and the recalcitrant scolded. I introduced the concept of 'poverty' into the project discourse. This meant looking for *thin* trainees in *shabby* clothes. On several occasions, I sat with a centre director at a recruiting session so that this type of applicant received priority. Disjuncture was uncomfortable. On one evening in Kordofan, a group of young women arrived to enrol at the centre. They were plump and cheerful, well-dressed, their arms covered with gold bangles. Definitely non-eligible until the centre director, eager to demonstrate the folly of my classificatory system, gleefully pointed out that none of these plump applicants could read and write and they all lived in a fourth-class housing area.

Geof Wood (this volume), commenting on that era, remarks that while targeting by people like me on the poorest appeared to be progressive, in the context of mass poverty it could be understood as regressive because of all the others it excluded. Indeed, this was the view of my project colleagues. The Sudanese training centre directors and my fellow expatriate 'technical' ILO colleagues equally complained that the new category of trainees I insisted on recruiting were unable to benefit from the curriculum and lacked the financial capital to use their newly acquired skills. My answer was that we had to change the curriculum to respond to the needs of illiterate people and to set up micro finance programmes and mini cooperatives for those completing training. The project became the biggest UNDP programme (in terms of budget) in Sudan.

Meanwhile, however, I discovered that my target population (at least the male part) was actually acquiring vocational skills more satisfactorily elsewhere. This was through informal apprenticeship arrangements in the industrial zone of every Sudanese town. Here, everyday household furniture was made and ancient lorries were repaired by illiterate but experienced artisans. By the time I left Sudan, I had reached the conclusion that the whole project had been a waste of time and money! On the other hand, it did not occur to me that the project might have had some utility for some young more educated people living in the first-class housing areas if ILO had never employed me to help the project reach its 'target population'.[3]

I continued to see the need to define and classify 'the poor', in the firm belief that without such effort the benefits of international aid would all go to the haves rather than the have-nots. In the 1970s the rationale for aid was largely in terms of helping less developed countries 'catch up' through technology and skills transfer. Thus for my ILO project colleagues, experts in metalworking or dressmaking, the issue of who got the chance to acquire those skills was largely irrelevant. And in the 1980s, when economists set the agenda, the case for reaching poor people was a largely disregarded alternative agenda to the prevailing theory of trickle-down.

For utilitarian economists everyone's utility gets the same weight in the maximizing exercise of the greatest happiness for the greatest number. No distinctions are made between individuals, symbolized by Bentham's famous panopticon 'a weapon against difference' (Bauman, 1998, cited in Wittel, 2001, p60). Thus it was difficult to persuade aid bureaucracies there *were* differences: that there were poor people and rich people; men and women; adults and children; until the 1990s, marked by an explosion of interest in differentiating intended beneficiaries. I now turn to that decade and discuss how, through the efforts of social analysts, such as myself when working as a social development adviser for DFID, the increased interest in differential beneficiary impact produced the unintended consequence of reinforcing the 'categorical imperative'.

From standardization to differentiation and back again

Poverty returned as a central issue in Aidland following the discrediting of structural adjustment policies in the 1980s – the 'lost decade' when aid-recipient governments were encouraged to cut government budgets, introduce user fees for social services and cut subsidies on basic goods and food supplies. Aidland began to learn about vulnerability and to understand that when there are shocks to the political economy those with least voice and least economic assets are the most severely affected. It appeared that structural reform of the economy was not sufficient for all people to move out of poverty, that some additional steps are required for that to happen.

Thus in the 1990s, as part of the wider currents of the time, civil society activists from the southern and northern regions of Aidland found the political space to promote categories of gender, age, disability and ethnicity as significant new ways of talking and thinking about 'putting people at the centre of development'.[4] Framed in terms of participation, empowerment and rights-based approaches, this achievement was to make visible the invisible in an effort to give voice to the voiceless. Hence, DFID's first White Paper stated that that one quarter of the world's population continues to live in extreme poverty, feeling 'isolated and powerless and often ... excluded by ethnicity, caste, geography, gender or disability' (DFID, 1997, p10).

Yet, bureaucracy has an extraordinary power for 'absorbing and turning knowledge to ends of its own' (Strathern, 2000, p291). By pointing out to the econometricians that people as well as countries should be differentiated, social analysts offered them the opportunity to classify, map, count and compare more different units of abstraction. We had created a boomerang effect. From inside the agency I became, for a time, complicit in that process.[5] It seemed the only way to get on to the agenda support to programmes that might bring benefits to poor people.

These categories of people became reified and subjected to measurement. Yet, those most interested in quantifying and measuring these categories were friends, not foes. These were the more radical economists in the bureaucracy who genuinely shared with social analysts a concern about poverty and inequality. Apthorpe (1996, citing Nyamwaya) comments that social analysts, just as much as development economists, identify social groups that may exist only in the imagination of the analyst. He suggests that social analysts are not necessarily unaware of the thin-ness and partiality of their descriptions, but are constrained by what Aidland bureaucracies are prepared to accept. I agree. Nevertheless, by insisting that difference is important – that how people live and make meaning of their lives is not necessarily the same in a Brazilian favela as in a Zambian mining town – social analysts made those people visible, but could not give them flesh and blood. They stayed as two-dimensional target populations, exposed to objectification and measurement, thin in description and thick in prescription (Apthorpe, 2003).

Thus, the 'poor', absent from the gaze of the World Bank in the 1980s, became the central focus for much of its regression analysis in the 1990s and 2000s. Previously 'invisible' women also started to appear because women's movements pressured for disaggregation of statistics. And what was defined as ethnic conflict in the years after the end of Communism led to an interest in exploring and measuring 'horizontal inequalities' (Stewart, 2002). Confusion and misunderstanding developed when econometricians used the term 'group', sometimes in terms of their own categories and sometimes as defined by sociologists, as a collection of people who in a particular context recognize themselves as having something in common. The bureaucratic drive for reductionism makes it difficult to communicate such a seemingly subtle point. Fluidity of identity is a problem for development practice because 'If group differences are to provide a useful basis for policy, group boundaries must be relatively clearly defined and have continuity over time' (Stewart, 2002, p6).

Complexity and diversity evade easy classification and are thus unwelcome in any bureaucracy, but the beneficiaries of aid agencies find it more difficult to object to the labels given them than those of public-sector bureaucracies in democratic regimes. Over the last decade DFID social development advisers have informally reported that people in aid-recipient countries do not like being described as 'poor' and that it is not a category around which people tend to organize themselves (Cornwall and Fujita, this volume). This information has not only been ignored but hints have been dropped by DFID's senior management that it is unwelcome.

Bureaucracies label people not only for allocative or fiscal efficiency. Labelling is linked to politicians' desire to keep issues simple. When working in Bolivia (2000–2002) I was responsible for drafting DFID's country strategy. To justify why Bolivia needed aid, this document had to include a basic description of the country with appropriate 'facts and figures'.

In Latin America the category 'Indian' was invented by European colonialism for fiscal purposes (Wilson, 2000), hiding the complexity and leaving indigenous populations with a diminished, uncertain social identity (Varese, 1989). Today, in Bolivia, census takers – recognizing the complexity of labels such as 'mestizo' or 'chola' – have started to ask people to categorize themselves rather than submit to predetermined classification schemes. Thus, aware of the trap of complexity but wishing to avoid essentialism, I wrote in my first draft of the country strategy:

> *There is conflicting data concerning the proportion of the population which is perceived/ perceives itself as 'indigenous'. According to UNDP it is 60%. While many Bolivians firmly believe in a society that is a single but multicultural and multi-ethnic nation, as expressed in the 1994 Constitution, others believe that Bolivia remains a dual society. The development of ethnic politics within the peasant movement became much more explicit in the 1990s.*

The then Secretary of State for International Development, Clare Short, told me this was not satisfactory and it was *not an issue of perception*. She required that I provide a concrete *figure* of the proportion of the population that was *actually* indigenous. As I felt this was impossible, I resolved the issue, at least to my own satisfaction, by redrafting the text. The published version simply notes that 'People of indigenous, pre-Colombian descent (the majority) incur a greater risk of remaining in poverty' (DFID, 2002, p2).

In this instance, despite Short's insistence that country strategy papers should be written to be read by people in aid-recipient countries, my experience suggests that she wanted to have at her fingertips some quick facts that can be used in answering Parliamentary Questions. Not just superficial categorization, but much of civil service practice responds to this pressure for making things simple. When I was a new civil servant, I was told that what cannot be written on one side of paper is not worth writing. While the search for simplicity is common to all public sector bureaucracies, aid organizations' extreme distance from the lives of their target populations and the inability for such populations to engage directly with the bureaucrats makes it particularly easy to construct a world of fantasy that suits politicians. The reluctance of aid officials to expose themselves to lives of poor people may possibly be explained by the fear of messy reality intruding into the planners' vision of how the world *should* be (Irvine et al, 2006).

Bureaucracies strike back?

Much of the effort by civil society activists, academics and their allies inside the bureaucracy to make different categories of people visible to aid agencies concerned getting the issue on the agenda. What took us by surprise was how it was then captured and converted into something else. In an interesting analysis on the difference between agenda setting and problem definition, Dery (2000) discusses how those in power learn and adapt in order to maintain the status quo, and the mechanisms they employ:

> It would thus seem that the political process does one thing when it determines whether or not an expressed public concern ... is an issue that deserves government attention, and quite another when it determines how the same issue will be conceptualized and how subsequent action, or inaction, may be legitimized. (Dery, 2000, p39)

Thus, our placing the subjects of aid on the agenda did not prevent the guardians of the status quo of Aidland from turning these subjects into new labels, exciting toys for further cross-country regression analysis. One contributory factor may have been the wider context of the 1990s with the growing popularity of 'targeted governance' linked to efficient, apolitical, evidence-based New Public Management. 'Targeted governance is ... highly optimistic in believing that good information can and will be collected to enable managers of all types to target their organisations' resources efficiently and with maximum benefit' (Valverde and Mopas, 2004, p246).

Wood (this volume) argues that public-sector bureaucracies evolved historically to allocate scarce goods. Thus, targeting may always be present, even within social policy regimes where certain benefits are universal rather than targeted. However, the question remains whether there are certain political and cultural conditions under which bureaucracies are capable of being informed more by relational requirements than by 'substantialist' concerns about the units or elements in the system.[6] This would mean shifting focus from allocation of scarce resources among differently labelled categories of people to a consideration of how best to support equitable relationships between people *without any a priori need for essentialist classification*. This would be a move from a distributional emphasis upon ensuring that people obtain access to goods and services to a relational emphasis upon guarding against social exclusion.

Bureaucratic organizations are arguably capable of a relational emphasis when they implement social welfare regimes that support solidaristic rather than individualistic approaches, for example in the case of blood donation, which is premised on giving a gift to a stranger.[7] Can *aid* bureaucracies make such a shift? How could we tell if an aid bureaucracy moves from a more categorical to a more relational approach to its activities? To answer this question, we must first consider what makes aid bureaucracies different from the wider category of public-sector bureaucracy.

In the next section I propose five characteristics that make aid bureaucracies different:

1   They are in a gift relationship with recipients of the resources they manage.
2   They are the generic heirs of colonial bureaucracies with a bigger spatial and social distance between them and the people they are administering.
3   Specific problems of racism remain unrecognized and unaddressed.
4   They are largely unaccountable to their clients – citizens of aid-recipient countries.
5   They often have an idealized understanding of their own organization and thus are particularly resistant to change.

The special characteristics of aid bureaucracies that reinforce the power of labelling

Thinking back on my time as a social analyst in Aidland, I reflect on my own appalling self-righteousness, the tolerance of my Sudanese, Indian and so many other developing-country colleagues – and their lack of choice in being polite about the way I was throwing my weight around. The aid relationship appears to be conducive to this kind of behaviour (Crewe and Harrison, 1998) and I have discussed elsewhere how the nature of a gift can imbue its donor with a moral righteousness absent from a more contractual (market-based) or entitlement relationship (Eyben, 2006a). The irony is that although modern bureaucratic systems are so significant in Aidland (and development itself is a modernist project), because aid is primarily a gift, much of our behaviour is shaped by 'pre-modern' social relationships best described as patronage.

It is noteworthy how the aid relationship is administered as a gift (dressed up by economists as a contract) by organizations that owe their history to the development of modern bureaucracy – which evolved in Europe simultaneously and not coincidentally with Europe's colonization of the rest of the world (Anderson, 1991).

Ideally, modern public-sector bureaucracy is an organization constructed on rational principles with staff recruited on the grounds of technical competency, making objective decisions concerning the greatest good for the greatest number. All bureaucracies construct systems of classification and quantify the units thus classified (Handelman,1995; Anderson, 1991). Colonial bureaucracies were, however, rather special, as they regarded people in the colonies differently from how their domestic counterparts treated people back home. Categories were abstract, not flesh-and-blood people. At home, especially as the working class captured political space, these units of accounting became also citizens with rights and entitlements. In the colonies this moderation of the bureaucratic process was absent.

It led to compartmentalization of attitudes within the public administration so that there was a 'disidentification' with the object of administration (De Swaan, 1997). Social and spatial distance allowed a process of 'othering' to take place.

The term 'othering' refers to the process whereby a dominant group defines into existence a subordinate group, for example, when an aid agency classifies its target population according to criteria that the people themselves would not employ. This process entails the invention of categories and of ideas about what marks people as belonging to these categories. By means of this 'objectification', those doing it can regard the moral rules of social relationships as inapplicable to those objectified (Schwalbe et al, 2000).

The process of 'othering' in the relationship between colonizer and colonized thus produced an extreme, unmoderated form of bureaucracy. Aid bureaucracies still sustain many of the old compartmentalizing attitudes. Until there is an open public recognition of development's historical amnesia such attitudes are likely to be sustained, even if more open to challenge by staff from recipient countries recruited into senior positions.

There is a very small but growing literature that attempts to explore the issue of race and development from the perspective of the practitioner (Noxolo, 1999; White, 2002; Goudge, 2003; Baaz, 2005; Crewe and Fernando, 2006). Noxolo, as a British black aid worker in Ghana, found herself in an ambiguous position of sometimes being ascribed whiteness and sometimes blackness. From the latter perspective she observed that white development practitioners were accorded privileges which they did not even notice as such. She refers to their racialized assumption that their knowledge is the universal knowledge, what she calls 'whiteness as "passepartout knowledge"' (Noxolo, 1999, p27). From interviews with DFID staff in the Caribbean she comments on their attempts 'not to be racist' but being forced within the bounds of the discourses to draw on racialized structures.

Next, compared with domestic line departments such as health or education, aid bureaucracies are unusual in the sense that their intended beneficiaries are neither citizens nor residents whose citizenship and taxation would in theory give them an 'organic' stake in the performance of government agencies and officials. On the contrary, they are very much outside of the public revenue streams on which claims for accountability and entitlement are commonly based. Despite the last decade's efforts at participatory consultation, an agency's goals remain ethnocentric in the sense that they must appeal to the public in the donor rather than the recipient country (Ufford, 1988).

Finally, aid bureaucrats idealize their own domestic bureaucracies into impartial rules-based organizations that make decisions on the basis of 'objective' evidence, and encourage recipient governments to reform and 'skip straight to Weber' (Pritchett and Woolcock, 2002). It is a case of 'do as we say' rather than 'do as we do back home'. Many aid bureaucrats may find themselves believing that this ideal representation is actually how they work, thus reinforcing resistance to suggestions that *they* need to change in order to meet their organizational goals.

Bearing all these characteristics in mind, what steps could be taken by those who see the current power of labelling as an obstacle to development? This is the subject of the following section, where I consider the generic characteristics of a formal organization that favours a relational rather than categorical approach and then look at the specific challenges and opportunities for change within Aidland.

Changing from a categorical to a relational approach

What would a relational approach look like?

The co-editor of this volume asked me what, with the benefit of hindsight, would I have done differently in that youth training programme in Sudan. The answer emerged during the 1980s with a growth among aid practitioners of interest in participatory approaches to development that could provide space for people to label themselves, rather than be labelled. Books like *Farmer First* (Chambers et al, 1989) influenced me to build on what I had already learnt when studying the informal apprenticeship system in Sudan, and promote approaches that support what people were already doing. Participatory approaches also changed my perspective on accountability so that 'the primary stakeholders' were no longer the donors but the people living in poverty for whom aid programmes existed.

Participatory approaches for any bureaucracy, including aid bureaucracies, require a shift in how it understands societal change, an openness to a diversity of views, and a preparedness to experiment, take risks and learn to change its mind. It diminishes its concern for orderliness, classification, effectiveness and rules, and strengthens its concern to be accountable to its diverse stakeholders, while facilitating deliberation among them (Bohman, 2000).

A category-based approach to aid is associated with understanding societal change as a linear progression in which specific causes produce specific effects. This paradigm of change, derived from the 'Newtonian' scientific model, assumes that it is possible to gain sufficient knowledge to engineer the desired result. Classification is a key instrument in securing that knowledge. This is the basis of conventional economics. The premise that society is a predictable machine provides an illusion of being in control and encourages governments to imagine they have more power than they actually do, often with unintended and unhelpful consequences (Ormerod, 1998).

In contrast the premise of complexity theory,[8] which is replacing the mechanistic paradigm in the natural sciences and is increasingly influencing the social sciences, is that change commonly occurs through self-organization of system elements that are in communication with each other. Anyone's diagnosis of a problem and its solution(s) is necessarily *partial*, because the information they possess about the complex system will be limited, and prior conceptions of how change happens will influence their knowledge.[9]

To overcome this problem of partial knowledge, a relational aid bureaucracy would need to recognize that unequal power relations in communicative interactions can result in one perspective or knowledge being privileged over others (Stacey and Griffin, 2005). It would want to facilitate and participate as just one stakeholder in processes that allow a deliberative dialogue on equal terms among diverse voices and understandings (Cornwall, 2004). Such aid bureaucracies would recognize that they might alleviate misery and promote social justice more effectively by taking small steps based on negotiation (Lindblom, 1990; Scott, 1999).

Exploring the relevance of complexity theory to the practice of UK government domestic machinery, Geyer (2003, p254) suggests that responsible political judgements require:

- respecting otherness and difference as values in themselves;
- gathering as much information as possible on the issue, notwithstanding the fact that it is impossible to gather all the information;
- considering as many of the possible consequences of the judgement, notwithstanding the fact that it is impossible to consider all the consequences;
- making sure that it is possible to revise the judgement as soon as it becomes clear that it has flaws, whether it be under specific circumstances or in general.

This would require bureaucracies to embrace a 'never-ending inconclusiveness' (Lindblom, 1990, p216), where issues are never resolved but regularly reframed, reviewed and renegotiated. Successful policy making would be understood not as the collection and control of 'objective evidence' but as building trust through active participation in collective action and problem solving (Hajer and Wagenaar, 2003), and providing space and resources for open-ended and challenging agendas to enter the debate (Long, 2004).

Implications for aid agencies

Are aid agencies moving in this direction? The current climate of targeted governance with results-based management, combined with an increase in the growth of horizontal but often exclusionary global networks, does not at first glance provide a conducive environment for reducing the power of labelling.

The profile of staff in aid bureaucracies is also changing. Those with long experience of working in Aidland are being replaced by New Public Management administrators with even less interest than their predecessors in contacting the messiness and complexity of the lives of their intended beneficiaries. There is little current evidence of top managements supporting any validation of the processes where 'before the rationality of choice comes the prior practical rationality of careful attention, careful listening, setting out issues and exploring working relationships as pragmatic aspects of problem construction' (Hajer and Wagenaar, 2003, p22, citing Forester, 1999).

At the same time, there is an increasing trend towards negotiating policy within informal transnational networks (Wedel et al, 2005). Here an individual may one day be an employee of the International Monetary Fund (IMF) and the next Minister of Finance in his (recipient) country of origin, while on the donor side an ambitious official will seek to move seamlessly between domestic and aid policy arenas. There is a distancing from the intended aid beneficiaries, expressed less in terms of formal bureaucratic 'othering' but more by constructing ideal visions of how Aidland should be, without checking how it might appear to the majority of the people who by no choice of their own find themselves living there.

However, the picture is far from negative. Some other processes are occurring which those seeking to reduce the power of labelling could seek to support and strengthen. The first of these is *growing spaces for deliberative policy making*. Concerns about more democratic processes and voice in Aidland's decision-making processes are growing. Ten years ago, the Organisation for Economic Co-operation and Development (OECD) Development Assistance Committee and its working groups reached decisions about aid policy by communicating with its members only. Today, it is routine to include a wider representation of spokespersons from recipient governments and civil society. The growing authority and weight of large countries living on the boundaries of Aidland, such as India, China, Brazil and South Africa, oblige donor governments and their aid agencies to start looking at the world from other perspectives.

Second, although there is a post-festivity hangover after the euphoria of the 1990s when *participation, empowerment and rights-based approaches* appeared to be successfully mainstreamed, some of the changes in understanding and attitudes from that time continue to be present and communicated to the next generation of aid bureaucrats.

The current emphasis on *country leadership* or ownership with broad-based consultation provides the possibility of including multiple voices and different perspectives on the problem of poverty.

There is a process of appointing many *more senior officials from recipient countries* than before. Indisputably, one's national origin does not necessarily imply a different perspective on the world (a fallacy of staff diversity policies), particularly if recruited from a cosmopolitan, transnational elite. Nevertheless, this trend certainly increases the likelihood of validating different ways of classifying and ordering the world and its populations.

While most research in recipient countries is still funded by donors, at least they are financing publications that highlight the problem of *whose* knowledge counts, and there are more active *efforts to give a stronger voice to the recipient party in research and knowledge programmes.* Similarly, there is increased interest in monitoring the implementation of programmes through *stakeholder accountability tools* such as social accounting or joint donor–recipient evaluations.

Finally, there is an *increasing recognition that the aid relationship has a history.* Connecting with the historical landscape of power[10] from which current practice has developed enriches our understanding and offers greater possibility of changing and of re-establishing relationships on a more honest footing.

All these trends offer the potential for aid bureaucracies to change to a more relational approach. However, more needs to be done. One measure is to expand timeframes of aid interventions so that recipients can define their situation and identify the labels that best suit them. The second is to challenge the definition of success and expand the understanding that aid workers can make a difference not only through formal targeted interventions, but through the relationships and influence they have on others. The third is directly exposing the issues of power and racism that characterize many of the daily relations in Aidland.

Conclusion

To be part of the solution we must recognize ourselves as part of the problem. I started this paper with a personal story and considered why labelling people was such an important part of what I then understood to be my task as a social analyst in Aidland. I followed this by considering certain aspects of the objectification process in Aidland. One was related to the general characteristic of modern bureaucracy to classify, simplify and measure. The other was connected with the various extreme features of aid bureaucracies, including their social and spatial distance from the objects of their labelling, their subordination to a single epistemic community of positivist thought, and the unequal power relations of the donor–recipient 'gift' relationship. All these make labelling in development, as distinct from normal bureaucratic practice, something special and arguably more pernicious. That donors and recipients are primarily in a gift relationship, with all its pre-modern ambiguities and contradictions, may offer one possible, unexpected avenue for regarding the ultimate beneficiary of aid no longer as 'object' but 'subject'. There are also opportunities (as well as dangers) in the new interpretative and deliberative approaches to policy making.

I have suggested that the current trends towards horizontal networking are influencing the bureaucratic forms of policy and practice observable in government aid organizations, but not sure whether for good or for ill. These trends may encourage aid organizations to learn more modesty about what it is possible to know and do, possibly resulting in greater receptiveness to dialogue beyond potentially exclusionary networks.

Networking provides opportunities if coalitions of those in positions of influence in Aidland (in both donor and recipient countries) encourage aid organizations to reinforce the potentially positive processes I have listed above, under 'Implications for aid agencies'. However, progress is likely to be through small steps and by a gradual shifting of understanding, rather than by any radical change for the better.

Finally, one more point about how I could have behaved differently as a young aid worker 30 years ago in Sudan. Then, I was full of missionary zeal. I never interrogated the foundations of my own knowledge and wisdom. Nor did I question the prerogatives that my whiteness and my expert status gave me. Perhaps one of the most important, yet most neglected, means for aid bureaucracies to voluntarily reduce their power of labelling and objectifying other people would be to encourage their staff to develop the capacity for reflection.

Notes

1   I am grateful to Raymond Apthorpe for his helpful comments on an earlier draft of this chapter.

2   By 'subject' I mean someone we understand and relate to as a complete human being like ourselves, as distinct from an 'objectified' other. Thus I am using the term in a quite different way from 'subject' in the sense of being subjected to authority (for example, 'colonial subjects') or to Foucault's disciplinary power.

3   Interestingly, when I made a brief visit to Khartoum nearly a decade later, I found the project head office still in existence with a skeleton staff of erstwhile colleagues. I was immediately taken to a room full of carefully kept box files stuffed with the many varieties of monitoring forms I had created.

4   It can of course be argued that our proposals for new categories were a means for social development specialists to assert influence and get promoted, because our technical expertise would be required to decide who was poor, indigenous or whatever. See Ufford's point that the definitions relevant for policy making 'do not change primarily because of new insights but because of successful penetrations into the arenas which determine access to funding (Ufford, 1988, p20).

5   I use my own personal experience here because I cannot speak for others and this account is an ex-post reflection.

6   See Emirbayer (1997) for this distinction. Substantialism is concerned with substances – elements or units; the relations between them are of secondary importance. Relational theorists, on the

other hand, consider individuals as inseparable from the relational contexts in which they are embedded. They reject the primacy of attributional categories and other substantives in favour of dynamic 'processes in relations' (Emirbayer, 1997, p298).

7   As Leadbetter (1997) points out in a review of Titmuss' classic work, of course it is not so simple. The bureaucracy of the welfare state can be a 'soulless system for shuffling round resources'.

8   Complexity theory postulates that change is emergent rather than predetermined. Organized efforts to direct it completely confront the impossibility of our ever understanding the totality of a system in constant flux. The system, composed of innumerable elements continuously shaped and reformed through interaction, is constantly creating new elements that in turn may affect (loop back) and change the existing ones. Thus we cannot predict all the effects that any of our actions may have on the wider system, or indeed on ourselves as initiators of the action. Small 'butterfly' actions may have a major impact and apparently significant ones may have very little (see Eyben, 2006b).

9   On the other hand there are formal organizations, for example the Catholic Church, where a relational approach (i.e. a concern for social cohesion and inclusion) is *not* associated with recognition that its knowledge is partial and limited.

10   I am indebted to Pfohl (2004) for this turn of phrase.

References

Anderson, B. (1991) (revised edition) *Imagined Communities: Reflection on the Origins and the Spread of Nationalism*, London, Verso

Apthorpe, R. (1996) 'Reading development policy and policy analysis: On framing, naming, numbering and coding', *European Journal of Development Research*, vol 8, no 1, pp16–35

Apthorpe, R. (2003) 'Virtual reality: An allegory of international aid-land and its peoples', unpublished paper presented at the Conference 'Order and Disjuncture', SOAS, September

Baaz, M. E. (2005) *The Paternalism of Partnership. A Post-colonial Reading of Identity in Development Aid*, London, Zed Books

Bauman, Z. (1998) *Globalisation: The Human Consequences*, Cambridge, Polity Press

Bohman, J. (2000) *Public Deliberation, Pluralism and Democracy*, Cambridge, MA, MIT Press

Chambers, R., Pacey, A. and Thrupp, A. L. (1989) *Farmer First: Farmer Innovation and Agricultural Research*, London, Intermediate Technology Publications

Chapman, J. (2002) *System Failure: Why Governments Must Learn to Think Differently*, London, Demos

Cornwall, A. (2004) 'New democratic spaces? The politics and dynamics of institutionalised participation', Introduction to *IDS Bulletin*, vol 35 no 2, pp1–10

Courpasson, D. and Reed, M. (2004)   'Introduction: Bureaucracy in the age of enterprise', *Organisation*, vol 11, no 1, pp5–12

Crewe, E. and Fernando, P. (2006) 'The elephant in the room: Racism in representations, relationships and rituals', *Progress in Development Studies*, vol 6, no 1, pp40–54

Crewe, E. and Harrison, E. (1998) *Whose Development? An Ethnography of Aid*, London, Zed Books

De Swaan, Abram (1997) 'Widening circles of disidentification: On the psycho-and sociogenesis of the hatred of distant strangers – reflections on Rwanda', *Theory, Culture & Society*, vol 14, no 2, pp105–122

Department for International Development (1997) *The Elimination of World Poverty*, Government White Paper, London, Stationery Office

Department for International Development (2002) *Bolivia. Country Strategy Paper*, London, DFID

Dery, D. (2000) 'Agenda setting and problem definition', *Policy Studies*, vol 21, no 1, pp37–48

Ellison, N. (2000) 'Civic subjects or civic agents?', *Theory, Culture & Society*, vol 17, no 2, pp148–156

Emirbayer, M. (1997) 'Manifesto for a relational sociology', *American Journal of Sociology*, vol 103, no 2, pp281–317

Eyben, R. (2006a) 'The power of the gift and the new aid modalities', *IDS Bulletin*, vol 36, p6

Eyben, R. (2006b) 'Making relationships matter for aid bureaucracies', in R. Eyben (ed) *Relationships for Aid*, London, Earthscan, pp63–79

Foucault, M. (1979) *Discipline and Punish*, Harmondsworth, Penguin Books

Gerth, H. and Mills, C. (1948) *From Max Weber: Essays in Sociology*, London, Kegan Paul, Trench, Trubner & Co.

Geyer, R. (2003) 'Beyond the third way: The science of complexity and the politics of choice', *British Journal of Politics and International Relations*, vol 5, no 2, pp237–257

Goudge, P. (2003) *The Power of Whiteness*, London, Lawrence and Wishart

Hajer, M. and Wagenaar, H. (eds) (2003) *Deliberative Policy Analysis, Understanding Governance in the Network Society*, Cambridge, Cambridge University Press

Handelman, D. (1995) 'Putting power into the anthropology of bureaucracy', *Current Anthropology*, vol 36, no 2, pp280–281

Hare, L. (1981) *Bentham and Bureaucracy*, Cambridge, Cambridge University Press

Irvine, R., Chambers, R. and Eyben, R. (2006) 'Learning from poor people living in poverty: Learning from immersions', in R. Eyben (ed) *Relationships for Aid*, London, Earthscan

Leadbetter, C. (1997) 'The gift relationship: From human blood to social policy, review of republication of R. Titmuss', 'The gift relationship', *New Statesman*, 18 July

Lindblom, C. (1990) *Inquiry and Change: The Troubled Attempt to Understand and Shape Society*, New Haven, Yale University Press

Lister, R. (2004) 'No more of "the poor"', 17 November, *Guardian*, www.guardian.co.uk/comment/story/0,,1352913,00.html

Long, N. (2004) 'Contesting policy ideas from below', in M. Boas and D. McNeill (eds) *Global Institutions and Development, Framing the world?*, London, Routledge, pp24–40

Mazlish, B. (2000) 'Invisible ties: From patronage to networks', *Theory, Culture & Society*, vol 17, no 2, pp1–19

Narotsky, S. and Moreno, P. (2002) 'Reciprocity's dark side: Negative reciprocity, morality and social reproduction', *Anthropological Theory*, vol 2 no 3, pp281–305

Noxolo, P. (1999) 'Dancing a yard, dancing abrard: Race, space and time in British development discourses', PhD thesis, Nottingham Trent University

Ormerod, P. (1998) *Butterfly Economics*, London, Faber and Faber

Pfohl, S. (2004) 'Culture, power, and history: An introduction', *Critical Sociology*, vol 30, no 2, pp190–205

Pritchett, L. and Woolcock, M. (2002) 'Solutions when the solution is the problem: Arraying the disarray in development', Working Paper 10, Centre for Global Development, Washington DC

Schwalbe, M., Godwin, S., Holden, D., Schrock, D., Thompson, S. and Wolkomir, M. (2000) 'Generic processes in the reproduction of inequality: an interactionist analysis', *Social Forces*, vol 79, no 2, pp419–452

Scott, J. C. (1999) *Seeing Like a State*, New Haven, CT, Yale University Press

Stacey, R. and Griffin, D. (eds) (2005) *Complexity and the Experience of Managing in Public Sector Organizations*, London, Taylor and Francis

Stewart, F. (2002) 'Horizontal inequalities: A neglected dimension of development', QEH Working Paper 81, Oxford, Oxford University Press

Strathern, M. (2000) 'Accountability and ethnography', in M. Strathern (ed) *Audit Cultures*, London, Routledge, pp279–304

Toyota, M. (2000) 'Border, mobility and contested ethnic identity: The case of the Hani/Akha in China, Burma and Thailand', *Anthropology in Action*, vol 7, nos 1–2, pp11–21

Ufford, van, P. Q. (1988) 'The hidden crisis in development: Development bureaucracies in between intentions and outcomes', in P. Q. van Ufford, D. Kruijit and T. Downing (eds) *The Hidden Crises in Development: Development Bureaucracies*, Tokyo, United Nations University, pp9–38

Valverde, M. and Mopas, M. (2004) 'Insecurity and targeted governance', in W. Larner and W. Walters (eds) *Global Governmentality: Governing International Spaces*, London, Routledge, pp233–248

Varese, S. (1989) 'The ethnopolitics of Indian resistance in Latin America', *Latin American Perspectives*, vol 23, no 2, pp58–71

Wade, P. (1997) *Race and Ethnicity in Latin America*, London, Pluto Press

Wedel, J., Shore, C., Feldman, G. and Lathrop, S. (2005) 'Toward an anthropology of public policy', *The Annals of the American Academy of Political and Social Science,* vol 600, pp30–51

White, S. (2002) 'Thinking race, thinking development', *Third World Quarterly*, vol 23, no 3, pp407–419

Wilson, F. (2000) 'Indians and mestizos: Identity and urban popular culture in Andean Peru', *Journal of Southern African Studies*, vol 26, no 2, pp239–253

Wittel, A. (2001) 'Toward a network sociality', *Theory, Culture & Society*, vol 18, no 6, pp51–76

3

The Politics of Representing 'The Poor'

Andrea Cornwall and Mamoru Fujita

The label 'the poor' is ubiquitous in development, a field of discourse and practice in which the power effects of labels and labelling are all too evident. Evoked in development policies and professions of intent, talk of 'the poor' affirms positions, lends moral purpose and creates as its object a mass of people with lives of abjection who are owed something better. For development workers, there is little more stirring than to invoke 'the poor' as the beneficiaries of one's compassion, one's indignation and one's assistance (Klouda, this volume). Yet if, as Geof Wood (this volume) argues, labelling becomes authoritative when it appears to be legitimate to those who are labelled, what are we to make of a label that few would comfortably wish to appropriate for themselves? Wood's critique of dominant forms of labelling 'the poor' in mainstream poverty measurements and classifications highlights the de-linking of structural explanations that link 'the non-poor' with 'the poor'. By labelling people as 'poor' within a narrative that casts them as responsible for their own 'empowerment', the inequities of existing social and economic relations that sustain poverty, vulnerability, insecurity and alienation are brushed out of the frame (Wood, this volume).

More proficient than any other development actor in the use of the label 'the poor' and in the kinds of discursive manoeuvres that Wood's analysis highlights, the World Bank came at the end of the 1990s to present itself as the Listening Bank, claiming responsiveness to those whom it regards as its 'clients'. Over the course of 1999, the bank embarked on an ambitious exercise to consult with an estimated 20,000 'poor people' in 23 countries to find out about their perspectives, experiences and priorities. This was published as *Crying Out for Change* (Narayan, Chambers et al, 2000b), the second in a three-volume series. The first volume in the series, *Can Anyone Hear Us?* culled a further 40,000 'voices' from the rather uneven but plentiful selection of Participatory Poverty Assessment reports and other such studies amassed by the bank (Narayan, Patel et al, 2000a).

In his address to the Annual Meeting of the Board of Governors of the Bank, on 28 September 1999, the bank's then president, James Wolfensohn, presented the rationale and results of this exercise:

My colleagues and I decided that in order to map our own course for the future, we needed to know about our clients as individuals. We launched a study entitled 'Voices of the Poor' and spoke to them about their hopes, their aspirations, their realities.

What is it that the poor reply when asked about what might make the greatest difference in their lives? They say organizations of their own so that they may negotiate with government, with traders, and with nongovernmental organizations. Direct assistance through community-driven programs so that they may shape their own destinies. Local ownership of funds, so that they may put a stop to corruption. They want nongovernmental organizations and governments to be accountable to them... These are strong voices, voices of dignity. (Reproduced on the flyleaf of *Can Anyone Hear Us?*)

These 'voices of dignity' lend an unimpeachable moral authority to the bank's intervention in developing countries. Used to justify a rise in lending to Community-Driven Development that reached 25 per cent of the bank's overall portfolio by 2003 (Irvine et al, 2004), these 'voices' provided the bank with the justification that they are responding to what 'the poor themselves' want and need.

Consultations with the Poor (World Bank, 1999) claims the authenticity of the voices of the people involved in it, who come to be cast as 'the true poverty experts'. But a number of questions arise about the ways in which the perspectives of those involved in this exercise on their own circumstances and their identification as 'the poor' were framed by the way in which the exercise was designed, conducted and distilled. In this chapter, we go back to the site reports and national synthesis reports from one of the regions involved in this study, Latin America. This was initially a pragmatic choice, driven by greater familiarity with this region and the sheer volume of material. Yet, as we went on to analyse what we found, it also became evident that the Latin American context is an especially interesting site in which to examine the bank's globalized prescriptions. This is not least because of the poverty-producing effects of neo-liberal reforms and the progressive alternatives to neo-liberal policies articulated not only by social movements, but also by influential figures within the governments in this region.

In this chapter, we trace quotes used in the 2000/01 World Development Report (WDR) (World Bank, 2000) and *Crying Out for Change* (Narayan, Chambers et al, 2000) back to the contexts in which they were voiced. We use what we find to explore the ways in which 'the poor' and their 'voices' came to be constructed, and go on to consider the implications of the uses to which the label 'the poor' comes to be put in mainstream development discourse. We begin by positioning ourselves. We go on to introduce the methodology used by the *Voices* exercise. From there, we go on to focus in detail on the key claims made by President Wolfensohn in the quote above, and on the politics of framing 'the voices of poor'.

Deconstructing the voices of the poor: Questions of positionality

Up to the end of the 1990s, surprisingly little attention had been paid to the implications of the positionality of those who carried out Participatory Rural Appraisal (PRA) exercises. Critics often conflated the methodology itself with shortcomings in terms of analysis – as in the much-cited account by David Mosse (1994) of his work with a team of Indian male technicians whose neglect of women's perspectives was ascribed to the methodology itself, rather than the dispositions of its users (Cornwall, 2002). Towards the end of the 1990s, there was growing recognition among those involved in the promotion of PRA that significant dangers of co-option and de-legitimation of participatory research were becoming evident in the enthusiastic take-up of PRA tools by institutions like the World Bank (Gaventa and Cornwall, 2001). The *Consultations with the Poor* polarized positions among those who had been active in the development and promotion of participatory approaches. For some, it was a triumph that lent a barely imagined visibility and legitimacy to a methodology that had been dismissed by development economists and social scientists alike as short-cut pseudo-science (Richards, 1995). For others, it was the Frankenstein that they had feared was in the making. We write this chapter from positionalities shaped by our engagement with these critical debates.

Our collaboration began when Mamoru Fujita approached Andrea Cornwall to supervise his MPhil thesis, in which he wanted to subject the use of participatory approaches in development to critical analysis. From a conversation with Ian Scoones came the idea of tracing the 'voices' used in the WDR 2000/01 back to the original site reports to find out what else they might have been saying. What Mamoru found made such interesting reading that we worked together to write this chapter, and take his original analysis further. His interest in critical analysis is strongly associated with the increasing importance of reflexivity in development. Have the interests in participation, power and reflexivity enabled researchers and practitioners to adopt new attitudes and change practice, including the scaled-up globalized processes like the *Consultations with the Poor*? How does reflexivity open possibilities of productive relationships between diverse positionalities? What is the role of critical analysis and engagement within the context of increased reflexivity, and how does it relate to practice? These questions were at the core of this research.

Having worked as a PRA trainer and facilitator since the early 1990s, Cornwall had facilitated many 'voice gathering' exercises using a similar methodology to that used in the *Consultations with the Poor*. As an anthropologist, Cornwall was acutely aware of the partiality of what comes to be said in the context of a PRA exercise and the frames through which the outcomes are read and reported (Cornwall et al, 1993; Cornwall, 1999). When the involvement of the IDS Participation Group (of which Cornwall was a member) in the *Consultations* exercise was first mooted, it prompted lively internal debate on the politics of engagement with an institution as powerful as the World Bank. It was evident that the *Consultations with the Poor* exercise was going to be a complex gamble. There was every possibility that it would result in what Cecile Jackson (pers. comm.) termed 'ventriloquizing the poor', to affirm the hegemonic development narrative of the moment. Increasingly sceptical of the politics of the use of the label 'participatory' to provide legitimation, Cornwall shared these concerns. Productive disagreement with close colleagues at IDS, especially Robert Chambers, focused on whether the window of opportunity for influence that this exercise offered should be enthusiastically embraced or sceptically rejected. Many committed people took the more positive view, and contributed to the *Consultations* exercise. This chapter is in no way a critique of their motivations, or indeed the quality of their work: under difficult circumstances, what they were able to achieve is nothing short of extraordinary.

What the *Consultations* exercise illustrates is that no methodology can be neutral to the relations of power that shape the ways in which 'results' come be framed and conveyed. This is as true of macro-economic analysis and micro-ethnographic studies, yet is a truth concealed by the residual positivism that characterizes the vast bulk of development research. Had the *Consultations with the Poor* been carried out by and for, say, Focus on the Global South or ActionAid, the frames of reference used to 'read' and distil what these 20,000 'voices' had to say would have been different ones, and a very different kind of message would have emerged from its 'findings'. Research is never value-neutral. At each stage in the process, researchers frame what is knowable. The choice of questions in a survey or the templates chosen for a PRA exercise preclude some answers at the same time as inviting others. The manner in which questions are asked evokes certain kinds of responses. What and who respondents think the researchers represent affects what is sayable. This much is obvious to any social scientist. The distinction that is often drawn between quantitative and qualitative *methods* obscures the important point that it is the choice of *methodology* that determines the ways in which any method comes to be used and the interpretive frame through which what emerges is read.

In the case of the *Consultations*, the presentation of the distilled findings from this exercise as the unmediated 'voices of the poor' is essentially little different from the use of certain kinds of statistics to make claims. The exercise itself gave rise to an enormous, rich and diverse body of 'data'. The representations of the 'voices of the poor' that emerged from this process are arguably less artefacts of the methods that were used, than of the dispositions of those doing the interpretive work. Our analysis, accordingly, focuses less on method – or indeed methodology – than on representation and on the politics of representing 'the poor'.

Garnishing touches? Representing the 'voices of the poor' in the WDR

The *Consultations with the Poor* was a stunning publicity stunt for the World Bank. It was also a coup for a number of those who sought to humanize the bank's operations. It achieved greater visibility for a set of arguments that advocates of participation had been making for years. And it brought some glimpse of the reality of ordinary people's lives into the field of view of the kind of development actors who live at such a remove from everyday life in the countries where their work is focused, that they are in need of reminding of what is happening 'out there' – or indeed, in some cases, in the worlds that surround the expatriate enclaves and air-conditioned meeting rooms in five-star hotels where donors spend much of their time. It was daring. And it was something that was able to make headlines within the development world, for doing what no one – or so it seemed from the way the exercise was presented – had ever done before: listening to the voices of actual, real Poor People.

As Chambers (2002) notes, policy makers and bank staff are likely to be more easily influenced by sound-bite-style headlines. There was an onus on those producing the 'voices' to find these sound bites and make the most of them. This is in itself a story-telling device that many qualitative researchers adopt, as it helps bring an analysis to life. But when the prerogative is to produce a 'global' one-size-fits-all narrative, it has a hazardous consequence: context disappears from view entirely.

Reading the WDR, it is striking how selectively these 'voices' came to be used. In the chapters under the theme of 'empowerment' – Chapter 6 (Making State Institutions More Responsive to Poor People) and Chapter 7 (Removing Social Barriers and Building Social Institutions) – only one of the 18 boxes is dedicated to the 'voices'.[1] In the main body of the text, three quotes appear in Chapter 6 and another three in Chapter 7. The findings from the exercise appear not to have made much of a dent on the overall thrust of the report. Rather, the 'voices' come to be, in McGee and Brock's words, 'treated as illustrations and flourishes' to 'humanise the analysis' (McGee and Brock, 2001, p34).

Outside the WDR report itself, the 'voices' came into their own. In the months following the release of the WDR, 'voices' were often cited in support of points that prominent World Bank officials wanted to make. They levered the kind of moral authority that the everyday fare of generalizing development narratives simply couldn't offer. They provided a refreshing aperitif that made the neo-liberal policy arguments they were used to affirm more palatable, imbuing the WDR's policy prescriptions with the smell of sincerity and the flavour of compassion. As Robert Chambers was later to comment, uttering and re-uttering quotes from A Poor Person could be regarded as having the power of a catechism: imprinting 'poor people's realities' in the speaker's sensibility.[2] Yet the selection of 'voices' to affirm policy positions arguably serves as much to enhance the authority of those who came to use them to speak on behalf of 'the poor' as it does to demonstrate their capacity to 'listen'.

Hearing voices

The *Consultations* study set about gathering its 'voices' on a scale that is quite extraordinary. The 23-country study operated at a cracking pace. The time allocated to fieldwork in multiple sites in each country was three months. The authors had just over three months to write a preliminary draft that synthesized the findings from the exercise as a whole. A staggering amount of documentary material was produced: 272 site reports and 21 national synthesis reports. This created a complex set of filters through which the 'voices' came to be narrated and read that mediated the synthesis that emerged.

The *Consultations* exercise sought to break new ground. It aimed to provide a way to systematize multi-site participatory research activities in such a way as to generate comparable findings. Grappling with issues of epistemological incompatibility – indeed, some might argue, incommensurability – preoccupied the design process, and its incomplete resolution permeates the Methodology Guide produced to structure the exercise.[3] In the opening letter to this guide, the leader of the Consultations process, Deepa Narayan, addresses the country teams with the following words:

> As this is a comparative study, we request that you work closely within the framework of the core themes, methods and reporting formats presented in the Guide. We fully appreciate, however, that the best open-ended and participatory field research is well tailored to local contexts and very dynamic. (1999, no page)

Much hinges on that 'however'. As can be discerned from this passage, there were two competing agendas at work: between standardization for comparative study and dynamic open-ended research tailored to local conditions. Reconciling the two is far from easy, and those involved in the design of the exercise made a brave attempt to do so. Significant in terms of our analysis, however, is that while the structuring of the exercise itself privileged standardization, the representation of its results made much of its 'participatory' nature – which became the hallmark of its claims to authority and authenticity, and the source of its cachet.

The 'voices' of the poor are presented in *Crying Out for Change* as if they arose unmediated from open-ended, participatory research. Closer inspection of the Methodology Guide, however, scotches any notion that this was an inductive, iterative process of listening and learning. Rather, it is peppered with pre-framed categories and circumscribed questions. Seven pages of the guide itemize methods to be used, activities to be done and further questions to be asked (MG, 1999, pp9–15). This is followed by a further 26 pages of methodology, which provide 'tips' on how to start the discussion, how to use the prescribed participatory tools, the format to be adopted, and sometimes precise questions to seek an answer to during the focus group discussions (MG, pp16–41). With time pressure, it is easy enough to imagine that seeking to adapt the terminology and discussions to local conditions and making time for reflection, analysis and further exploration might well be sacrificed to getting through all the questions. It needs to be remembered that in some sites the teams spent only two days and that the average time spent in each site was only ever envisaged to be four or five days.

The MG has little to say on the question of who participates in these exercises, and whether this has any influence on what emerges – particularly, one might imagine, how those who were asking the questions presented what they were doing, for whom, and why. It is not that the issue is not mentioned at all (MG, pp42–43, 46, 49); the teams are told to seek out 'the poor' and women, told to practice triangulation by comparing what different groups have to say and to think about why different results emerge, and to record who participated in the analysis, 'older men, younger women, children, boys not in school, better-off women etc.' However, the emphasis is rather on accurate documentation of the visuals and following the format for reporting. As we go on to suggest, this had implications in terms of simplification and decontextualization.

One of the distinguishing features of participatory research is its emphasis on exploring people's own categories and meanings, and using these as an entry point for analysis (Chambers, 1997). By defining a pre-determined list of topics, loaded with conceptual categories ('vulnerability', 'social exclusion', 'gender', and indeed 'the poor') that have a very particular origin and framing power, the MG frames what is possible for respondents to say and limits the opportunity for participatory analysis. It is not difficult to imagine how this might stifle the space for the creative improvisation and iterative learning that has been deemed so important in participatory research (Chambers, 1997). This is reflected in the site reports, many of which came to resemble a list of answers to pre-determined questions. The reports typically consist of short answers and a few potentially useful quotes in response to individual questions, sometimes accompanied by a brief description of group dynamics.

An indicative example of how a pre-existing set of preoccupations worked to frame one of the much-publicized results of the *Consultations* exercise appears on page 37 of the Methodology Guide. This illustrates, again, the tension between open-ended enquiry and sticking with the agenda prescribed by the bank's analytical and conceptual categories and associated policy preferences:

> *Allow the group to generate their own criteria. Once they have done so, check whether the following criteria have been included:*
>
> – *which of these institutions are considered important by them*
> – *people's trust in these institutions*
> – *their effectiveness*
> – *provide help when needed*
> – *people have a say in their decision-making process.*
>
> *If these have not been included, ask the group to consider them as well, and if they are willing, include them on the visual, These indicators are crucial for this study and may have to be prompted by the facilitators. Make a note of criteria decided by the group and the ones introduced by the facilitators.* (MG, p37)

It is perhaps hardly surprising that the much-touted 'finding' that poor people trust their own institutions more than those of the state was to emerge from this exercise. As we go on to suggest, a closer reading of the reports from which the vivid quotes that substantiated this 'finding' were extracted reveals a rather different story. It is to this, and some of the other stories that a closer inspection of reports from the *Consultations* exercise tell, that we now turn. We begin, however, by exploring how 'the poor' came to be constituted as the objects/subjects of this study in order to contextualize how their 'voices' came to be represented.

Creating 'the poor' as a category for analysis

> *They cannot represent themselves; they must be represented.*
>
> Karl Marx, *The Eighteenth Brumaire of Louis Napoleon*

'The poor', as we note earlier, is not a category that many people living in poverty would claim for themselves; it is not a social identity around which it is common for people to organize, nor is it a label people would readily identify themselves with. Rather, it is a label used to designate *others*. In a well-turned critique of *Can Anyone Hear Us?* Richard Pithouse argues that in it 'the poor emerge as The Poor – a de-individualised and othered category' (Pithouse, 2003, p123). Pithouse goes on to point out 'familial connections between this project and colonial discourses that sought to other people via a process of racialisation' (p118). Reflecting on their experience of working on *Can Anyone Hear Us?* Rademacher and Patel describe how 'voices' were turned into catchy quotes, 'largely stripped of their original social and political context' (Rademacher and Patel, 2002, p275). For all their talk about 'listening', Rademacher and Patel ask whether the bank was ever able to receive what 'more contextualised, actual "voices"' (2002, p176) might have to tell them.

Bundling together a disparate collection of snatches of narrative, each labelled by country but lacking anything that might distinguish them further, the analysis produced by the bank in these volumes demarcates 'the poor' as an object for 'our' intervention, and 'our' compassion. Pithouse (2003) notes the curious absence of any sense of indignation: 'the poor' are produced as 'inert and resigned', presented 'in a strange mixture of corporate-speak and the very same contrived archaism that colonial writers consistently attributed to the colonised' (p127). Their commentaries on change, Pithouse notes, are very selectively editorialized and they are presented as people that exist in another time: their very abjectness, their tales of misery, violation and abuse redolent with sorrow, but never with ire. The causes of this misery are never sought in actually existing political processes that have disenfranchised them, processes that may, after all, have been instigated by the very institution who seeks to make 'the poor' their 'clients'. Pithouse argues, 'the poor' become, in the bank's narrative, *them*: not-us.

Reading the site reports (SR), it becomes apparent that the way in which the category 'the poor' is understood and deployed varies according to each site, and by each individual within that site. The technique of wealth ranking, popularized in the early 1990s as a PRA method used for gaining insights into local classifications of wealth and well-being (Scoones, 1995; Welbourn, 1991), was one of the prescribed techniques in the Methodology Guide. Its outcomes provide interesting reading. In Vila Junqueira, Brazil, for example, one group of young men and women categorized inhabitants into three groups: 'better living conditions' (12 per cent), 'more or less' (64 per cent) and 'poor' (14 per cent, defined as only being able to afford necessary groceries, cannot eat beef, children don't study, incomplete houses with second-hand furniture) (SR-Vila Junqueira, pp7–12). It is implied, if not explicitly stated, that the majority of the participants perceived themselves as belonging to the 'more or less' category, discussing what it meant to be poor with reference to a group who were not 'us', even if they shared certain conditions of life and insecurities.

In some sites, difficulties were noted by facilitators of getting people to make these classifications. In Chota, Ecuador, researchers reported that at the stage of identifying different levels of well-being within the community, the participants (adult women) resisted, saying that they all eat the same food, and that nobody owns cars. The facilitators had to insist, and ask about any group of people who had less before obtaining a further set of categories, older members of the community, those who own their own land, and younger members of the community who were often recently married, those who own less land and often sharecrop (SR-Chota, pp6–7). In Isla Talavera, participants were opposed to referring to themselves as 'poor' and argued that they didn't face problems of malnutrition or illness (SR-Ilha Talavera, p21). The facilitators first tried to persuade them that they were talking about poverty in general, but met further resistance. They finally agreed on 'deficient quality of life' but the facilitators mention that the discussion hardly took off. In *Crying Out for Change*, a quote from this group discussion among people who were evidently unwilling to class themselves as 'poor' – 'there is no unified community, there is no unity, when they have to speak with authorities, they are afraid' – is labelled as having come from a 'group of poor women' (Narayan, Chambers et al, 2000, p219). Another example of labelling the speaker as 'poor' comes from Atucucho, Ecuador:

> In Atucucho, Ecuador, a 23-year old poor mother says that the situation of women is difficult because of extremely low wages. Some mothers work as domestic employees for 250,000 sucres per month. You know how much bus fare costs these days; they have little money left for anything else. (*Crying Out for Change*, p112, our emphasis)

The site report reveals that the speaker worked in a community day-care centre, and is interviewed as a person who is capable of presenting an overview of the community (SR-Atacucho, p55). Whether or not she herself would have termed herself 'poor' is another question.

The dangers of the blanket application of the category 'poor' to all the people involved in the process are evident. These examples point to the arbitrary and slippery nature of the way in which the category 'poor' is deployed in the global reports. The politics of representing the heterogeneous people involved in this exercise as 'the poor' comes into particularly sharp relief in relation to the core policy arguments that the *Voices* exercise sought to advance: affirmation of the bank's neo-liberal governance prescriptions.

'The Poor' as victims of the state

The analysis of the *Consultations of the Poor* evades discussion of positional power and differentiation amongst those who are labelled 'the poor'. Yet when those 'voices' speak of the state, there is no such ambiguity. One particular quote, from a discussion group in Esmeraldas, Ecuador (SR-Nuevas Brisas del Mar, p52) appears to have captured the imaginations of the writers of the WDR as well as of *Crying Out for Change*:

> *Eight women and two men in a discussion group in Esmeraldas, Ecuador describe their helplessness in the face of abuse and unfair treatment by the mayor and municipal staff: 'Some receive us, others don't. It's awful... They are abusive... They treat one almost like a dog... The municipality only serves the high-society ones... The mayor even slapped a woman who asked for help...'* (WDR, 2000, p100; *Crying Out for Change*, p205)

The emphasis in the global narrative is on 'good governance' and any evidence of bad government becomes grist to a narrative in which the state appears as profoundly hostile to 'the poor' either because of active abuse or by neglecting their needs. In line with this narrative, it is notable that aspects of the discussion that the quote above is drawn from simply disappear. Closer inspection of the site reports reveals that this same group of people viewed the government as potentially capable of giving the necessary external help in terms of the infrastructure of the community (SR-Nuevas Brises del Mar, p53) and, when discussing the problems of the community, stated that all the problems need the support of the municipality in order to be resolved (pp40–42).

Another example comes from a women's discussion in La Matanza, Argentina that is cited in *Crying Out for Change*:

> *It [local government] is non-existent... They do not give you any results... They must get involved in areas they rule; they must look at the small part of Argentina under their scope and fulfil their role, and they don't do it.* (*Crying Out for Change*, p209; SR-La Matanza, pp45, 48)

Yet there is no mention of the fact that participants in the same discussion group also mentioned that the government is the place to run for support, especially as the last resort (SR-La Matanza, p51). Nor do the affirmations of the role of government in supporting the poor that appear in the National Synthesis Reports from this region find their way into the global synthesis. The National Synthesis Report for Brazil notes, for example: 'despite the pervasive criticism of government in the groups, many governmental institutions were highly ranked in terms of their role in assisting people in times of crises' (p72).

Indeed, for all the claims that were subsequently made about 'the poor' calling for 'community-driven' programmes – presumably of the kind that the bank had been promoting and continued to promote with some vigour in the years to follow – site-level and National Synthesis Reports for this region suggest a rather different story. In Brazil:

> *Overall the groups showed a surprising disbelief in their capacity to solve problems by themselves. In a very few cases, the groups agreed that the problem being discussed could be solved by the community without external assistance... A number of important findings on the role of institutions on people's life [sic] were drawn from the site reports. The institutions listed were very heterogeneous in nature but surprisingly there was a prevalence of governmental institutions vis-à-vis non-governmental or market ones.* (Brazil National Synthesis Report, p86)

In Argentina, the National Synthesis Report notes, in the section 'Solving the Problems':

> *With relation to who is responsible for solving the problems of the community, most of the groups attribute it to the Government. The most common answer was: 'If the Government doesn't solve this, who is going to solve it?', referring to their own Government, unemployment, health services, the Police, prices. In most of the groups, Government–Community partnerships arose as the way to solve some problems related to addictions, health, malnutrition, housing, family violence, filthiness, empty plots of land, discrimination, thefts, fights, rapes, places for the children, fear, lack of culture, family planning. Also, although in connection with few problems, they decided that the community itself was able to address them – family problems, abandonment and negligence, suicide, relationship problems with their neighbours, lack of solidarity.* (Argentina National Synthesis Report (ANSR), p38)

As in Brazil, state-administered social policies were seen as an important part of the solution: 'The problems raised are perceived as mainly structural, which can only be solved through external support (Government) by implementing social and economic policies that will help to overcome this Poverty [sic] situation' (ANSR, p38). And in Ecuador, amidst complaints about the government being slow to respond, ignoring petitions, workshop participants are reported in the Ecuador National Synthesis Report (ENSR) as saying: 'The Municipality cares for the interest of the population', 'It is at least doing something to benefit the people...' 'Municipalities help our people who really need it. It is an institution that the poor need for economic support' (Workshop Urban area of Paján, Report Paján, ENSR, p88).

Indeed, the very fact that those interviewed were so often to give their terrible experiences of state institutions might be interpreted as *confirming* the importance that these institutions have in their day-to-day lives. The quotes that are selected to speak about governmental institutions affirm the neo-liberal arguments that the bank has consistently promoted. It is easy indeed to fall into line with the implied conclusion that poor people regard the government as useless and that their communal institutions are those that better serve their everyday needs. What the synthesis doesn't convey is the ambivalence that emerges in some of the site reports about the leadership of community associations, as in the case of Nuevas Brisas del Mar, Ecuador – from which a quote appears in *Crying Out for Change* (pp147–148) in which a woman mentions a lack of unity in the community and points out that unity is needed before they could approach the municipality to gain support. The quote is editorialized: 'Poverty of time, political indifference and lack of unity present further obstacles to organizing at the local level' (p147). Yet there is little in the site report to suggest this conclusion: rather, it suggests that people had mixed attitudes toward the current leadership of the community. From this evidence, it seems to be politics itself rather than political indifference that is at work.

The way in which the state and local non-state institutions come to be represented in these narratives needs to be traced back to the artefacts from which they came to be constructed: to the questions asked in the MG. Researchers were charged with finding out what qualities 'the poor' identify as important in institutions. And the criteria listed in the Guide offered a broad spectrum of such qualities: mutual trust, participation, accountability, ability to resolve conflicts, respect, honesty and fairness, listening, hard work, timeliness, access, among others (*Crying Out for Change*, pp180–195). As noted earlier, the Guide enjoins researchers to include specific criteria in the ranking if they are not mentioned; it is therefore unsurprising that the criteria listed in the guide are reproduced here, even if in different words. Questions like 'do people feel that [they] have any control or influence over these institutions' are clearly not 'open-ended' and 'participatory': they elicit certain kinds of answers, which were duly received and used to elaborate the very arguments that framed the questions in the first place.

Not only are certain issues selectively edited, and editorialized, in the overall synthesis of the Consultations. Others are selectively omitted. One such example – addressing a structural issue par excellence, that of land – arises from the consultation in Los Juries, Argentina. *Crying Out for Change* (p206) picks up on an example of 'poor women' complaining that municipal authorities held a festival to generate funds for road repair, which were never put to this use (SR-Los Juries, p32). Yet the overriding theme that emerges from the site report is the issue of land ownership, which is given first place in the ranking of problems. In the parts of the text that surround the quote used in *Crying Out for Change*, discussion group participants talk at length about the failure of the police to take up their claims against a local firm, who acted on the provincial government's legal measures on unproductive lands to send in bulldozers to reclaim land and destroy everything on it (SR-Los Juries, p32). Later in the site report, the issue of land looms large in the account given by the president of the peasants' union, which he attributes as the key factor inhibiting a better relationship between villagers and government (SR-Los Juries, pp38–43). Negative perceptions of privately owned companies voiced by 'the poor', equally, find little mention in the global narrative.

Whose solutions?

The overall narrative of *Crying Out for Change* seeks to 'reform the state' through 'community-driven' programmes, 'accountability' and 'inclusion' (p232). The overall message is the need for institutions (state or otherwise) to adopt different values and behaviour, so that poor people can establish a meaningful engagement with them (Chapter 9). These issues gain increased significance when these quotes appear in the WDR, in Box 6.1. Presented in a highly simplified form, scattered within the text of the report, these quotes convey the impression that complaints of 'the poor' are an invitation for the kinds of recipes for improvement purveyed by the bank. A sentence appears at the beginning of the same chapter that makes no bones about what the bank has in mind: 'most important is to streamline and "rightsize" public administrative entities and privatise public enterprises and other operational public programs [sic]' (WDR, p100).

Little mention is made in the WDR or *Crying Out for Change* of the effects of these kinds of reforms on 'the poor' that are more than evident from quotes like these, from the Ecuador National Synthesis report (ENSR):

> *The government raised the price of gasoline and now it costs us more to transport and we no longer make a profit. We don't make enough money ... the currency is worth less... Poverty affects us because of the foreign debt...* (Chota Report, Tablas Workshop, ENSR p24)

> *We don't have money to buy fertilizer, seeds, everything is in dollars ... we don't have anything to eat... The Government should reconsider and not raise so much the price [of] basic commodities... The Government should have more compassion for the poor and not increase the price of electricity... They should pay the teachers to come teach. They should give the poor jobs...* (Cañal Report, Juncal Workshop, ENSR p24)

Indeed, the ENSR begins by contextualizing the study in a setting 'sunk in a deep economic crisis where the policies of adjustment had been the most frequent solution'. The report went on to give an account of drastic measures taken by the president, including the urgent pursuit in the National Congress of bills seeking privatization of state enterprises. 'These actions', the report goes on, 'have had serious effects not just on the economic standing of all Ecuadorians but also on the political instability and on the loss of credibility of democratic and even financial institutions' (ENSR, p5). These are also, unmistakably, the very neo-liberal policies so forcefully advocated by the Listening Bank.

It is this kind of contextualization that is most strikingly absent from the homogenizing narrative of the global synthesis, and the disembodied quotes that are scattered throughout the WDR. It becomes erased in the labelling of all of those who participated in these exercises as 'the poor'. This has two effects. The first is of reinstating the legitimacy of an 'us' who reads what 'they' have to tell us – and who are then imbued with moral authority of being the ones who need to respond, to give 'them' what 'they' are asking for. The second is the dislocation of 'the poor' from the political economies in which they are located. 'The poor' come to be represented within the global narrative not just as victims, but also as their own saviours. Whether represented as abject, inert, lacking in agency, needing our compassion and attention (Pithouse, 2003) or as heroic survivors, whose struggles for self-improvement merit our admiring support (de la Rocha, 2007), these representations of 'the poor' echo others in contemporary mainstream development discourse. 'The poor' appear within them as responsible for their condition, living out a destiny that it is up to them to seek to better – through survivalist self-help (Pithouse,

2003; de la Rocha, 2007), forming 'organizations of the poor' that can better provide for their needs because they embody all that the 'social capital' and 'civil society' discourses would have us believe (Fine, 2000; Chandhoke, 2003), or by seeking 'empowerment' through self-employment (Batliwala and Dhanraj, 2004).

Contests over the normative frame through which these representations come to be read and interpreted are clearly at play in the WDR itself, with a tension between those who argue for 'pro-poor coalitions' between poor people, their organizations and the public sector, and those who advocate cutting back the state even further. Stripped of context, editorialized, and with significant elements of the conversation missing from the frame, 'voices' can be levered in support of either narrative. The emphasis in both is on poor people taking responsibility for their condition and taking on the task of helping themselves to survive: and in both 'social capital' and 'empowerment' become the panacea. Both deflect attention from the structural conditions – at the micro or macro levels – that produce and sustain poverty. Indeed, as Mick Moore (2001) points out, the very notion of 'empowerment' that is deployed in the WDR is insistently localized: either in the individual or in small-scale self-help groups that enable people to cope with their poverty rather than mobilize to transform the structures that keep them poor.

Conclusion

Reading through the site reports, a veritable cacophony of views, experiences and perspectives emerges. *Crying Out for Change* captures these 'voices' in a residual category of 'the poor', and the 'voices' are editorialized so as to tune out any discordant sounds and present an overarching narrative that is in perfect harmony with the bank's own policies: their 'cries' for change are harnessed to support a particular set of highly normative prescriptions. In order to obtain quotes that could pack a punch, *Crying Out for Change* obscures other linkages, other perspectives, other parts of the conversation that provide less convenient a justification for the overall narrative.

Writing about participation at the end of a decade in which the label 'the poor' began to be popularized in development, Cohen and Uphoff (1980) contend:

> Their [the rural poor] being considered as a group is not, indeed, something they would themselves be likely to suggest. There are significant differences in occupation, location, land tenure status, sex, caste, religion or tribe which are related in different ways to their poverty. To talk about 'the participation of the rural poor' is to compound one complex and ambiguous term with another, even more complicated and amorphous. (p222)

The power effects of using a term that is, as Cohen and Uphoff argue, complex, ambiguous and amorphous bears further reflection. One of these effects is to domesticate a diversity of people into a category that holds within it a normative appeal for intervention on their behalf. Not only, then, are the 'they' who are 'the poor' not the 'us' who read such accounts and identify ourselves with the mission of development (Pithouse, 2003). They are a residual category formed precisely of that which 'we' are not. The deployment of the term 'the poor' works to dissociate those engaged in 'poverty reduction' efforts from addressing the underlying structural issues that produce poverty; targeting 'the poor' exacerbates this distancing and dissociation, deflecting attention from the poverty-producing role of institutions like the World Bank and the governments that resource its operations.

The *Consulations with the Poor* exercise epitomizes the power effects of labelling; its synthetic outputs provide excellent examples of the kinds of framing devices that Moncrieffe draws attention to in the introduction to this book, and the dislocation between the condition of poverty and structural explanations for its persistence that Wood highlights. But it also reveals that, as Foucault points out, discursive domination is never total and that within every discourse exists the possibility of 'strategic reversibility' (1991, p5).Our reading of the site reports reveals a multiplicity of sites of resistance: from the group of women who refused to be labelled as 'poor', to the contextualization of one of the national synthesis reports in terms that were clearly critical of the macro-economic prescriptions of the Bank that commissioned them. It also reveals other stories that might be told using these materials, read through other frames of reference – stories that suggest altogether different policy framings, and affirm an altogether different approach to the structural inequities that hegemonic 'poverty reduction' policies often serve to exacerbate in the name of 'the poor'. Finally, it stimulates us into reflexive imagination on something better – for example, a more equal and reciprocal process that might have been/be possible – which is one of the major roles critical analysis plays in the studies of development.

Acknowledgements

We're very grateful to Karen Brock, Rosalind Eyben, Irene Guijt, Rosie McGee and Joy Moncrieffe for comments on an earlier version of this chapter. We owe special thanks to Ian Scoones for having suggested the idea of tracing the quotes from the WDR back to the original site reports.

Notes

1 Box 6:1 Poor people are often harassed by public officials.
2 Robert Chambers, seminar presentation, IDS, October 2001.
3 The Methodology Guide can be found at www1.worldbank.org/prem/poverty/voices/reports/ method/method.pdf.

References

Batliwala, S. and Dhanraj, D. (2004) 'Gender myths that instrumentalise women: A view from the Indian frontline', *IDS Bulletin*, vol 35, no 4, pp11–18
Brock, K. and McGee, R. (eds) (2002) *Knowing Poverty: Critical Reflections on Participatory Research and Policy*, London, Earthscan
Brock, K. (2000) 'In the Frame: Critical reflections on knowledge production', Unpublished paper, IDS
Chambers, R. (1983) *Rural Development: Putting the Last First*, Harlow, Longman
Chambers, R. (1997) *Whose Reality Counts? Putting the First Last*, London, Intermediate Technology Publications

Chambers, R. (2001) 'The World Development Report: Concepts, content and a Chapter 12', *Journal of International Development*, vol 13, no 5, pp299–306

Chambers, R. (2002) 'Power, knowledge and policy influence: Reflections on an experience', in K. Brock and R. McGee (eds) *Knowing Poverty: Critical Reflections on Participatory Research and Policy*, London, Earthscan, pp135–165

Chandhoke, N. (2003) *The Conceits of Civil Society*, Delhi, Oxford University Press

Cohen, J. and Uphoff, N. (1980) 'Participation's place in development: Seeking clarity through specifity', *World Development*, vol 8, pp213–235

Cornwall, A. (1999) 'Making sense of community wellbeing: Processes of analysis in participatory wellbeing assessments in South London', *PLA Notes*, vol 34, pp63–67

Cornwall, A. (2002) 'Whose voices, whose choices? Reflections on gender and participatory development', *World Development*, vol 31, no 5, pp1325–1342

Cornwall, A., Guijt, I. and Welbourn, A. (1993) *Acknowledging Process: Challenges for Agricultural Research and Extension Methodology*, Brighton, IDS Discussion Paper 333

De la Rocha, M. (2007) 'The construction of the myth of survival', *Development and Change*, vol 38, no 1, pp45–66

Fanon, F. (1967) *Black Skin, White Masks*, New York, Grove Press

Fine, B. (2000) *Social Capital Versus Social Theory: Political Economy and Social Science at the Turn of the Millennium*, London, Routledge

Foucault, M. (1991) 'Governmentality', in G. Burchell, C. Gordon and P. Miller (eds) *The Foucault Effect: Studies in Governmentality*, Chicago, University of Chicago Press

Gaventa, J. and Cornwall, A. (2001) 'Power and knowledge', in P. Reason and H. Bradbury (eds) *Handbook of Action Research: Participative Inquiry and Practice*, London, Sage Publications

Irvine, R., Chambers, R. and Eyben, R. (2004) 'Learning from poor people's experience: Immersions', Lessons for Change Paper 13, IDS

McGee, R. and Brock, K. (2001) 'From poverty assessment to policy change: Processes, actors and data, IDS Working Paper 113, IDS

Moore, M. (2001) 'Empowerment at last?', *Journal of International Development*, vol 13, no 3, pp321–329

Mosse, D. (1994) 'Authority, gender and knowledge: theoretical reflections on the practice of Participatory Rural Appraisal', *Development and Change*, vol 25, no 3, pp497–526

Narayan, D., Patel, R., Schafft, K., Rademacher, A. and Koch-Schulte, S. (2000) *Voices of the Poor: Can Anyone Hear Us?*, Washington DC, Oxford University Press for the World Bank

Narayan, D., Chambers, R., Shah, M. K. and Petesch, P. (2000) *Voices of the Poor: Crying Out for Change*, Washington DC, Oxford University Press for the World Bank

Pithouse, R. (2003) 'Producing the poor: The World Bank's new discourse of domination', *African Sociological Review*, vol 7, no 2, pp118–148

Rademacher, A. and Patel, R. (2002) 'Retelling worlds of poverty: Reflections on transforming participatory research for a global narrative', in K. Brock and S. McGee (eds) *Knowing Poverty: Critical Reflections on Participatory Research and Policy*, London, Earthscan, pp166–188

Richards, P. (1995) 'Participatory rural appraisal: A quick and dirty critique', *PLA Notes*, vol 24, pp13–16

Said, E. (1995) *Orientalism*, London, Penguin

Scoones, I. (1995) 'Investigating difference: Applications of wealth ranking and household survey approaches among farming households in southern Zimbabwe', *Development and Change*, vol 26, pp67–88

Spivak, G. (1988), 'Can the subaltern speak?', in C. Nelson and L. Grossberg (eds) *Marxism and the Interpretation of Culture*, Basingstoke, McMillan

Welbourn, A. (1991) 'RRA and the analysis of difference', *RRA Notes*, no 14, pp14–23

World Bank (2000) *World Development Report 2000/1, Attacking Poverty*, Oxford University Press for the World Bank, Washington DC

World Bank (1999) *Consultations with the Poor: Methodology Guide for the 20 Country Study for the World Development Report 2000/1*, Washington DC, Poverty Group, PREM

4

Disjunctures in Labelling Refugees and Oustees[1]

Jaideep Gupte[2] and Lyla Mehta[3]

Labels versus reality

Uprootedness and forced displacement, due to conflict, persecution or even 'development', are conditions that characterize the lives of millions across the globe. The international development community has largely been concerned with refugees crossing borders to flee persecution,[4] violence, impoverishment and brutal regimes. But less attention has been paid to displaced populations that experience refugee-like status in their own countries for similar reasons or those displaced as a consequence of infrastructure projects such as mines, dams and roads, often known as 'oustees'. This chapter examines the prevailing labels that are used in refugee and oustee contexts by revisiting questions such as who is a 'refugee', who is an 'oustee', what does it mean to be displaced, or even the more fundamental question of what violence, persecution and protection mean to the refugee or oustee. Introducing such enquiry to both oustee and refugee issues has the potential to overturn the injustices encountered by refugees and oustees, while protecting them from the violations of basic rights that they encounter almost daily. It can also award them with agency to shape their own life-choices around settlements, livelihoods and social networks in their new homes.[5] Why is it important? Ignoring the complexities of labelling refugees and oustees can only lead to increased resistance on the part of displaced people and the failure to integrate them into wider developmental efforts.

In this chapter we demonstrate that a large part of the stigmatization around forced migrants comes hand-in-glove with the processes of categorization which impose labels upon them. Refugees are labelled as 'problems' for host countries and interventions are focused on 'durable solutions': voluntary repatriation back to their home country, resettlement in another country or, in some cases, integration into the host society (Harrell-Bond, 1986, p1). Oustees often are labelled as the unfortunate victims of development projects that are necessary for a country's prosperity or for the greater common good (see

Roy, 1999). Traditional approaches treat the uprooted at best as recipients of charity and welfare, or at worst, as victims or problems. The approaches that have tried to accord agency to the refugee and oustee, as they make the best of their adverse conditions and mobilize around their rights, are few and far between. This chapter recognizes any act of labelling, while being an inescapable reality, as a non-benign, ontologically unstable act 'made up of human effort, partly affirmation, partly identification of the Other' (Said, 2003, p3). It thus examines the active role played by policy frameworks and laws in determining the status, rights, livelihood options and future of oustees and refugees at the national and international level.

We acknowledge that states face considerable challenges in meeting their international obligations concerning the protection of refugees (e.g. under the 1951 Convention relating to the Status of Refugees and the subsequent 1967 Protocol, which we turn to shortly). These include difficulties caused by the mixed nature of migratory movements, increasing costs and resource constraints, along with the pressures of other overlapping international alliances. However, with respect to oustee displacement, the ambiguities are fewer. The chapter demonstrates that resettlement and rehabilitation guidelines laid down by the World Bank and bilateral agencies as well as national and local policies around forced displacement caused by 'development projects' are often fundamentally flawed when it comes to determining who an oustee is, and their rights and losses are not adequately reflected in compensation packages. This is because oustee populations often represent the most marginalized groups of a nation and were traditionally considered to be disposable in the name of the greater common good. Notwithstanding the challenges that states face, the chapter argues that it is problematic when such pressures cause a heavy-handedness in adopting a cookie cutter approach to labelling large cohorts of forced migrants together – simple categories to make short-term policy options 'simpler'. Such categorization is often justified under a result-oriented framework that works on short political horizons and primarily seeks evidence of completion. By dissecting the labels imposed on forced migrants and examining their implications for policy and practice, we demonstrate that the simplified labelling of refugees and oustees bears the risk of decontextualizing suffering, devaluing personal understandings, and de-emphasizing the material, non-material and cultural factors that need to be addressed to mitigate suffering. Specifically, the chapter uncovers that such categories have often proved inadequate in informing the precise strategy or method of intervention. Another important consequence of generalized categorization is the inadvertent increase in stigmatization, which reinforces inequalities and undermines efforts at social reintegration.

The chapter thus argues that there is a disjuncture between how forced migrants view themselves and how current policy frameworks view them. While categorizing refugees and oustees in certain ways may highlight their abnormal conditions of stress, trauma and difficulty, there is also a danger it inappropriately presupposes a condition of vulnerability that justifies top-down, needs-based interventions that often almost border on social engineering. It blinds the methods of intervention to the resilience and resourcefulness of the forced migrants, having direct bearings on their livelihood and reconstruction options. Finally, the almost arbitrary categorization of who constitutes a 'refugee' or an 'oustee' and what constitutes 'nation', 'home', 'loss', 'livelihoods' and 'land' leads not only to a gross violation of rights but to the systematic exclusion of large groups of people who would like to see themselves as 'refugees' and 'oustees'. The chapter explores all these issues both conceptually as well as empirically by drawing on examples from both refugee and oustee experiences worldwide.

Nomenclature

Before we begin to examine labels in forced migration, a few words on nomenclature are in order. Studies on refugees and oustees broadly fall under the umbrella of 'forced migration' even though they rarely speak to each other. Forced migration is largely concerned with people who are compelled or forced to move, when they would rather choose to stay; 'the force involved may be direct, overt and focused, or indirect, covert and diffused' (van Hear, in Robinson, 2003, p5). The labels given to populations encountering forced uprootedness/migration are varied. The refugee, according to the UN Convention Relating to the Status of Refugees (1951), 'must be outside his or her country of nationality and unable or unwilling to return due to a well-founded fear of persecution for any one of five reasons: race, religion, nationality, membership of a social group or political opinion' (cited in Robinson, 2003, p5). Subsequent formulations by the Organization of African Unity and the Latin American Cartagena Declaration have a wider scope. Largely, refugees have the protection of international law that internally displaced people (IDPs) lack even though they might be affected by refugee-like conditions resulting from violence, violations of human rights, and natural or human-made disasters. The number of IDPs, defined by the UN as 'persons who have been forced to flee their homes suddenly or unexpectedly in large numbers, as a result of internal strife, systematic violations of human rights, or natural or man-made disasters, and who are within the territory of their own country' (UN, 1992, para 17), were estimated at about 20–25 million worldwide in 2002.

The term 'oustee' is borrowed from the Indian literature on involuntary population displacement, where it is commonly used to describe people 'ousted' from their habitat through government intervention, generally for the purpose of some development-required change in land or water use (see Lassailly-Jacob, 2000). While being a label in its own right, we prefer the term oustee to 'development-induced displaced' people, 'resettlers' or even IDPs, since the latter terms do not highlight the unjust and coercive nature of forced uprooting.

Labelling as a non-benign act

So what are labels? Geoff Wood describes them as 'the way in which people, conceived as the objects of policy are defined in convenient images' (Wood, 1985). Their purpose is therefore to simplify the complexities to which they refer. From the very outset then it is important to recognize that labelling is an inevitable part of any development and policy discourse. Labelling is also 'a way of referring to the process by which policy agendas are established' (Wood, 1985). That is, labels share a recursive relationship with policy-making processes in that they are tools to aid the policy-making processes which themselves have bearing on how labels are formed, and what meaning they hold. Lacan (1994) views this ontological instability as the 'politics of the unconscious' wherein a vital part of social categorization is to be understood in terms of repression or obliteration. That is, labelling,[6] or ideological practice, does not merely obscure, but it also inscribes in and enables the very construction of social reality.

Consequently, their necessity should not in any way preclude labels from being subject to scrutiny. Questions probing the motivations behind and consequences of labelling, whether inadvertent or intentional, are paramount to successful policy analyses (as is argued in the various chapters throughout this book). A useful frame to keep in mind is Scott's (1998) unpacking of the 'high modernism' employed by centrally planned social-engineering projects in the pursuit of an ordered utopia. In the present context we might equate the state's necessity to order, to its need to label and compartmentalize social, political and economic realities. In tow with Scott, we take the view that 'the bureaucratic planner with a map does *not* know best, and can *not* move humans and their lives around the territory as if on a chessboard to create utopia; that the local, practical knowledge possessed by the person-on-the-spot *is* important; that the locus of decision making *must* remain with those who have the craft to understand the situation; that any system that functions *at all* must create and maintain a space for those on the spot to use their local, practical knowledge (even if the hierarchs of the system pretend not to notice this flexibility)' (DeLong, 1999, p245).

That is in a Foucauldian sense, the main mechanisms of disciplinary power need to be deconstructed to reveal their footprints in their entirety – 'by themselves simplified rules [codes of discipline and power] can never generate a functioning community, city, or economy. Formal order, to be more explicit, is always and to some degree parasitic on informal processes, which the formal scheme does not recognise, without which it could not exist, and which it alone cannot create or maintain' (Scott, 1998, p310). The power of labelling, coupled with its self-perpetuating necessity within development policy, might also be equated to Jeremy Bentham's 'Panopticon',[7] which contorts power relations to allow 'seeing without ever being seen' (see 'Panopticism' in Foucault, 1995, pp195–228). Those readers familiar with refugee camps and resettlement villages will perhaps agree that these are present-day sites of 'panopticism' where displaced people are subjected to bureaucratic surveillance and control.

Labelling and the inadequacies of need

It is evident that labelling in refugee and oustee policy has been closely related with a needs-based approach to assistance. When short-term political horizons demand quick, measurable and visible responses, labels provide easy categories to compartmentalize results. If unchecked, the label of 'refugee', 'displacee' or 'IDP' is easily equated with the negative connotations of a dependent, troubled or helpless person. Past experience has shown top-down, label-led policy to feed from such labels to deliver basic needs-driven interventions, limiting efforts therefore to physical protection at best.

> *Why are refugees and displaced people defined as a welfare problem requiring 'relief' or 'care and maintenance', rather than as people who have problems, but who also have the determination to survive and who are ready to put their energies into productive work that could also benefit their hosts?* (Harrell-Bond, 2002, p9)

The reality is that refugee and displacee policy in the South has been largely driven by the demands of donors and humanitarian organizations (Karadawi, 1984; Harrell-Bond, 2002). The pressure to see results is overwhelming and is interpreted as seen through the satisfaction of immediate needs like food, water, shelter and sanitation. This, added to knee-jerk reactionism, has lead to the adoption of a confinement strategy, keeping large numbers of refugees in settlements or camps, and dependent on relief (Voutira and Harrell-Bond, 1995; Hyndman, 1997). In a critique of UNHCR practices, Stein (1994) articulates that efforts have been aimed at ameliorating the situation of the refugees, the host community and the state, pending the day those refugees returned to their country of origin, rather than promoting settlement and eventual reintegration of refugee populations in countries of asylum. As is all too evident from past and present examples, these encampment strategies that view refugees as a 'problem' and that are aimed at satisfying their 'immediate needs', present several shortcomings.

For example, the inadequacies of supporting only basic-needs programmes have for long been evident in the large-scale relief camps set up for the Bangladeshi (East Pakistani) refugees in eastern India, where efforts were centred around the provision of the 'five major necessities ... of space, the construction of shelters on this space, provision of medical assistance, supply of water and the supply of food' (Luthra, 1971). Even though the refugees were provided with numerous services, stretching government resources to the extreme, insofar as the refugees were concerned, they were economically isolated and therefore, according to a refugee testimonial, had 'hardly any rights' (Mukherji, 1974a). As Jeff Crisp of the United Nations High Commissioner for Refugees (UNHCR) Evaluation and Policy Unit articulates:

> ...it is now time to reconsider the wisdom of using scarce resources to feed, shelter and generally 'warehouse' refugees who are deliberately prevented from establishing livelihoods and becoming self-sufficient. Notions such as 'integrated zonal development' and 'refugee aid and development' may be forgotten or discredited. But the principles on which they are based – that refugees should enjoy productive lives and contribute to the development of the areas where they are settled – could usefully be revived. (Crisp, 2001, p16)

Moreover, it has long been known that focusing assistance on camps can ignore the needs of the majority of the refugees or displacees who are self-settled (Chambers, 1979; Hansen, 1982) or who have chosen to self-exclude themselves from resettlement programmes (Harrell-Bond, 2002).

Labels of exclusion and inclusion

Problems of exclusion

Just as poorly thought-out categories provide easy escape valves to vent short-term pressures, they can also be used as powerful implements of exclusion. Labelling inherently creates exclusive divisions given that once labelled, there are clear ideological constructions of 'us' versus 'them', or even 'them' versus 'another-them'. That is, labels are *a priori* exclusionist. Said (2003) potently characterizes this as 'the very core of traditional Orientalist dogma' (p3), where a relatively unknown 'them' is weighed against 'us' and 'our values'. In this light, a label that is often thrust upon refugees sees forced migrants as 'spongers', an alien burden on the host society.[8] As Zohry and Harrell-Bond (2003) point out, while signing on to the 1951 Convention, Egypt entered reservations to Articles 12 (personal status),

20 (rationing), 22 (access to primary education), 23 (access to public relief and assistance) and 25 (labour legislation and social security), making them inapplicable in Egypt. Thus, refugees were explicitly excluded from recourse to public funds, creating refugee islands isolating the displaced within.[9] Egypt is a further signatory of the 1989 UN Convention on the Rights of the Child, but refugee enrolment in public schools, for example, is only possible through specific Presidential decrees (like the decree for Sudanese refugees), such that 'primary and secondary education for most refugees is not allowed' (Zohry and Harrell-Bond, 2003, p26). Furthermore, Palestinian refugee students have been specifically excluded by decree from studying medicine, pharmacy, dentistry and engineering, and must pay university fees in foreign currency at overseas rates. Zohry and Harrell-Bond surmise that Palestinians in Egypt are probably the least educated amongst the Palestinian diasporas worldwide. Here, the refugee label acts as a clear tool for exclusion. It is non-benign in that it views the refugee as an encumbrance and, more poignantly, therefore limits the forced migrant's own capacity to realize better life choices.

Victims of violence who are displaced within their own country also suffer from exclusionist labels. Several thousand displacees of the continued communal violence and rioting in Ahmedabad and Mumbai, India, have often been misrepresented in policy dialogue. For example, riot victims who flee from the fear of future targeted or retaliatory rioting and violence are not recognized by government policy as those who are forcibly displaced, as there is an apparent element of choice involved. Here, there is particular need to question what 'persecution' and 'displacement' truly mean to the victims of communal violence. The displacees either have had to fend for themselves or relocate to several makeshift transit camps, some without facilities or any government support. In recent years, the worst spates of communal rioting have resulted in such huge numbers of displacees, that the government has been forced to officially recognize them. However, this has been piecemeal, as recognition of the displaced has been under grossly generalized labels. For example, entire camps are labelled either 'Hindu' or 'Muslim', without differentiating income, occupation or gender of the displaced (Gupte, 2006). This has prevented policy interventions from providing nuanced care to the displaced, let alone recognizing their capacity as fully functional members of an economy who, only momentarily, happen to be victims of urban violence. Clearly, this has worsened the situation for those displacees who ostensibly require only minimal, but properly directed support to restart their livelihood.

Similarly, when it comes to development-induced displacement, the declaration of who an 'oustee' is, is a highly political charged exercise which often reveals the biases of policy makers. But this label can exclude vast populations who should be included as the project affected. For example, there is frequently a marked lack of recognition of the fact that customary rights of indigenous and tribal people and women, including their access to common property resources, are often enshrined in informal arrangements recognized by customary law that is rooted in local understandings of property regimes. In particular, women largely have rights and control over resources in customary arrangements which may be corroded in newly created formal institutions to govern resources which may be male dominated and also ignore local dynamics (Mehta, forthcoming). This manifests itself in official categories such as the 'landless' for those who lack official titles, despite the fact that they may control and cultivate vast tracts of forest and so-called 'waste' land (for extensive documentation of this in the Indian context see Morse and Berger, 1992). These groups thus may be excluded from receiving compensation or project benefits. A further example of labels misrepresenting ground reality can be seen in relocation efforts connected with the Yacyretá Hydroelectric Project on the Paraná River on the Argentine–Paraguayan border – generalized compensation schemes overlooked a particular section of ousted brickmakers who were uniquely effected since the clay deposits, their primary source of raw material, had already been completely flooded by the reservoir (Mejia, 2000).

Problems of inclusion

So labels *ex*clude. However, generalized labels are also problematic when they lead those labelled to reject the categories that have been stamped upon them. Given the top-down nature of policies and programmes, it is little wonder that both refugees and oustees often reject official 'catch-all' settlement programmes. In 1989 only 25 per cent of all refugees lived in settlements where they would receive aid (Cuenod, 1989). Instead, the majority had found their own way within the host society. Studies have repeatedly shown that despite the availability of food aid and services in places of encampment, people prefer freedom and the autonomy to decide and rebuild their own lives (Harrell-Bond, 1986, 2002; Kibreab, 1996). Bangladeshi (East Pakistani) refugees in India quickly returned home after the liberation of Bangladesh, even though the actual ground-improvements were scant. '[I]n comparison to the prospect of a free life in a newly independent country, camp life appeared to be like bondage which had suddenly become intolerable. The impatience with which they awaited release was notable' (Mukherji, 1974b, p450). A less dramatic, though similar example of refugees refusing formal settlement schemes is that of Tibetan refugees in Bhutan, where a significant number refused the offer of citizenship by the Bhutanese government (Roy, 2001).

While relocation and resettlement are largely physical and economic initiatives, rehabilitation is more protracted and difficult since it involves restoring a community's and individual's livelihood, income, dignity, well-being and the capacity to interact in the new environment as an equal. According to Asif (2000, p205), in India between 1951 and 1991, about 213,000 were displaced due to 'development' schemes, of which nearly 30 per cent were 'tribal'. Nearly 75 per cent of the 'tribal' populations had not been settled at all and the author suspects that most of them refused resettlement. In part, this has to do with the resettlement experience, a classic social engineering exercise where oustees are often exposed to control from project officials and have little or no say in site selection or on questions around land, grazing, water provision and so on. No wonder that many refuse resettlement. This has less to do with the physical problems around resettlement (i.e. inadequate land, water sources, poor civic amenities), than with the fact that oustees woefully lack the ability to participate as equal actors around compensation procedures, around determining solutions to the problems of resettlement and in the protection of their human rights. This rejection of assistance points to a further disjuncture in the labelling of forced migrants – inaccurate labels *in*clude those who see themselves as better off not being thus labelled.

Capacity, resilience and need

A common thread between this problématique of exclusion and inclusion is the failure to adequately understand refugee and oustee capacity. Simplified labelling presupposes a condition of helplessness and the provision of standardized policy interventions then comes hand-in-glove, leaving out particular needs whilst misallocating resources to functions better performed by the forced migrants themselves. For example, the capacity of social networks is often left out by traditional labelling. To illustrate: In answering the question of how the self-settled refugee or oustee makes ends meet, Harrell-Bond describes refugees in Guinea (cf. Van Damme, 1999) and in Nakivale, Uganda (cf. Human Rights Watch, 2002) strategically deploying 'members of their households to take advantage of services or food distributions available in camps' (Harrell-Bond, 2002, p6). Refugees do not appear out of a historical vacuum lacking in social networks, skills and experience, and they are not necessarily a group of traumatized people whose social norms have disintegrated. Neither do they form uniform groups, with each family and each individual being shaped by different opportunities, experiences and capacities.

Examples of self-settled or self-excluding refugees relying on their social 'safety net' abound: the Eritrean refugee community in Sudan displayed strong social networking, a capacity gained through the collective experience of hardship, and because this emerged as a response to the war, it gave birth to 'new social organisations [which] transcended the old kinship networks or ethnic affiliations' (Kibreab, 2001, p7). The powers of traditional leaders declined, while new leaders emerged with strong links to the liberation movement. The community then relied on their collective and cooperative efforts in dealing with aid agencies and the Sudanese authorities as well as for evolving a coping strategy for overcoming hardship and social disorientation. Similarly, Roy (2001, p27) provides evidence of Bangladeshi refugees that 'settle down on their own by using their resources [of] kinship nets and the accommodative social atmosphere in West Bengal'. Numerous such examples (like the Sri Lankan Tamils, Chakmas, Tibetans and Lhotshampas, to name a few others in South Asia) all point to the heavy reliance on social networks by self-settled refugees, particularly when the host community displays cultural, religious or lingual commonalities. Kibreab contrasts such examples with those from Liberia, Rwanda and the former Yugoslavia, where the social trellis was weakened by divisions of ethnicity, tribe, religion and/or language.

Another illustration of the collective efforts of refugees being a source of much protection and empowerment is seen in the collective efforts of the refugees from the Chittagong Hill Tracts (CHT) which enabled them to withstand pressures to return. Despite the Bangladeshi government promising to improve local conditions and applying considerable pressure to extradite refugees, the refugees were able to collectively put forth a charter of demands, which they demanded be met before any repatriation (see CHT, in Chimni, 1994). Similarly, the people's movement in Nagarnaar, in Chhattisgarh, India is also an example of how collective action and good knowledge of one's constitutional rights can be empowering: For years now the indigenous peoples of Nagarnaar have been battling with the recommendations of the National Mineral Development Corporation (NMDC) for establishing a steel plant in Nagarnaar. Strong social connectivity among the people of Nagarnaar has allowed them to sustain a high level of protest, and collectively demand for their rights to be upheld.[10]

Though an important resource, reliance on social interconnectedness does not encapsulate the entire gamut of coping strategies displayed by refugees and displacees. Of the Eritrean refugee population that returned home from the Sudan and elsewhere in 1991, approximately 200,000 came without external assistance. Even though the self-returnees did not have access to entitlements of, for example, the PROFERI[11] Pilot Project, they shared whatever service opportunities were available close to their settlement area. 'Those who self-settled generally did better than those who settled under government schemes' (Kibreab, 2001, p12) by combining a diversity of income-generating activities including agriculture, and working in construction or collecting and selling water, firewood, building materials and thatching grass or engaging in petty trade during the slack season.

It is worth noting that when refugees take advantage of the situations they are placed in, they are not exhibiting dependency so much as a capacity for changing their livelihood strategies (see Bakewell, 2003). By not engaging with individual as well as social capacities, top-down labelling inherently fails to adequately address ground reality.

The forgotten and the overlooked

The literature in both refugee and oustee studies is unanimous about the top-down nature of settlement schemes. Questions of what 'adequate protection' or resettlement and rehabilitation mean to the refugee or oustee are seldom asked. Their centrality ironically forgotten, the labelled are forgotten in favour of the label itself. The local host's and refugees' perceptions of asylum are hardly taken note of or involved in decision making (Karadawi, 1983; also see Harrell-Bond, 2002). A case in point is the inadequacy of policies, programmes and studies in addressing the hazards of being landless. As recent studies have shown, for both refugees and oustees alike, regaining access to productive land is essential in the process of regaining their livelihoods, minimizing their risks and therefore rebuilding their coping strategies (see Cernea, 2000). Apart from having disastrous economic, ecological and political effects, becoming landless also has far reaching impacts on an individual's sense of well-being and socio-cultural identity. These are rooted in local and culturally specific perceptions. Thus, there is a great need for a 'local dimension' to any refugee or displacee assistance effort (see, for example, the traditional land tenure system in Eritrea, in Kibreab (2001), and the deprivation of society's norms, values, morals and beliefs caused by landlessness in the Kisan tribe of India, in Nayak (2000)).

Furthermore, top-down labels homogenize the oustee/refugee experience. The forced migrant is usually made out to be a male householder and the varied experiences of different categories of women and men are blanked out. For instance, although men might be more actively involved in organized fighting, women may need to flee to refugee camps, be subjected to violence, assume non-traditional responsibilities, and intensify their efforts to secure food, shelter and security for their family (see UN Department for Disarmament Affairs (DDA), 2001). These dissimilar experiences need to be recognized in order to have programmes catering to actual, rather than assumed refugee needs. In the same vein, and because dislocation drastically reworks social norms and necessitates the uptake of new responsibilities for daily survival, the experiences of oustees too have been different for women and men. Research on the gender impacts of forced displacement due to 'development' is slowly emerging. It has highlighted the several male biases that underlie the design and implementation of resettlement and rehabilitation policies and programmes (see Thukral, 1996; Indra, 1999; Mehta, forthcoming). For instance, compensation is usually directed to men, while women are rarely involved in decision making and implementation processes of resettlement schemes. Thus, resettlement programmes often exacerbate gender inequalities among displaced people. Moreover, as research amongst displaced women and men of the Sardar Sarovar dam in India shows, women largely have rights and control over resources in customary law or informal arrangements: for example, in the forest villages along the banks of the Narmada River, women earned an independent source of income from the sale of minor forest produce. But in Gujarat, the resettlement programme neither grasped, nor compensated them, for this loss. As a result, women's economic dependence on male members increased upon resettlement (Mehta, forthcoming). Colson's 40-year study of the Gwembe Tonga communities in the Zambezi Valley also shows how interventions largely ignored women and resulted in a loss of autonomy for them. Any gains that accrued to women were more of an incidental character and not due to any planned form of intervention (Colson, 1999).

Similarly, resettlement research has largely focused on the highly negative social, economic and cultural impacts of resettlement and its various impoverishment risks. However, it has been less vocal on the need to understand the dynamics around realizing the rights of displaced women, children and men. This is because mainstream research has largely been interested in the perspective of the planner or the researcher, using broad and standardized labels which are incapable of picking up the variable nature of forced migration. Take the Impoverishment Risk and Reconstruction (IRR) model of sociologist Michael Cernea (Cernea, 1997, 2000). Cernea's work has been path-breaking in identifying the relatively visible impoverishment process. Still, it needs to be complemented by a contextual analysis that takes into account certain relatively latent dynamics. For example, it intends to redress the inequities of forced displacement and achieve resettlement based on the principle of equity. It refers to the risks encountered by sub-groups within a community (such as the landless and women) who suffer specific losses that might not be predicted by policy makers and planners and thus suffer a more severe impact. But it does not go far enough in teasing out the dynamics of social differentiation among resettled populations, especially with respect to the reconstruction phase. For example, it is argued that the risk of landlessness can be eliminated through land-based relocation schemes. But the elimination of risks for one group may increase the vulnerability and risks of another group. As the Narmada experience shows, the resettlement package in Gujarat endows major sons (over 18 years of age) with five acres of land. But major daughters receive nothing and married women face growing insecurity, given that in the past it was common for women to have control over forest resources and forestland. Conflicts over land have also intensified, given the struggle for survival due to the poor quality of the land endowed and the absence of forest and other common property resources to meet basic subsistence needs. Land has now achieved a monetary value previously unknown. Thus while sons may welcome being considered beneficiaries of the compensation package, many women bear greater risk (see Mehta, forthcoming).

In order to address inequities within communities, the IRR model may need to advocate explicit partisan interventions for vulnerable groups within displaced communities (ibid). It may also need to develop mechanisms whereby displaced people can provide their own definitions of loss, impoverishment and development and thus become respected stakeholders in the displacement and planning process. In sum, it is evident that top-down processes of labelling lead to top-down policy making. Data, figures, results, policy frames are all presented in abstractions of the label, while the messier vicissitudes of individualized experience (pain, suffering, loss, and also resourcefulness, ability etc) are left by the wayside. The emphasis on the risks and impacts of displacement often ignores the need to create institutions to protect and strengthen the rights of oustees as defined by them, even in cases where these might contest the whole exercise of forced displacement.

Re-thinking the labels we must live with

Being a refugee doesn't mean that I am helpless and in need of assistance. I want UNHCR to know that yes, I am a refugee as long as I am living in exile as one who had to flee persecution and problems in my country, but I don't want one dollar of their help. Don't give me material assistance. Give me economic opportunity so that I can help myself...

Liberian refugee in Accra, Ghana (as quoted in Dick, 2002)

On account of the continued use of top-down labelling, there is a need to conceive of new imaginings and practices of development. One significant effort to enhance the agency of those disenfranchized by displacement is the 'risks and rights' approach of the World Commission on Dams (WCD) (2000). Its report was the result of a two-year stakeholder dialogue between industry, affected groups, governments and NGOs concerned with large dams that, amongst other things, highlighted the magnitude and dynamics of dam-based displacement worldwide. Critical also was the development of a 'rights-and-risk' approach to be used as a tool for decision making, which contrasts sharply with balance-sheet approaches. This approach explicitly links risks with the concept of rights by advocating an approach that recognizes rights and assesses risks (in particular rights at risk). The rights include constitutional rights, customary rights, rights to livelihoods, legislated rights and rights to property. By distinguishing between 'involuntary risk bearers' and 'voluntary risk bearers', the approach seeks a way for all stakeholders to negotiate together in a transparent manner so that risks and benefits are spread in an equitable manner (WCD, 2000, p208). Unlike conventional balance sheet approaches, it also seeks to give more voice to those who face the greatest risk and whose rights and entitlements are the most negatively affected. Thus the WCD seeks to move towards processes whereby displaced people are viewed as respected stakeholders who agree to move without force and coercion. Thus their resettlement would take place through mutually agreed and legally enforceable mitigation and development provisions. If countries and agencies accept the WCD guidelines, they would need a radical rethinking of the way in which resettlement programmes are planned and executed, making it virtually impossible to pursue current programmes that are largely divorced from the needs, rights and aspirations of refugees and oustees. The guidelines are thus a significant step to show how poor people's lifeworlds, aspirations, rights and values can be respected and built on in forced migration research, policy and practice.

Traditionalist dogma still lingers however. As Michael Cernea has shown in recent work, there is an inherent incompatibility between the goal of providing a compensation package that will improve incomes and livelihoods and the lack of means to do it. Thus he calls for additional investment financing that could help lift the uprooted above their pre-displacement livelihood status (Cernea, 2002, p3). Whether or not agencies will run with this is open to debate. Existing signs indicate that in practice there is very little incentive for agencies to invest in reconfiguring traditional labels to treat oustees as 'investors' who, by giving up land as livelihoods, are entitled to an equal share in the benefits of a project. Moreover, as lawyer Dana Clark has demonstrated, the World Bank's revised resettlement policy of 2001 waters down some of the strengths of its 1990 policy, which clearly states that displaced people should benefit from the project and should have their original standard of living improved or at least restored (Clark, forthcoming). The revised 2001 policy introduces new language, which can potentially weaken the strengths of the 1990 policy, thereby placing people at greater risk of impoverishment. For example, the revised policy no longer applies to those affected by the 'indirect' impacts of a project (e.g. downstream impacts of a reservoir). Similarly the focus on the restoration of past incomes is a step back from embracing development-oriented objectives of improving life styles and livelihoods of project affected people (see criticisms by Scudder (1996)). It may also seriously disadvantage indigenous peoples, women and ethnic minorities, who often lack formal legal rights to land, but whose rights are enshrined in customary arrangements. To underscore the point, these measures are a step back from the previous provisions that provided compensation mechanisms to those without formal titles to the land.

Conclusion

The chapter has aimed to demonstrate that traditional labelling of refugees and oustees bears the risk of decontextualizing suffering, devaluing personal understandings, and de-emphasizing the material, non-material and cultural factors that need to be addressed to mitigate suffering. More poignantly, such categories have often proved inadequate in informing the precise strategy or method of intervention. Another important consequence of generalized labelling to the forced migration experience has been the inadvertent increase in stigmatization, which reinforces inequalities and undermines efforts at social reintegration. The chapter thus argued that there is a disjuncture between how forced migrants view themselves and how current policy frameworks label them. While labelling refugees and oustees in certain ways may highlight their abnormal conditions of stress, trauma and difficulty, there is also a danger it inappropriately presupposes a condition of vulnerability that justifies top-down, needs-based interventions that often almost border on social engineering. It blinds the methods of intervention to the resilience and resourcefulness of the forced migrants, having direct bearings on their livelihood and reconstruction options. Finally, the almost arbitrary categorization of who constitutes a 'refugee' or an 'oustee' and what constitutes 'nation', 'home', 'loss', 'livelihoods' and 'land' leads not only to a gross violation of rights but to the systematic exclusion of large groups of people who would like to see themselves as refugees and oustees.

As the era of monstrous state-planned development initiatives has been widely recognized as a bygone development frame, it is paramount that we simultaneously re-examine current practices of top-down labelling within development policy, particularly with respect to forced migrants, and welcome the arrival of more nuanced efforts. This chapter has looked at a wide span of issues within forced migration. As Geoff Wood wrote '...the issue is not *whether* we label people, but *which* labels are created, and *whose* labels prevail to define a whole situation or policy area, under what conditions and with what effects?' (Wood, 1985, p349). Thus, the labels embedded in forced migration policy and practice need to be either discarded or radically rethought in order to buttress the experiences, local efforts and knowledges of forced migrants with national and international systems that promote democratic mooting.

Notes

1   This chapter is based on research conducted for the DFID-funded Development Research Centre (DRC) on Migration, Globalisation and Poverty at the University of Sussex and draws on Mehta and Gupte (2003). We are grateful to our DRC colleagues, especially Richard Black and Meera Warrier, for their support and encouragement.
2   Doctoral student, Department of Politics and St Antony's College, University of Oxford.
3   Research Fellow, Institute of Development Studies, University of Sussex.
4   The number of refugees in the world at the end of 2000 stood at 16 million, of which 12 million are under the mandate of the United Nations High Commissioner for Refugees (UNHCR) and 4 million under the mandate of the United Nations Relief and Works Agency for Palestine Refugees in the Near East (UNRWA). The largest numbers of refugees are found in Asia, 9 million, followed by Africa with 4 million. Three million refugees are located in developed countries (UN Press Release POP/844).
5   A recent strand of literature has argued for bridging the divide between refugee and oustee studies. See Harrell-Bond, (2002); Mehta and Gupte (2003).
6   or 'symbolisation' in Lacanian terminology.
7   Jeremy Bentham's Panopticon Letters (1787) reprinted as Bentham, J. (1995) *Panopticon Letters* Ed. Bozovic, M., London, Verso, pp29–95.
8   There are parallels here with northern debates on immigration: For example, in the UK in the late 1960s, Enoch Powell, a Conservative politician, became infamous for anti-immigrant speeches, predicting 'rivers of blood' if immigration continued. Powell labelled 'aliens' as being such a severe burden that British social and economic systems would collapse into violent anarchy.
9   'Refugee Islands' are the lowest tier in a three-tiered spectrum of assimilation, beginning at 'local settlement' where refugee services can be provided for while completely ignoring the local host populations, isolating the refugees within settlement camps. 'Local integration' constitutes the second tier wherein resources are shared by the host and refugee populations, leading to the third tier where the refugees become full participants of the host community by gaining citizenship and political rights (Merkx, 2000, p15). In the context of this chapter, it is apparent however that merely acknowledging this gradient in assimilation strategies does not address the disjunctures inherent in labelling refugees and oustees.
10 For details see PESA e-discussion group on www.panchayat.org; also see 'A report on terror, repression and criminal conspiracy against tribal people' on www.ambedkar.org.
11 Program for Refugee Reintegration and the Rehabilitation of Resettlement Areas.

References

Asif, M. (2000) 'Why displaced persons reject project resettlement colonies', *Economic and Political Weekly*, 10 June, pp2006–2008
Bakewell, O. (2003) 'Community services in refugee aid programs: A critical analysis', Working Paper no 82, Evaluation and Policy Analysis Unit, Geneva, UNHCR
Barry, C. and Pogge, T. (2005) *Global Institutions and Responsibilities: Achieving Global Justice*, Oxford, Blackwell Publishers

Cernea, M. M. (1997) 'The risks and reconstruction model for resettling displaced populations', *World Development*, vol 25, no 10, pp1569–1588

Cernea, M. M. (2000) 'Risks, safeguards, and reconstruction: A model for population displacement and resettlements', in M. M. Cernea and C. McDowell (eds) *Risks and Reconstruction: Experiences of Resettlers and Refugees*, Washington DC, World Bank

Cernea, M. M. (2002) 'For a new economics of resettlement: A social critique of the compensation principle', *International Journal of Social Sciences*, no 175, Paris, UNESCO

Cernea, M. M. and McDowell, C. (eds) (2000) *Risks and Reconstruction: Experiences of Resettlers and Refugees*, Washington DC, World Bank

Chambers, R. (1979) 'Rural refugees in Africa: What the eye does not see', *Disasters*, vol 3, no 4

Chimni, B. S. (1994) 'Symposium on the human rights of refugees: The legal condition of refugees in India', *Journal of Refugee Studies*, vol 7, no 4, pp378–401

Clark, D. (Forthcoming) 'An overview of revisions to the world bank resettlement policy' In L. Mehta (Forthcoming)

Colson, E. (1999) 'Gendering those uprooted by "development"', in D. Indra (ed) *Engendering Forced Migration: Theory and Practice*, Oxford, Berghahn

Crisp, J. (2001) 'Mind the gap! UNHCR, humanitarian assistance and the development process', Working Paper no 43, New Issues in Refugee Research, *Journal of Humanitarian Assistance*, www.jha.ac/articles/u043.htm

Cuenod, J. (1989) 'Refugees: development or relief?', in G. Loescher and L. Monoham (eds) *Refugees and International Relations*, Oxford, Oxford University Press

DeLong, B. (1999) 'Seeing one's intellectual roots: A review essay', *Review of Austrian Economics*, vol 12, pp245–255

Dick, S. (2002) 'Liberians in Ghana: Living without humanitarian assistance', New Issues in Refugee Research, Working Paper no 57, Geneva, UNHCR

Foucault, M. (1995) *Discipline and Punish: The Birth of the Prison*, New York, Vintage Books

Fraser, N. (1996) 'Critical theory and "globalisation": Toward a transnational perspective', invited presentation at conference on 'Critical Theory and International Relations', University of Aberystwyth, Wales, June

Fraser, N. and Honneth, A. (2003) *Redistribution or Recognition?: A Political-Philosophical Exchange*, London, New York, Verso Books

Gupte, J. (2006) 'Labelling violent Mumbai: Urban infra-power and charisma.' Paper read at Contemporary South Asia Seminar Series, 9 February, at University of Oxford

Hansen, A. (1982) 'Self-settled rural refugees in Africa: The case of Angolans in Zambian villages', in A. Hansen and A. Oliver-Smith, *Involuntary Migration and Resettlement: The Problems and Responses of Dislocated People*, Boulder, CO, Westview Press, pp13–25

Harrell-Bond, B. (1986) *Imposing Aid: Emergency Assistance to Refugees*, New York, Oxford University Press

Harrell-Bond, B. (2001) *Imposing Aid*, Brighton, Sussex Centre for Migration Research

Harrell-Bond, B. (2002) 'Towards the economic and social "integration" of refugee population in host countries in Africa', Discussion Paper, Stanley Foundation conference on 'Refugee Protection in Africa: How to Ensure Security and Development for Refugees and Hosts', 10–14 November

Human Rights Watch (2002) *Hidden in Plain View: Refugees Living Without Protection in Nairobi and Kampala*, New York, Human Rights Watch

Hyndman, M. (1997) 'Geographies of displacement: gender, culture and power in UNHCR refugee camps, Kenya', PhD thesis, Faculty of Graduate Studies, Department of Geography, University of British Columbia

Indra, D. (ed) (1999) *Engendering Forced Migration: Theory and Practice*, Oxford, Berghahn

Karadawi, A. (1983) 'Constraints on assistance to refugees: Some observations from the Sudan', *World Development*, vol 11, no 6, pp537–547

Kibreab, G. (2001) 'Displaced communities and the reconstruction of livelihoods in Eritrea', Discussion Paper no 2001/23, Tokyo, United Nations University

Lacan, J. (1994) *Speech and Language in Psychoanalysis*, Baltimore, MD, Johns Hopkins University Press

Lassailly-Jacob, V. (2000) 'Reconstructing livelihoods through land settlement schemes: Comparative reflections on refugees and oustees in Africa', in M. M. Cernea and C. McDowell (eds) *Risks and Reconstruction: Experiences of Resettlers and Refugees*, Washington DC, World Bank

Luthra, P. N. (1971) 'Problem of refugees from East Bengal', *Economic and Political Weekly*, vol 6, no 50, pp2467–2472

Mehta, L. (Forthcoming) *Displaced by Development: Confronting Marginalisation and Gender Injustice*, New Delhi, Sage

Mehta, L. (Forthcoming) 'The double bind. A gender analysis of forced displacement and resettlement', in L. Mehta (Forthcoming) *Displaced by Development: Confronting Marginalisation and Gender Injustice*, New Delhi, Sage

Mehte, L. and Gupte, J. (2003) 'Whose needs are right? Refugees, oustees and the challenges of rights-based approaches in forced migration', Working Paper T4, Brighton, Development Research Centre on Migration, Globalising and Poverty, University of Sussex

Mejía, C. M. (2000) 'Economic recovery after involuntary resettlement: The case of brickmakers displaced by the Yacyretá Hydroelectric Project', in M. M. Cernea and C. McDowell (eds) *Risks and Reconstruction: Experiences of Resettlers and Refugees*, Washington DC, World Bank

Merkx, J. (2000) 'Refugee identities and relief in an African borderland: A study of Northern Uganda and Southern Sudan', *New Issues in Refugee Research*, Working Paper no 19

Morse, B. and Berger, T. R. (1992) *Sardar Sarovar. Report of the Independent Team*, Ottawa, Resource Futures International Inc.

Mukherji, P. N. (1974a) 'The great migration of 1971: Reception', *Economic and Political Weekly*, vol 9, no 10, pp399–408

Mukherji, P. N. (1974b) 'The great migration of 1971: Return', *Economic and Political Weekly*, vol 9, no 11, pp449–451

Nayak, R. (2000) 'Risks associated with landlessness: An exploration towards socially friendly displacement and resettlement', in M. M. Cernea and C. McDowell (eds) *Risks and Reconstruction: Experiences of Resettlers and Refugees*, Washington DC, World Bank

Robinson, C. (2003) 'Risks and rights: The causes, consequences, and challenges of development-induced displacement', Occasional Paper, May, Washington DC, The Brookings Institution-SAIS Project on Internal Displacement

Roy, A. (1999) 'The greater common good', *Frontline*, vol 16, no 11

Roy, S. (2001) 'Refugees and human rights: The case of refugees in eastern and north-eastern states of India', in S. Roy, *Refugees and Human Rights: Social and Political Dynamics of Refugee Problem in Eastern and North-eastern India*, New Delhi, Rawat

Said, E. (2003) 'Preface to Orientalism', in E. Said (ed) *Orientalism*, 2003 edition, London, Penguin, x–xxiii

Scott, J. (1998) *Seeing Like a State: How Certain Schemes to Improve the Human Condition Have Failed*, London, Yale University Press

Scudder, T. (1996) 'Development-induced impoverishment, resistance and river-basin development', in C. McDowell (ed) *Understanding Impoverishment*, Oxford, Berghahn Books

Stein, B. (1994) *Returnee Aid and Development*, Geneva, UNHCR

Thukral, E. (1996) 'Development, displacement and rehabilitation: Locating gender', *Economic and Political Weekly*, vol 31, no 24, pp1500–1503

United Nations, Commission on Human Rights (1992) *Analytical Report of the Secretary-General on Internally Displaced Persons*, 14 February, E/CN.4/1992/23

UN Department for Disarmament Affairs (2001) 'Gender perspectives on disarmament, demobilization and reintegration', New York, UN DDA and Office of Special Adviser on Gender Issues and the Advancement of Women

Van Damme, W. (1999) 'How Liberian and Sierra Leonean refugees settled in the forest region of Guinea (1990–96)', *Journal of Refugee Studies*, vol 12, no 1, pp36–53

Voutira, E. and Harrell-Bond, B. (1995) 'In search of the locus of trust: The social world of the refugee camp', in E. V. Daniel and J. C. Knudsen (eds) *(Mis)Trusting Refugees*, Berkeley, CA, University of California Press

Wood, G. (1985) 'The politics of development policy labelling', in G. Wood (ed) *Labelling in Development Policy. Essays in Honour of Bernard Schaffer*, London, Sage Publications, pp5-31

WCD (World Commission on Dams) (2000) *Dams and Development: A New Framework for Decision Making*, London, Earthscan

Zohry, A. and Harrell-Bond, B. (2003) 'Contemporary Egyptian migration: An overview of voluntary and forced migration', Forced Migration and Refugee Studies Programme, American University of Cairo

5

When Labels Stigmatize:[1] Encounters with 'Street Children' and 'Restavecs'[2] in Haiti

Joy Moncrieffe

Introduction

We rarely speak about class inequalities, external domination or dependence; this language is unfashionable now – and is often dismissed as 'unsophisticated'. However, back in the 1970s, this was rousing political language throughout much of the Caribbean. Academics and activists such as Walter Rodney and Michael Manley explained, in most accessible terms, the ways in which colonial and neo-colonial power was often exercised as domination and repression. They exposed the legacies of racial and class inequalities and encouraged 'people power', which they defined in terms of collective resistance to secure 'liberation'. 'People power', as these leaders conceptualized it, required independence, initiative and self-belief. With respect to the latter, they recognized that slavery and colonization had left a lasting, though not necessarily irreversible, imprint on the minds of the people. As Palmer (1989, p114) describes in the context of Jamaica, one of the more harmful by-products of European domination was the effect of that rule 'on the minds of sections of the Jamaican populace':

> *A white bias had come to prevail and with it a concomitant devaluation of the sense of self of the citizens of African descent who, interestingly enough, comprised the vast majority of the people.* (Palmer, 1989, p114)

'Mental slavery' – as Bob Marley famously depicted it – had many dimensions and could result in tacit compliance with various forms of injustice.

As a student in Jamaica in the 1980s and 1990s, I was familiar with this political language. Despite the limitations to that discourse, I am persuaded that many of the broad observations about how power actually works were as relevant then as now: power, in practice, can be repressive and even lend itself to violence; conversely, power is crucial for producing healthy changes in social relations, such as would profit those subsisting in conditions of poverty or those subjected to various forms of injustice; repressive power is most potent and durable when people accept and uphold the (mis)perceptions and conditions that underpin their own inequality; therefore, much hinges on the extent to which, in the emerging social contexts, people are adequately challenged to recognize, confront and transform the socially acquired dispositions that allow for repression, both of others and of themselves.

Historical (social) dispositions are not easily changed. Forty years after independence in much of the English-speaking Caribbean (Haiti gained independence in 1804), analysts still contend that experiences of inequality and poverty are, in no small part, rooted in long-standing beliefs about – and socially acquired attitudes to – race, ethnicity, wealth, class, age and gender, among others. Historical (social) dispositions inform many current practices; many current practices, in turn, reinforce these dispositions. This synergistic relationship can persist even where there are comprehensive institutional reforms and economic development.[3]

This is uncomfortable terrain for many development actors. There is perceptible silence on critical issues such as racial prejudice and other substantive concerns such as how relationships of power – and the socially acquired dispositions that underpin them – influence inequalities and impair social justice. This silence is, in part, rooted in a sense of incapacity: it is difficult to make sense of and plan for intangible factors such as 'socially acquired dispositions'. It is also rooted in frameworks that simply cannot conceive of individuals as social beings and, accordingly, focus solely on satisfying people's rational, egoistic utility-maximizing tendencies. However, the silence may well be rooted in cowardice or even dishonesty. As development actors, we tend to downplay our own biases (assuming we do recognize them) and to assert our objectivity. Yet, our own socially acquired dispositions, including our prejudices, infiltrate our practice and are consequential for outcomes. Development actors, through their actions and inaction, can have a role in upholding the adverse power relationships that sustain inequalities and injustices.

In this chapter, I use a case study of select groups of children – 'street children' and 'restavecs' – in Haiti to reflect on how negative dispositions can be reproduced, including how these dispositions are reinforced and challenged by extant social relations and structures; and how development actors – with their own socially constructed dispositions, including biases and prejudices – intervene in these social contexts, and with what consequences. Haiti is an important country for study. It is one of the most stigmatized both within and outside of the Caribbean and there is increasing evidence that some Haitians also hold very negative views of themselves. (Stigma, particularly self-stigmatization, is consequential for development.) The focus on children is deliberate. Children have comparatively little space on the development agenda, yet the power relations that shape their lives have enormous short and long-term implications.

Section 1 of the chapter provides a brief background on Haiti. Section 2 uses aspects of Bourdieu's theory of society – particularly his deliberations on 'habitus' – to outline a framework for analysis. Section 3 delves into the case study, exploring how various authoritative state and non-state actors label and treat 'street children' and 'restavecs' in Haiti; how these children view themselves; and the ways in which they resist or comply. Section 4 outlines the challenges to the development expert and emphasizes the importance of self-reflection.

Section I

They think of us as people who were once good but not anymore. They treat us as people who are not worth anything and they have forgotten that we used to be good. (Interview, Priest, Maurice Sixto)

From 'victor' to 'vanquished': Changing dispositions in Haiti

Anyone familiar with Haiti's history of resistance, revolt and strong defence of its independence will be struck by its tragic decline and the dramatic reversal both in the way Haitians are recognized and in how many Haitians now recognize themselves. Two centuries ago, after executing the first successful slave revolts, Haiti was widely celebrated as the first black republic (Dayan, 2004), inspiring pride among would be revolutionaries and nervous apprehension across colonizing countries. Conversely, today's headlines commonly depict Haiti as a 'wretched place on Earth'; a place of 'unending and worsening agony' (Daniels, 2004), which some suggest confirms the dangers of premature independence as one missionary explained:

> *The physical chains may have been removed, one resident missionary explained, but the mental chains remain. The people have never had the opportunity to see what a family unit looks like. The masses of the people are uneducated – not meaning unschooled or untrained – but ignorant. Children, from the time they are able to walk, have to do so much work – especially girls – and so much of a child's learning before being able to read and write is stolen from children in Haiti.[4]* (Interview, Missionary to Haiti)

Haiti still evokes 'fear' (Maignot, 1996) but now of a different sort: there is fear of being bombarded by Haitian 'boat people', fear of being infected with 'Haitian diseases' and, across the Caribbean countries that once desired to be like Haiti, unspoken fear of suffering the same unfortunate fate. Haiti's long and seemingly irreversible decline is now used to frame the ways in which Haitian people, on the whole, are regarded: from 'poor and wretched' Haiti come 'poor and wretched Haitians'. The poverty and decline are represented as the people's whole stories and the persistent suffering as retribution for their own wrongdoings. Thus, labelled as poor, wretched and even ill-deserving people, Haitians, particularly those in poverty, are subjected to discrimination and abuse within the Caribbean and in countries external to the region. The Minority Rights Group and Anti-Slavery International have documented the gross treatment of Haitians – including children – who labour on estates in the Dominican Republic. They equate the labour conditions to a modern-day form of slavery. In Guadeloupe, Haitians are commonly treated as second-class citizens; many are denied French citizenship and legal status. Between November 1991 and 1993, Haitian men, women and children were imprisoned on the United States naval base in Guantanamo Bay, the 'world's first and only detention camp for refugees with HIV'.[5] As one interviewee explained, 'They think of us as people who were once good but not anymore. They treat us as people who are not worth anything and they have forgotten that we used to be good.'

Rather than being protected by their state institutions, Haitians have become accustomed to appalling abuses within their own country. There is a long history of violent repression, though certainly of some Haitians more than others: Haiti is, after all, a highly unequal society, with a legacy of racism.[6] From day to day, various forms of victimization create and harden differences across segments of the population. Class and racial distinctions are prominent: visible and even vulgar displays of wealth and consumerism coexist much too easily with some of the worst forms of depravity, and people from designated 'underclasses' are regularly treated with the disrespect that 'suits' their station. Foucault's description of the process of objectification and re-socialization that typifies modern day prisons is pertinent here for, in Haiti, the use of force against various groups does punish the body and compel conformity but it is the pervasive and systematic discrimination that 'punishes the soul', such that some eventually accept and even endorse the negative perceptions of themselves. Self-defamation is pervasive in Haiti and is projected, quite commonly, in regular conversations: 'nothing good can come to us Haitians, it's we sin why we're suffering'; 'Haitians are stupid, we behave like animals'; and according to one popular proverb, 'we have been trying to make "dough" since 1804 but it will still not sit evenly; that's how stupid we are'. However, this is merely one part of the story. Those labelled as the 'underclasses' still have and exercise their capacity to resist and even dominate in particular spaces. Some trade upon the labels assigned to them and act in the violent ways expected, while others persevere with stubborn resilience:

> *People may be shooting and killing but the people will continue with business. The thieves will burn down the market today but tomorrow you will see people again. This is their form of resistance. In some countries, people would not go out. We Haitians are not passive people.* (Interviewee 1)

In summary, Haiti's post-independence decline – economic, social and political – has produced substantial changes, both in how Haiti is regarded, and in how many Haitians now regard themselves. Haitian children are growing up in a context where their country is stigmatized regionally and internationally, a situation which is then compounded by multiple and pervasive forms of prejudice, discrimination and inequalities within the country; particular labelled groups – such as 'restavecs' and 'street children' – are most at risk. For the majority, who live in conditions of poverty, their social worlds breed negativity and futility, which coexist with instances of stubborn resilience. How are the prevailing social dispositions reinforced and challenged by existing social relations and structures? How do various development actors – with their own socially constructed dispositions, including interests biases and prejudices – intervene in these social contexts, and with what consequences, particularly for 'restavecs' and 'street children' in Haiti? Bourdieu's concept of 'habitus' provides a useful analytical framework.

Section 2

Habitus: What is it and why is it significant?

As Wacquant (2005, p316) explains, Bourdieu's conceptualization of habitus 'helps us to revoke the duality between the individual and the social by capturing the "internalisation of externality and the externalisation of internality"; that is, the way society becomes deposited in persons in the form of lasting dispositions, or trained capacities and structured propensities to think, feel and act in determinate ways, which then guide them in their creative responses to the constraints and solicitations of their extant milieu.' Because 'habitus' is socially acquired, it varies across contexts (time and space) and, significantly, 'across distributions of power'; it can also be transferred across different domains, producing consistency in consumption patterns (such as in music or food) and in other lifestyle choices, such as in political or cultural preferences within and among different social classes. Thus, we construct our social world by applying socially derived categories of judgement, which we share with others who were exposed to the same conditions and experiences. However, as individuals, we have a unique set of experiences and, therefore, internalize and project 'a matchless combination of schemata' (Wacquant, 2005, p317). Habitus, then, is both 'structured by the past and structuring of the present'. It is not derived from a single social structure but from the diverse environments that one encounters. Contrary to economic approaches, which conceptualize individuals as rational, egoistic and bent on maximizing utility, Bourdieu emphasizes that these socially derived dispositions can produce unpredictable and seemingly 'irrational' actions. Correspondingly, Kabeer (1999), in her reflections on measuring women's empowerment observes that there is an 'intuitive plausibility' to equating power and choice, when the disempowered use their power to improve their welfare.[7] In contrast, analysts have much more difficulty accommodating those instances when women not only accept but choose their inequality[8] (cited in Moncrieffe, 2004a). Thus, people can be socialized in ways that cause them to become complicit in their own poverty and inequality.

However, while habitus is 'enduring', it is not 'static or eternal'. Socially derived dispositions can be challenged, eroded, and even dismantled when there is exposure to effective counteracting external influences. Yet, habitus has what Wacquant describes as 'inbuilt inertia': there is a tendency to reproduce practices that are 'patterned off the social structures that spawned them' and to use this frame of reference to 'filter' subsequent experiences. Bourdieu accounts for the tensions and contradictions that arise when people encounter and are challenged by different contexts. His theory can be used to explain how people can resist power and domination in one domain/social arena and express complicity in another. For example, in one interview, a prominent Member of Parliament in Uganda, a female Muganda, expressed pride in women's achievements and her own efforts to gain authority in what was long regarded as 'male domain' (her public face). However, she also described her acceptance of her husband's domination at home: she was not allowed to eat high protein foods, could not sit at the table with him and was required to kneel before all male visitors to her home (her private face) (see Moncrieffe, 2004b).

Bourdieu's theory has other noteworthy applications to development. Here, it is critical to reiterate that, as development actors, we invariably bring our own mindsets/ frameworks, which inform how we interpret and work within different contexts. We inevitably make assumptions about individuals and categorize and label them based on our own socially acquired preferences and perceptions and/or based on the (mis)information we obtain. Typically, Goffman (1963, p12) notes, we are unaware of the assumptions we hold 'until an active question arises as to whether or not they [the assumptions] will be fulfilled'. Where we persist in labelling at a distance, we circumvent the encounters that can potentially challenge our assumptions. Correspondingly, when we are unduly fixed in our assumptions, we may fail to recognize and accept the challenges that encounters may bring. Meaningful encounters may reveal discrepancies between self-perceptions/self-labelling and the perceptions and labels that others hold. They may expose divergences between what frames and labels formally signify in high policy-making circles, and what they mean for the persons charged with managing policy on the ground; communities and the sub-groups among them; and for the labelled groups themselves. Following Bourdieu, discrepancies such as these can produce symbolic, social or cultural struggles, since people may gain or lose depending on how they are categorized. Conversely, struggles may fail to ensue where people accept – willingly or unwillingly, consciously or unconsciously – and endorse the labels they are assigned. In other circumstances, people may object and desire to contest labels but lack the skill and capacity to do so – where, when and how this matters. Often, stigmatized individuals and groups are so discredited –'reduced in our minds from whole and usual persons to tainted, discounted ones' (Goffman, 1963, p12) – that they are excluded from the spaces that would allow for encounters and from real opportunities to contest. Persons who accept or feel unable to confront the stigma may opt to exclude themselves.

Bourdieu emphasizes that 'genuine science' demands reflexivity, meaning 'systematic and rigorous self critical practice' (Swartz, 1997, pp10–11).[9] This is crucial for exposing and tackling the symbolic struggles that we are all involved in and for then producing real knowledge about a given context (Navarro, 2006). Reflexivity necessarily involves examining the extent to which the social contexts, and the ways in which we as development actors – with our differing socially constructed dispositions – mediate them, offer real scope for transforming the durable negative dispositions that may obstruct empowerment.

The case study below describes how some 'street children' and 'restavecs' in Haiti experience labelling. It highlights the attitudes of various development actors and the consequences of such labelling.

Section 3

Constructing children's social world: Authoritative state labelling and non-labelling

As in many other countries, children and their concerns have very low priority at all levels of the Haitian society. Particular groups of children – those who are stigmatized – often suffer gross abuses, including from state representatives who ought to act in their interests; otherwise, they are ignored when human rights infringements occur. There are huge implications for accountability and for citizenship over the long term. Influenced by this wider social disregard for children and facilitated by a long history of unaccountable and irresponsible leadership, successive governments have helped to create and sustain social structures and practices that reinforce children's lack of rights.

All respondents confirmed that the Haitian government is weak, ineffective, unable and, in large part, unwilling to commit to dealing with matters such as child protection and child rights:

Haitian governments are not stable. You hardly find any kind of child policies. Even where isolated policies exist, there is no plan of action.

Children are not a priority for the government. What government does is very negligible.

(Interviewees 2 and 1)

Certain groups of children are seemingly dismissed, even by prominent government representatives. For example, 'restavecs' are children who come principally from the rural areas to live and work in urban homes. Many of these children are promised food, shelter and education opportunities. There are a number of reasons for this migration:

Poverty is not the only reason why these children leave their homes. Some leave because there are no schools in their local area. Others leave because of their parents' superstition: parents believe that if children stay in the rural areas, something diabolical will happen to them. Some leave because of their perception that conditions must be better on the other side.

(Interviewee 1)

While some children are treated well or moderately well in the receiving families, the majority are treated badly, enduring merciless beatings, rape, very hard workloads and long working hours.

Foyer Maurice Sixto is a private organization that was established to provide for the educational needs of these children and to ensure temporary security in the periods they are allowed to leave their homes. The organization also attempts to work with the receiving families to reduce and ultimately prevent child abuse. 'When we started this project, every week we had children with marks on their bodies. We always had to meet with families. Now, we rarely see these.' However, abuse does continue in other forms:

There is a lot of evidence of rape, particularly of girls, within homes that take them in. Children are considered as things. This is a taboo subject. The children won't tell what they are going through easily, even if they are being ill-treated or raped. A lot of times, children prefer to be victims rather than being embarrassed.

(Interviewee 1)

One major difficulty for organizations such as Foyer Maurice Sixto is that there are widely diverging views on the true costs of the restavec system. Within government, for example, there are members who consider the system 'a huge sore for Haiti'; there are also prominent political leaders who consider it a useful arrangement, given the economic situation. According to one respondent:

The President is not categorically against the restavec system. Rather, he thinks it is good that if parents see that they cannot take care of their children, they give them to someone else. The President has said that as NGO workers, we should make the effort to help families to come out of misery. He would support us but we should do the work. I was flabbergasted to see that at the highest level of government, our representatives had totally resigned themselves from responsibility to the population.

(Interviewee 3)

Thus, at the level of government, the label 'restavec' has different meanings. While there is a contingent of representatives who desire to eradicate the system, this group does not have sufficiently strong support from some of the more powerful leaders and has not managed to frame the issues in ways that engender serious attention to the plight of the majority of children who are suffering as a result of the system. Consequently, ambivalence and non-commitment continue.

Conversely, in many circles the label 'street children' evokes a firmer response. One NGO representative reported that in one meeting, a ministry official argued that 'the only way to deal with street children is to build a big jail and put them inside'. Street children are the most reviled of the groups within Haiti, the NGO respondent contended. 'Across the majority of government institutions, even those concerned with social affairs, street children are regarded as thieves and killers.' This stigma gives licence to abuse, particularly from the police.

> Yet, street children do not choose to be where they are. The reasons for their situation are deep and the solution is to develop the communities they are coming from. When responsible decision makers think that the only solution is a big jail, we have a very difficult problem.
>
> (Interviewee 2)

Habitus: Missionaries' mindsets and attitudes

Stigma has the power to produce what Goffman describes as a 'discrepancy between virtual and actual social identity'. Likewise, unqualified (including self) beliefs in the moral superiority, objectivity, fairness and unguarded commitment of development actors can serve a similar function; that is, they can mask actual social identities. For example, it is naive but not entirely unreasonable to assume that missionaries to and within Haiti would not display many of the prejudices described. However, interviews revealed that relations between missionaries and various labelled groups of Haitians vary considerably.

In Haiti missionaries (local and expatriates) have prime roles in providing child services, particularly through schools and orphanages. There is little coordination among them and according to all former and current missionaries interviewed, little effectiveness:

> Missionaries are notorious for being independent. We don't branch out and join with others; we create our own thing each time. Missions would make a better impact if we cooperated.
>
> Missionaries, particularly those of us from America, have not been effective. There is an inability to build true relationships with Haitians. We have come in and given a lot and that is a great thing. However, we have not given Jesus Christ. We come in saying we have this wonderful God and when things get bad in the country, we are the first to leave.
>
> Missionaries go everywhere we're comfortable. When I came to this country, I resided with a missionary family who had been here for about 8 years. None of the family could speak Creole; none knew the names of the people in the church. This family had so many walls that they had never allowed Haitian people in.
>
> (Interviews, various missionaries)

Misperceptions and labelling come from both communities. There is a view that while many Haitians distrust Americans, including missionaries, they also regard them as wealthy, clever and racially superior. Conversely, while one missionary reported being intimidated by the 'beauty and pride of the Haitian people', there is agreement that especially in their private circles, many missionaries speak about the people in very derogatory ways and that particular groups, including street children, are stigmatized.

According to one missionary:

> *I have seen missionaries act in ways that keep Haitian people below them. For example, there was one occasion when some Haitians came to the door of this couple I was visiting. They sent their workers out to them as they didn't like Haitian people coming in. On another occasion, a number of missionaries visited me and was surprised that we had Haitians eat with us. They said, 'You have Haitians at your table!'*
>
> *I will give our (emphasis added) girls [meaning servants] things they need to do because we run a guesthouse. Other missionaries give their (emphasis added) girls a job and say, 'they'll never get it right'.*

Even the most benevolent of respondents (from among the missionaries) spoke of her resentment towards street children:

> *I have myself got angry at these kids begging me. I don't like it. It's just that bother of someone peeking at your window and getting in your space and the guilt of not knowing what to do.*

There was agreement that most orphanages are run as 'businesses', which means that many parents who are unable to pay are excluded. There are complaints, too, that children are frequently mistreated: 'I started this orphanage after working in eleven others. None of these orphanages provided a home setting. Most times, the children were treated like pigs' (Interview, 26 May 2005). Further, street children, in particular, are not accommodated in many faith-based orphanages (whether they are run by local or foreign missionaries), as there is genuine fear that they (street children) will 'corrupt' the 'normal' children in their care. Interviews conducted at one of the few reputable orphanages indicated that while the responsible missionary was convinced that she had received a special commission from God to help children in Haiti, she was not persuaded that this involved street children. She outlined practical reasons:

> *There are two categories of street children in Haiti: children of the street and children in the street. Those in the street left home for different reasons and have come to search for a better way of life. Some, such as former restavecs, have been severely mistreated. Those of the streets were born there. Their parents are people in the streets. Both groups of children need attention; they didn't choose to be in that position. However, I wouldn't take in any of them because they have been their own government and will not accept to be told to do anything. They do a lot of bad things in the streets and they will spoil your own children if you invite them in.*

As the account below shows, this stigma is pervasive throughout the society.

Mark's account

Mark[10] is an immigrant from the United States who, having heard reports about child slavery in Haiti, decided to visit the country 'to check out the situation'. The conditions, he explains, are even worse than he thought. He decided to help in the best way he could and, therefore, rented a shack to house five street children. After two months, he had responsibility for 36 children. Currently, he claims, there are about 2000 children who come to him when they are in crisis.

> *The police will beat and even kill them. The orphanages won't take them in. All get razor slashes while they are sleeping. They are treated as animals. The teachers victimise them because they are street kids. They beat them for not understanding. Teachers call them coco-red, which is a name used in Haiti for little insects that come out of the garbage. Since I have been here, not one Haitian has offered to help.*

Habitus: Elite perceptions and attitudes

One common assumption is that elites inevitably discriminate against lower segments of the society. However, there is no one elite perception of poverty or standard reaction to stigmatized groups. There is, instead, a diversity of responses. Goffman notes that 'the attitudes we normals have towards a person with a stigma' include 'varieties of discrimination, through which we effectively, if often unthinkingly, reduce his life chances' (Goffman, 1963). People can also respond with benevolent social action. Interviews conducted among select elite groups, including school children in Haiti, revealed both unawareness and unconcern about the conditions of these 'other' children as well as acts of kindness and acknowledgement that street children and restavecs are victims of the dire social and economic conditions in Haiti. Of course, without sufficient cross-group encounters, the dominant perception is that all elites characterize street children as 'little vagabonds who are on the street because they want to be there'. Interviews indicate that this is how many street children believe they are perceived and that the more common experience is that of elite prejudice.

Reginald's account

Reginald was the most eloquent of the boys interviewed. He explains that he was forced to leave home when he was nine years old because his parents did not have the means to provide for him. He reports that Mark had paid for four of them to have piano lessons. All the other children in the music school were racially mixed and wealthier. Though his elderly teachers did not treat them unfairly, the children were especially cruel. 'They didn't want to come near us. They say we are black pigs because most of the pigs in Haiti are black.' Reginald decided not to pursue piano lessons. However, 'I would have been good at the keyboards if I had stayed. Then I would have found a band and played for them.' Therefore, as Reginald sees it, 'bourgeoise people do not want to speak to us. Bourgeoise people have a complex when it comes to poor people. Bourgeoise only speak to bourgeoise.'

Normalized cruelty

However, the focus on class distinctions and inter-class discriminations can downplay the everyday cruelties than children who survive on the streets experience. Daniel is 14 years old, though he is of such small stature that he has the appearance of an average nine-year-old. Throughout the interview, he appeared shy and withdrawn and frequently fell asleep, as did a number of the boys. (One of the boys explained that if there is nothing to do and nothing to eat, the best recourse is to sleep.) Daniel has nine fingers. He explained that when he was nine years old, he stole a cake, as he was very hungry. The vendor grabbed him and severed his finger with a machete. Other respondents reported being beaten, chopped and attacked in other ways by various community members and by older children.

From social conditionings to social dispositions: How the stigmatized respond

Labels that have the power to stigmatize are propped up by discourses (Goffman's stigma theory) that dehumanize and discriminate, and that explain the labelled group's inferiority in terms such as inherent/essential biological differences, status/breeding or just reward for prior action. Stigma theories can be used in ways that generate fear. As Reginald explained, 'there is a general feeling that all children in the streets will steal from you'. Thus, even benevolent social action is best conducted at a safe distance, avoiding an encounter: Missionaries restrict themselves to 'comfortable areas'; development agents with responsibility for improving child rights and welfare may complete years of work without venturing into areas where street children and restavecs actually subsist. There is also the fear of being touched, contaminated by those considered less human. Consequently, children from the 'superior classes' may reject social associations with the underclasses; religious personnel continue their missions but would prefer that their personal space is not invaded.

Stigma theories often give licence to rights abuses. Persons considered 'not quite human' can suffer physical and psychological torture, seemingly without recourse. For restavecs in Haiti, sexual and physical abuses continue without serious acknowledgement in policy debates and little commitment to fundamental change. The government conceives its mandate as to 'regularize' the system rather than to uproot it.

It would be simplistic to suggest that there is no justification for fearing children on the streets in Haiti. As interviews with the children indicated, there are politically supported gangs of youth on the streets who specialize in kidnapping for ransom or who kill 'on order'. Foreigners and prominent members of the society are prime targets. The groups of children who were interviewed for this study insisted that it is important to differentiate between gang members and ordinary street children. Gang members do try to influence them, they explain; however, there are many street children who recognize that 'while gangsters are well paid, they will die'.

There is ample evidence that the alienation, forced exclusion, poverty and the techniques learnt for survival on the streets substantially increase the opportunities for 'anti-social' behaviours. These behaviours are, in turn, taken as justification (prime proof that the labels are not misplaced) for the categories and the labels. Similarly, children who are dehumanized and suffer sexual abuses have been known to abuse other children in turn.[11] Sexual abuse is often 'licensed' on the streets (such as through group initiation rights, by paedophiles and as part of normal everyday 'interactions'). As described, it is also common within restavec host families, where many children have no effective rights. This learnt behaviour is then perpetuated in other contexts. Thus, the director of the orphanage who feared that street children and former restavecs would 'spoil' her own children based this conclusion on a single case in which a street child – known to have been sexually abused – who was admitted, against advice, to an orphanage reputedly raped a young girl, who then left that orphanage in disrepute.

Therefore, while critics of original labelling theories are in large part correct – 'the label does not create the behaviour; there are other causal factors that may remain and continue to incite [particular actions], in spite of the labels'[12] – labelling processes that stigmatize can help to sustain the conditions and living experiences that teach behaviours that are consistent with the labels. This need not mean that people accept the meanings associated with the labels. For example, Reginald explained that 'even when I am called coco-red, I don't care. I believe that through education, anyone can become great. After all, Aristide was an indigen just like me.' Reginald's response is perhaps much too easily classified as indicative of his capacity to resist (Scott, 1985), aspire (Appadurai, 2004) and exercise his agency. The 'weak' may indeed have weapons to counter the stigma but public resistance and bravado can coexist with private shame, which may be revealed, as Goffman notes (p18), 'when only he and a mirror are about'. Thus, despite Reginald's public bravado, he was susceptible to the taunts from his classmates and left music lessons as a consequence.

Importantly, 'the weapons of the weak' need not be used to productively change circumstances. People may respond by wielding power in the spaces they are allowed to dominate. Mark reports that many of these boys who appear docile in the daytime become tough contenders at night or on occasions when they are forced to defend their turf. Similarly, representatives from Volontariat pour le Développement d'Haïti (VDH), a local organization that works with street children, note that children often attend their local meetings armed with guns and other weapons, as these give them a sense of power. Therefore, labels that stigmatize can produce a perverse sense of empowerment that then corroborates the labels.

Stigma is most effective when persons come to accept the negative perceptions of themselves. This 'tacit consensus' was most visible among the young female restavecs (some only eight years old) who were interviewed for this study. Maria is 13 years old and has been living with her aunt for five years. Her responsibilities are to wash clothes, wipe floors, cook, carry water and go the market. Victoria is eight years old and lives with a woman who is not related to her. Victoria has a heavy workload and goes to school in the evening. She tries unsuccessfully to hide the scars on her neck, which she eventually explains came from beatings with a belt. When asked how she felt about her circumstances, she stated:

> I don't feel good. They are always shouting at me. If I was with my mother's family or in a good family, it wouldn't be the same. I feel low because I am going through a lot of trials. I want to go back home.

All the girls concurred that they felt like nothing. The director from Foyer Maurice Sixto explained that the 'children – particularly girls – feel as if they are zombies. They feel there is no hope. They are not living for tomorrow; just for today.'

Section 4

Enter the development expert

These encounters with street children, restavecs and various authoritative state and non-state actors in Haiti depict the power of stigma. Authoritative actors have the power to label people and to (mis)recognize them in ways that can have long-standing influence on how they perceive themselves, respond to opportunities, make claims and exercise agency. There are substantial and very troubling long-term implications when children are the object of this stigma. In the absence of 'effective counteracting external influences', learnt behaviours and socially acquired dispositions are reinforced and reproduced, even over generations. These stubborn dispositions and the social relationships that buttress them can dislodge and disrupt development initiatives, including those that seek to 'empower' while overlooking or underestimating the more and less obvious ways in which power relationships can underpin inequalities and injustice.

It is the responsibility of the development expert to seek to understand deep power relationships and to work towards cultivating conditions where socially derived dispositions can be 'challenged, eroded, and even dismantled'. The honest and judicious starting point ought to be 'systematic and rigorous self critical practice' (Swartz, 1997, pp10–11): reflexivity. Critical questions might include:

- How do our socially constructed dispositions influence how we frame issues and conceptualize categories of people?
- Do we have deep knowledge of how social relations on the ground contribute to differing poverty experiences?
- How do we as development actors intervene in social contexts, such as Haiti, and with what consequences?
- What is required to improve social conditions such that people can develop the capacity to contest, resist and transform the dispositions that block their own empowerment?

Should we strip away the virtual social identities (such as those of rational, objective and committed managers) of many of us who are involved in development, would we discover actual social dispositions that are not unlike those of many of the kind missionaries within Haiti? As expert researchers, policy makers, programme managers and evaluators, we all harbour biases that are not displayed publicly but may be the subject of our private conversations or become much more evident 'when only [we] and a mirror are about'. Our own socially acquired meanings (stated or unstated) that we then assign to labels – which may conflict with the meanings that our respective organizations publicly adhere to – influence how we perceive issues and shape the encounters that we willingly or less willingly engage in.

Development agencies and donors in Haiti are in very authoritative positions, since the government has effectively allowed them to 'develop the country' without much guidance/constraint. There is a perception that the agencies are in an especially commanding position as the government is effectively more accountable to them than it is to the population. All the agency representatives interviewed described the inadequate coordination among them, the competition and the lack of accountability for outcomes. According to one representative:

> *It is really catastrophic how things are being done by the NGOs, international agencies and the government. We all have different starting points and methodologies. Everybody is free to do what they want. There is no focus point and no regulation. The government is totally absent and so there is no accountability.*
>
> (Interviewee 4)

Without strong direction, many agencies focus on areas or projects that are likely to secure funding and show short/medium-term results. For some, this inevitably excludes Port-au-Prince and its myriad problems, including the plight of street children and restavecs. There are a number of agencies that have specific plans and programmes for these children; however, there are questions, including from agency representatives themselves, about their effectiveness, and complaints that agencies lack real knowledge of the children's experiences. (Too) many respondents were sceptical of the development agencies' long-term goals. (It is important to note that this includes some former and current agency employees.) One interviewee summarized what appeared to be a fairly common perception:

> *These agencies have no interest for there to be changes in Haiti. If they changed the way they do things, a lot of them would not eat or drink. It's an industry; without countries such as Haiti, the industry would not exist.*

Encouragingly, one of the agencies interviewed, PLAN Haiti, has started a process of reflecting on the way it exercises power in Haiti, particularly its own – unintentional – role in perpetuating dependency and poverty among children. It has revised its programme approach in order to transform the ways in which children and youth, on the whole, are perceived and how they perceive themselves. One agency representative was convinced that 'PLAN's programmes, through its Child Centred Community Approach, are now getting to the heart of the matter'. Though it is important to study what claims such as these mean in practice, it was clear from the interviews that not all child development agencies and their representatives were as committed even to this 'stated' goal of transformation. One development expert explained her reluctance to engage in debates about the restavec system: 'We are not in any country to destroy the culture. We have to work within it. We have commissioned some studies on the restavec system and some findings are very positive: some former 'restavecs' are now ministers of government!' Meanwhile, another development expert reflected on his 16 years of work in Haiti and on the outcomes of the numerous studies on street children and 'restavecs': 'I think we have failed in breeding a new day for children, as we stated in our mission.'

Notes

1   I am enormously indebted to Marcia Petit-Frère for her research assistance in Haiti.
2   '*Restavecs*' (which literally means stay with us) are children who come principally from the rural areas to live and work in urban homes. Normally, these children are promised food, shelter and education opportunities. While some are treated acceptably, many are subject to gross abuses.
3   In Cuba, for example, Fidel Castro's post-revolution government followed the founding ideologies of the 19th-century nationalist movement and made considerable efforts to uproot discrimination. The government systematically destroyed the public organizations that supported overt racism, such as segregated clubs. Furthermore, by stipulating free access to education and health services, it succeeded in improving living standards, including among 'black' Cubans. By 1962, Castro's government concluded that the race problem – which it viewed as rooted in economics – had been resolved and the matter was, accordingly, virtually banned from public debates. However, covert forms of racism continued and, particularly since the 1990s, racial and ethnic prejudices have become much more blatant. Similarly, France's strategies for building 'raceless equality' have masked or, perhaps more appropriately, circumvented similar tensions. Départmentalization – which allows French Caribbean people to claim the same rights as other French citizens – has, in principle, extended social benefits but has not managed to prevent discrimination in areas such as employment. The ANC government in South Africa has adopted a similar strategy. The government contends that open discussions of inter-ethnic rivalries are likely to inflame tensions in a context where substantial structural programmes are required, and must be prioritized (Moncrieffe, 2004b, pp32–34).
4   Interview, former missionary to Haiti, May 2005.
5   Dayan, 2004, p2.
6   According to Max Paul (1996), these inequalities originated with the inappropriate land tenure system that Pétion adopted, for while neighbouring Saint Domingue, under Henri Christophe's leadership, used land to benefit the entire state, Pétion parcelled out land for the mulatto elite, which entrenched inequalities and racial divisions.
7   For example, various reports reveal that some women in Uganda have used the new political spaces offered by the Movement's affirmative action policy to improve their economic and political standing. See, for example, Goetz and Hassim's *No Shortcuts to Power*.
8   Uganda's second participatory poverty appraisal (PPA2) depicts some of the ways in which women defend unequal gender norms. The Kasensero, Rakai site report notes that while some younger women are beginning to challenge the norms that sustain gender inequality, many older women tend to enforce traditions and sanction those who flout the rules. Thus, younger women protested that they were banned from the lakes, to their detriment: 'we have to rely on men all the time because we cannot go to get the riches ourselves... Our poverty will be continuous until we are allowed to go the lake.' Meanwhile, many among the older women interviewed were firm: 'women should not go into the lake at all because they are always dirty'. Since the young women had begun to challenge this instruction, the gods were now punishing the community; thus, 'the fish stock has already begun to deplete' (Moncrieffe, 2004a, p28).
9   There are a number of multi-disciplinary texts (such as from Social Anthropology, Social Archaeology, Psychology, Philosophy, Education) on reflexivity, which explore its implications for qualitative research and include recent critiques. See, for example, Nightingale and Cromby, 1999; Hodder, 2003; Robertson, 2002; Lynch 2000.
10   Names have been changed to protect the respondents' identities.
11   This is not to suggest that it is only sexual abuse that causes children to abuse others.
12   See discussion in the introduction to the chapter.

References

Appadurai, A. (2004) 'The capacity to aspire: Culture and the terms of recognition', in V. Rao and M. Walton (eds) *Culture and Public Action*, Stanford, CA, Stanford University Press

Bourdieu, P. (1980) *The Logic of Practice*, Stanford, CA, Stanford University Press

Brodwin, P. (2003) 'Marginality and subjectivity in the Haitian diaspora', *Anthropological Quarterly*, vol 76, no 3, pp383–410

Crewe, E. and Fernando, P. (2006) 'The elephant in the room: Racism in representations, relationships and rituals', *Progress in Development Studies*, vol 6, no 1, pp40–54

Daniels, A. (2004) 'A wretched place on earth: The agony of Haiti, unending and worsening', *National Review*, vol 56, no 6, pp27–29

Dayan, J. (2004) 'A few stories about Haiti or stigma revisited', *Research in African Literatures*, vol 35, no 2, pp157–172

Ferguson, J. (2003) *Migration in the Caribbean: Haiti, the Dominican Republic and Beyond*, London, Minority Rights Group International

Foucault, M. (1991 edition) *Discipline and Punish: The Birth of the Prison*, London, Penguin Books

Gaventa, J. (2003) 'Power after Lukes: An overview of theories of power since Lukes and their application to development' (draft)

Gaventa, J. (2006) 'Finding the spaces for change: A power analysis', *IDS Bulletin*, vol 37, no 6, pp23–33

Goetz, A. and Hassim, S. (2003) *No Shortcuts to Power*, London, Zed Books

Goffman, E. (1963) *Stigma: Notes on the Management of Spoiled Identity*, Englewood Cliffs, NJ, Prentice-Hall; reprinted (1968) Harmondsworth, Penguin

Haugaard, M. (ed) (1997) *The Constitution of Power*, Manchester, Manchester University Press

Haugaard, M. (ed) (2002) *Power: A Reader*, Manchester, Manchester University Press

Hodder, I. (2003) 'Archaeological reflexivity and the "local" voice', *Anthropological Quarterly*, vol 76, no 1, pp55–69

Kabeer, N. (1999) 'Resources, agency, achievements: Reflections on the measurement of women's empowerment', *Development and Change*, vol 30, pp435–464

Kothari, U. (2006) 'Critiquing race and racism in development discourse and practice', *Progress in Development Studies*, vol 6, no 1, pp1–7

Lynch, M. (2000) 'Against reflexivity as an academic virtue and source of privileged knowledge', *Theory, Culture and Society*, vol 17, no 3, pp26–54

Maignot, A. (1996) 'Haiti and the terrified consciousness of the Caribbean', in G. Oostinde (ed) *Ethnicity in the Caribbean*, London, Macmillan

Moncrieffe, J. (2004a) 'Ethnic diversity and state response in the Caribbean', Background Paper for the Human Development Report 2004, http://hdr.undp.org/publications/papers.cfm

Moncrieffe, J. (2004b) 'Beyond categories: Power, recognition and the conditions for equity', Background Paper for the World Development Report 2006, http://siteresources.worldbank.org/INTRANETSOCIALDEVELOPMENT/Resources/Conditions_for_Equity_Uganda_Moncrieffe.pdf

Navarro, Z. (2006) 'In search of a cultural interpretation of power: The contribution of Pierre Bourdieu', in R. Eyben, J. Pettit and C. Harris (eds) *Exploring Power for Change*, IDS Bulletin, vol 37, no 5, pp11–21

Nightingale, D. and Cromby, J. (eds) (1999) *Social Constructionist Psychology*, Buckingham, Open University Press, retrieved 2 January 2007 from www.psy.dmu.ac.uk/michael/qual_reflexivity.htm

Palmer, C. (1989) 'Identity, race and black power in independent Jamaica', in F. Knight and C. Palmer, *The Modern Caribbean*, Chapel Hill, The University of North Carolina Press

Paul, M. (1996) 'Racial ideology and political development: The cases of Haiti and Bermuda', in G. Oostinde (ed) *Ethnicity in the Caribbean*, London, Macmillan

Robertson, J. (2002) 'Reflexivity redux: A pithy polemic on "positionality"', *Anthropological Quarterly*, vol 75, no 4, pp785–792

Scott, J. (1985) *Weapons of the Weak: Everyday Forms of Peasant Resistance*, London, Yale University Press

Swartz, D. (1997) *Culture and Power. The Sociology of Pierre Bourdieu*, Chicago, The University of Chicago Press

Wacquant, L. (2005) 'Habitus', in J. Becket and M. Zafiovski (eds) *International Encyclopedia of Economic Sociology*, London, Routledge

White, S. (2002) 'Thinking race, thinking development', *Third World Quarterly*, vol 23, pp407–419

Wood, G. et al (1985) *Labelling in Development Policy*, London, Sage Publications

6

Poverty as a Spectator Sport

Tony Klouda[1]

A partir des années 1960, le triomphe de la télévision a provoqué une centralisation et une standardisation extrêmes de l'information destinée au grand public. La concurrence féroce pour l'Audimat pousse les chaînes de télévision à privilégier l'information-spectacle. Pour intéresser les gens, il faut les toucher en leur montrant constamment des victimes : victimes des catastrophes, de la grippe du poulet et, surtout, de la violence, car il n'y a rien de plus spectaculaire que la mise en scène de la guerre, des attentats, des voitures qui brûlent.[2]

Les nouveaux parias de la République
Stéphane Beaud et Gérard Noiriel
Le Monde, 23 October 2004

Being led to or from the sacrifice?

It is of course impossible to say whether the growing need for victims on the television had any link to the parallel growing need for 'victims'[3] in the development industry, but by the end of the 1970s, many development agencies were getting worried. Field staff were complaining that the work they were trying to do bore little relation to the advertising campaigns for the industry which focused on victims – the hungry, the maltreated, the dispossessed, the sick. Those organizations that tried to change their tack, to 'educate the public' about the real nature of the work they were doing, suddenly found themselves in financial crisis. Very few people were interested in providing money for what looked like a long drawn-out process of negotiation with community groups about improving utilization of resources, or legal advocacy or of thinking about the implications of power imbalance. So the agencies went back to the startling images of victims – images (either positive or negative) of individuals (looking distressed or happy, depending on the assessment by the advertiser of the donor audience) whose situation would be changed by the experienced intervention of the agency concerned.

Since that time, development agencies have learned how to target particular donors with particular interests, as well as stabilizing their funding base so as to allow for a variety of approaches in their work. Many have converted the negative images to positive ones – building on the hope that their intervention will help particular people realize their potential. But the fundamental truth remains: the majority of people who want to contribute their money want to do so for some immediate form of suffering or want, and the images building on hope are easily recognized as a substitute for 'there are negative forces impeding this person's development which we will alleviate'. Such images rarely include any political, cultural, social or personal context. It is a hard sell, and lies completely at odds with the idea that people have their own identity and dignity – agencies have to make the case that they will put that dignity and support into place in lieu of local social forces whilst implying that those local forces have been wrong, evil or mistaken.

What does this have to do with 'labelling'? Well, clearly the development agencies make the maximum use of categories and labels that they think will attract the greatest funding. Put in a kinder way, they hold out the promise that they will help people in the categories that the public want to help. In this respect, 'victims' and 'poverty' rank high as labels designed to attract funds. But there are many more insidious labels in use referring to supposed situations as much as to people – examples include 'gender-based violence', 'exploitation', 'power', 'orphans and vulnerable children', 'risk behaviour', 'genocide' and 'rights' – whose use implies not only an agreed understanding of such terms (which does not exist) but also the possibility of the immediate action that will meet the short-term needs of donors.

The *purpose* of labelling is more important than the labels

The discussion leading up to this publication suggested that labelling[4] of people and situations needs to be challenged,[5] or at least that those who are labelled need to participate in the discussion as to the relevance and utility of the labels. This is a very old argument indeed, as will be discussed later in the chapter. However, one aspect that has been covered neither by the old nor new debates is the *purpose* behind such a challenge.

A debate about labels and about the framing of a problem would only have relevance if the goal of development were agreed – since each set of labels applies only to a particular type of framing of a problem and the end point to be achieved – but this is very far from being the case. Not only is there a multitude of visions of what 'development' has as a goal but there are also a multitude of reasons for helping and being helped. Whoever determines the purpose of development, there can never be such a thing as a single purpose. Matching (a) these desires to help with (b) the desire to be helped provides the basis of the game of development.

The desire to help those who seem to be suffering or in need is deeply embedded in perhaps the majority of people. As has been mentioned in a previous article,[6] the desire for and debates about such benevolence[7] were already clearly articulated in the 3rd century BC in Chinese writings. It is also a desire that is associated with great virtue in many, if not all cultures. Unfortunately, this generalized wellspring of benevolence conceals many different types of motivation and understanding, and it is this diversity that has led in many cultures to ferocious debates through the centuries about who it is that should be supported, whether it is people or their situations[8] that should be tackled, with what criteria and how that should be done. These debates are essentially unresolved today, and the absence of agreement makes it absurd to make grandiose calls for the elimination of poverty, or the establishment of rights or whatever is fanciful on the current catwalks of development agencies.

The basis of the argument of this paper is that the variety of labels, frames or categories applied to people and their situations in terms of 'the poorest, most marginalized, least powerful' reflects the variety of interests hidden in the idea of benevolence, and that unless there be clarity concerning the end point of this benevolence there is little point in arguing about labels or frames. There are three main types of motivation that lead to the variety of acts of benevolence. On the one hand, as Confucius was quick to spot, there is the muddle of compassion, selflessness[9] and selfishness which are often combined in benevolence. On the other hand, as Arthur Schopenhauer clarified, there is not only this muddle, but the idea of benevolence is intrinsically linked with, in his terms, our 'will' and power, which, following Kant, he linked with the ways in which we create categories – categories and frames being created by our interests and by the language games of groups that determine culture.[10] This problem affects as much those, such as individuals, who believe they just want to help others, as it does governments who may be acting with entirely different motives when they say they are attacking questions of 'poverty' or 'powerlessness' or 'marginalization' or 'rights'. Thus the questions addressed in this paper are about the motivations[11] for using those labels, categories of problem or frames, and the acceptability or other of such motivations.

The danger in the debate about labels and frames is that by pretending that a unified or consistent approach is possible to a condition labelled or framed in a particular way (such as 'poverty' or 'inequality'), the debate gives a spurious validity to the actions of development agencies that identify either a cause for action, or people grouped by labels (such as 'poor'), to support. This paper tries to undermine such validation and proposes instead an acknowledgement of the chaos of the current range of acts of benevolence which have simultaneous legitimacy and illegitimacy.

Development is not a logical business, but an emotional one, based on conflicting values that can never be resolved. This is one reason why it is impossible to leave the range of people's motivations[12] outside the equation. All development aid is ultimately founded on the interest of individuals to give aid for the purpose they define, and since these purposes vary it is important to consider this diversity and understand how best it can be managed. The motivation[13] determines the way the problem is identified, the categories of people or situations that are to be 'improved', and the ways in which the approach is adapted to the realities that are revealed once the work is started.

Parallel strands

The three main types of motivation for benevolence (compassion; personal or national benefit; control) are worth keeping distinct even though they are rarely separate. Thus it is quite possible that the majority of individuals who give to donor agencies directly or through their taxes do so predominantly out of some kind of compassion for others, whether or not that compassion has been studiously generated by clever marketing.

Against this apparently simple desire, there is the wide variety of practices of modern 'development' agencies. Some of them either closely relate to this desire for compassion by singling out particular individuals and supporting them directly. Others work in more general terms. Some of these latter work for a general goal such as the provision of particular services (armaments, roads, infrastructure, schooling, health, education, loans), or generalized reconstruction after a disaster. Some try to work to reduce the impact of or to prevent particular types of social or economic inequality. Some try to advocate for or promote particular rights. Many base their work on a rather hazy idea of 'empowerment', the nature of which may be derived from the Enlightenment philosophy at the end of the 18th century – when the French decided to follow Rousseau and liberate people in the rest of the world from their supposed chains.[14] There is very little, if anything, in common between these various approaches. Furthermore, in working through this variety of mechanisms, the simple idea of compassion very quickly is subsumed to the self-interest, personal or national benefit, or control that take over – as has been detailed in a very large number of studies of the development industry.

The problems behind this multitude of approaches have been very extensively debated by economists and others since the 18th century, together with debates about the theoretical basis for work with 'the poor' or else against 'poverty'. As has been so well charted by Gertrude Himmelfarb,[15] the central debates of the time were:

- the extent to which a 'scientific' approach based on verifiable indicators should replace the personalized, subjective, moralistic approach;
- whether the focus should be on pauperhood (and therefore on individuals, their capacity to cope and their dignity) or poverty (however defined);
- whether providing aid or support increases dependency.

One argument of this paper is that these debates are still relevant today – *all* approaches being hamstrung by the values that are behind them.

Different perspectives of the truth

This particular debate about labels is a very old one. Turn, for example, to the *Anti-Jacobin Review* of 1797 where James Gillray (writing in the aftermath of 'the Terror' of the French Revolution in a parody of Southey's humanitarian poem *The Widow*) depicted intolerance, fanaticism and violence masquerading as enlightenment and virtue.[16] It exposes what it considers the hypocrisy and naivety of the faith of the Jacobins in their interpretation of the condition of 'the poor' and in the agreement by 'the poor' with that interpretation.

The picture by Gillray shows a richly dressed person talking with a knife-grinder clad in rags who is holding his wherry, or wheelbarrow with a knife-grinding attachment. The commentary is as follows:

The Friend of Humanity and the Knife-Grinder
Scene, The Borough

Figure 6.1 *The knife-grinder*[17]

Friend of Humanity: 'Needy Knife-grinder! Whither are you going? Rough is the road, your Wheel is out of order. Bleak blows the blast; your hat has got a hole in't, So have your breeches! Weary Knife-grinder! Little think the proud ones, Who in their coaches roll along the turnpike-road, what hard work 'tis crying all day "Knives and Scissors to grind O!" Tell me, Knife-grinder, how came you to grind knives? Did some rich man tyrannically use you? Was it the Squire? Or Parson of the Parish? Or the Attorney? Was it the Squire for killing of his Game? Or Covetous Parson for his Tythes distraining? Or roguish Lawyer made you lose your little All in a law-suit? (Have you not read the Rights of Man, by Tom Paine?) Drops of compassion tremble on my eye-lids, Ready to fall, as soon as you have told your pitiful story.'

Knife-grinder: 'Story! God bless you! I have none to tell, Sir. Only last night a-drinking at the Chequers, This poor old Hat and Breeches, as you see, were Torn in a scuffle. Constables came up for to take me into Custody: they took me before the Justice. Justice Oldmixon put me in the Parish Stocks for a Vagrant. I should be glad to drink your Honour's health in A Pot of Beer, if you would give me Sixpence; But for my part, I never love to meddle With Politics, Sir.'

Friend of Humanity: 'I give thee Sixpence! I will see thee damn'd first. Wretch! Whom no sense of wrongs can rouse to vengeance. Sordid, unfeeling, reprobate, degraded, Spiritless outcast!' (Kicks the Knife-grinder, overturns his Whell, and exit in a transport of republican enthusiasm and universal philanthropy.)

This parody is valuable not only because it attacks the comfortable romantic imaginations (or labelling) of the poor and the consequent hypocrisies inherent in that position, but also because it represents the divergences of view about the label 'poverty' itself[18] – divergences that have continued to the present day – and because it suggests that the label of poverty may be entirely uninteresting to the knife-grinder himself, even though he may be doing a variety of things to ensure the quality of his life.[19]

Labels are valid principally for the creator

As Kant so clearly identified, the validity of labels is never with reference to some possible external 'truth' since the labels are a creation of human beings – so the validity can only be for the creators of the labels and to their utility in categorizing actions in a manner satisfactory to the creators. It is commonplace to say that the 'terrorist' for one person may be the 'freedom fighter' of the other. And since people of different environments, backgrounds and education will see the same picture in different ways it is quite clear that the different labels they bring may only be reconciled with one another by mutual interest. This therefore also means that there is much scope for disagreement about the nature of a situation, the factors that lead to the situation, or the actions that might lead to its improvement. But, whether help is requested or not, people remain wanting to do something.

In addition to their merely transitory and subjective validity, labels also have the problem of isolating only a particular aspect of a person's life. They may in fact be very independent, happy, intelligent and fulfilled people despite also carrying around with them the label of 'poor', 'oppressed', 'marginalized', 'criminal', 'sex workers' or whatever.

The cracks appear

Much of the debate concerning the validity of various types of development practice has not really reached the general public who give their money or volunteer their time. As a result, with the enormous increase in the numbers of the development organizations in the post Second World War period, and the growth of the development industry as a career path, there have been widening gulfs between:

1   the expectations and motivations of those who contribute money to agencies;[20]
2   the aims of those who represent the agencies to the public and who manage the programmes; and
3   the understanding and perspectives of those who work for the agencies in the field.[21]

Figure 6.2 *The Brueghel peasant wedding dance speech*

There are a number of possible reasons for these gulfs. The people who give in general do so in the trust that the agencies do what they seem to suggest with their advertising. But, as has been suggested, there are increasing questions as to:

- whether the interventions are truly benevolent (i.e. that the interest of the work be not so much in serving others, as in seeking profit, curiosity, pleasure, employment, travel or even, as in Booth's words, a motivation to find 'their own salvation while seeking vainly to bring salvation to others');[22]
- whether the aims as stated to the public are in fact being met;
- whether the analysis (framing) of the problem matches the complex realities influencing the situation of the person being targeted by the beneficence.

Poverty, injustice, suffering

Most people working for development agencies are used to the idea that there is no one type of poverty, no one form of inequality, no one type of injustice. Thus:

- President Nyerere of Tanzania was famous for his espousal of a 'human dignity' approach to development.

- The Millennium Development Goals provide an economic measure of poverty.
- There are a number of different 'Quality of Life' Indices.
- Different people and agencies target the particular inequalities, sufferings or injustices in which they have an interest.
- There are those who espouse relativistic definitions, and those who go for a fixed level.

This range has existed for centuries. The range follows the motivations for compassion. Most people who act out of compassion do so because they do not like the thought that some people (invariably of a particular type) undergo some particular form of suffering whilst being unable to do much about it. Inevitably, the reason for their having a particular form of compassion is subjective – embedded in their own experience of life as well as in their cultural framework that determines what is right and what is wrong. This in turn implies that there are particular types of people who they believe deserve support more than others, and particular types who 'deserve what they get' – the 'deserving' and the 'undeserving'. Different cultures, groups and communities will have very different perceptions as to who deserves support and who does not.

A very simple example of the failure of communication this can lead to is the use of the word 'marginalization'. Many agencies have found that when they try to find out who in a community is 'marginalized', the people they talk to are mystified. What exactly does that mean? Some people deliberately keep themselves apart from the main group, and different sub-groups choose not to mix with other sub-groups. Who marginalizes whom? Similarly the concept of 'vulnerability' – ask who is more vulnerable and there is confusion since all people can be considered vulnerable in one way or another at different times or in different situations.[23]

This type of problem is a very common one for development workers to face. When working with any particular group, members of the group are in general far quicker to spot what the workers want and the ways in which workers use categories than is the worker to have even a glimpse of local realities. The group invariably exploits the worker for its own benefit by using the language the worker tries to use. So if the workers want poverty, they'll get poverty. If they want gender imbalance, they'll get that. If they want injustice, that can be thrown in for no extra effort. Another scenario, of course, is that there is a battle of wits or even that the group just says yes and pads off to do their own thing. It is in this way that the different purposes are matched – the same language is used, but each side can claim they are achieving something different.

The moral maze

The centrality of moral judgement and attitude in the labels accorded either to individuals or their social environment is just as problematic when considering the 'scientific' or supposedly morally neutral view of poverty. In order to avoid subjective and emotional bases for aid, the idea here is to apply morally neutral policies for its provision (i.e. generalized provision of services, of support, of legislation).

The most recent proponents of a supposedly morally neutral approach, which in public policy terms can be traced back to the Elizabethan Poor Laws of the late 16th and 17th centuries, are Rothstein and Uslaner,[24] whose starting point is the centrality of trust:

> At the individual level, people who believe that most other people in their society in general can be trusted, are also more inclined to have a positive view of their democratic institutions, to participate more in politics and to be more active in civic organisations. They also give more to charity and they are more tolerant towards minorities and to people who are not like themselves ... Cities, regions and countries with more trusting people are likely to have better working democratic institutions, to have more growth in their economy and less crime and corruption.
>
>   ... Trust also is part of a social conscience – the belief that the various groups in society have a shared fate and that it is the responsibility of those with more resources to provide for those with less ... Yet, helping those with fewer resources does not simply involve taking from the rich and giving to the poor ... Instead, we argue, the policies most effective in reducing inequalities are universal social policies.
>
>   ... Our argument is that universal programmes that cater to the whole (or very broad sections) of society, such as we find in the Scandinavian countries especially, lead to a greater sense of social solidarity which spurs generalised trust which then lead to more equality in turn.

The universal programmes of which Rothstein and Uslaner speak are the improvements in economic equality and in equality of opportunity – the latter being seen in relation to public education, labour market opportunities and gender equality. They contrast this approach with selective welfare programmes whose disadvantage they see as follows:

> Selective welfare programmes on the other hand, tend to stigmatise recipients as 'welfare clients'. They demarcate the rich and the poor very clearly and those at the bottom are made to feel that they are less worthy, not least because of the bureaucratic intrusion felt in the process of implementation. Universal programmes are connected to citizens' rights, while selective welfare programmes have trouble with legitimacy because they have to single out the 'deserving' from the 'non-deserving poor'.

Whilst this kind of argument is very alluring, it suffers from two main problems.

The *first* is that the society generated is just more willing to give charitably. This may in fact be a worthwhile conclusion (or at least more honest) in that it suggests that the aim is not to eradicate 'poverty' or any other form of suffering, but to allow the continuation of the multiple ways in which individuals and states choose to understand the problems of others and react. In other words, those feeling good are those who are giving and they will continue in their own ways to select their particular categories of deserving from the non-deserving. A rather odd argument for a policy that is supposed to be values-free!

The *second* is that it is unclear which is cause and which effect – trust or equity – and in their conclusions they point to the pessimism of their vision as they claim that lack of equity and lack of trust are locked in a never-ending vicious cycle. So if they are in a vicious cycle they fail to suggest how policy can break it.

They also fail, though, to deal with the issue that dogged the approach of the Elizabethan Poor Laws, notably that the generalized measures never had an effect on the existence of poverty and that more and more resources had to be channelled from the state to cover the support of those deemed as 'poor'.[25]

The labels in the above example are quite subtle in their application – they are more often implied rather than stated – but no matter how value-neutral they are purported to be they none the less reflect a very particular set of values.

Values, trust and hypocrisy

Return now to the more overtly values-laden approaches.[26] For some people there is nothing problematic about a values-laden approach. All it means, after all, is that those who give aid or support do so on their own terms. It is their perception that counts, and especially as, according to them, they are the owners of the resources or privilege, it is theirs to dispense with as they please. Furthermore, since they will claim they can't help everyone in the world, they could say it is inevitable that some form of selection must occur, and that their particular means of selection is as good as any other. It should be noted that this argument does not depend for its validity on whether those being helped agree with the way their situation is defined.

The problem with this is the fact that purported benevolence (by governments, NGOs or individuals) is so often in one way or another *hypocritical* that it leads to deep-seated unease amongst those working in the industry with a large proportion of current development practice, supposed philanthropy and ostensible compassion.

Few if any agencies care to talk openly about their own hypocrisies. This might be understandable to some, but this makes it difficult to trust the openness of their criteria for giving aid. To what extent are they accountable and to whom? To what extent are they honest about their results? To what extent are they honest about their motivations?

It could be argued that most development agencies are clear about their criteria for selection or analysis. The current American governmental policies on aid are clear not only about their moral standpoint, but also about which types of person and country can benefit from their aid – agencies wanting American funding have to sign contracts not only that they will not benefit specific types of people, but also that they won't work with any that do. Many religious agencies are clear that only the people belonging to their religion should benefit. A wide variety of targeted programmes exist only for people with some specific disease, or who are members of a particular ethnic group, or who have a particular gender, or who have a particular age range or even a particular occupation.

Unfortunately, whilst the criteria for selection are clear, the realities faced by the workers often make it impossible to match those criteria, or else a lot of invention has to go on to make it seem they are applied. Very good examples abound in programmes for people with AIDS, or for children supposedly made vulnerable because of AIDS. Similarly, groups are quite ready to claim for themselves the criteria for aid whether or not there is a match.

But there is real suffering

Whatever the argument about labels, victims do exist. People suffer disasters, and are exploited, abused, neglected, expelled, terrorised and killed.[27] Countless treatises on the art of development, after they have made their criticisms on the basis of a variety of failures, come back to this point and the authors beat their breasts in anguish over what positively can 'be done'.[28]

... and many people do benefit

Undeniably, many people in the world have benefited from the development industry. Some have got medicines for some of the time, some have set up small businesses, some have had access to water and to other resources, some have survived another day, some have received the armaments necessary to blow to pieces those they see as their oppressors, homes have been rebuilt after disasters. It would be madness to deny this. And of course there are the millions of people who are benefiting directly from the development business as a result of employment and the foreign exchange and commercial opportunities brought in the train of the expatriates who still dominate the industry.

But many situations evade easy categorization

Whenever I have started to probe the reasons for differences between people and households in a variety of urban and rural communities, I am nearly always drawn to the sheer complexity of the processes that lead to a particular situation. Take, for example the problem of chronic illness and disability, which is very strongly associated with poverty because the amount of time that has to be devoted to the care of the person concerned, as well as because that person finds it hard or impossible to work, or to interact with others. In every community there are households with chronic illness that are well supported by others around them, and households with the same chronic illness that are not well supported. Why this difference? Every time I have asked this question the first response has been '*It depends what that person or family were like before their illness*'. In other words if the family or person had been seen to be pulling their weight in the community, being kind, fulfilling their obligations, they would be supported. If not, then mostly they would be helped only if they gave payment or their inheritance. I have heard the same response when asking the question why some households look after foster children well, and others do not. The situation is therefore not one of simple stigmatization, fear or whatever, but one based on human interactions and the perceptions of those interactions. The challenge then becomes for the society 'Even if you do not like a person or household, can you change the support mechanisms that exist to include that person?' And there is no easy answer to that in any society. Again, the question of motivations crops up.

So the problem of labels begins to look not as a problem for achieving consensus on labels, since no easy labels are applicable, but on how to resolve complex situations that everyone recognizes but which few are prepared to resolve.

Spectator sport

There is a fundamental mismatch between two sets of reality. On one side there is the set of desires of people to contribute money or resources or expertise which are channelled through professional agencies to remove or alleviate poor conditions. On the other is the set of complex realities of the people they believe they are helping – realities that fail to be captured by the labels or frames currently in use, and that are so complex that current and past policies are woefully inadequate.

The generalized goals of aid or development agencies that talk of the war against poverty, or the mitigation of poverty, or empowerment of women, or human rights are mostly cant – pious words used insincerely – and they are also used hypocritically. The labels that are used can never reflect the range of realities of people, their interactions and their environments. Whipping up public anger on the basis of such labels is deceitful manipulation. But the expectations of people are so high about the spending of their money that the agencies can hardly do otherwise, and so both the public that give money and the agencies are locked into a mutually reinforcing cycle of the maintenance of 'development' programmes using descriptions of situations that are so clearly inadequate and misrepresentative. The viciousness of this cycle is fuelled by the competition between agencies for funds from the public.

It is this aspect that is suggested in the title of this essay in referring to poverty as a spectator sport – one in which people pay for and contribute to an event in which they play no part, and to which they have no accountability. It is a theatrical event in the sense that a series of artfully contrived pictures or presentations are provided to a public that demands a certain type of show. Those that give are removed in every possible way from the situation they believe they are benefiting, and the agencies make sure they are even more removed by keeping the descriptions simplistic and the reporting minimal. As a result the agencies themselves have little accountability either to the people who contribute money or to those supposed to be benefiting. If situations get a bit difficult, or funding dries up, they just move on.

A possible defence by the implementing aid agencies is that they are professional, that they employ people with experience of local situations who make judgements on the basis of extensive exploration with the people they serve and that detailed explanation of these processes is simply not wanted by the donating public. Unfortunately, although this is true at one level – that professionals are employed – it is equally true that the great bulk of their work is with little value in relation to the changes they claim to be making. Again this is a problem of the great generality of the labels tied to the objectives. There is no *one* poverty, no *one* inequality, no *one* injustice, no *one* power, no *one* exploitation. There are countless types of each category resulting from the myriad types of human interaction even within one small group of people.

... and the competition of the analysts

There is therefore another aspect to 'poverty as spectator sport': it is the competition between professionals about the analyses they apply – which drives them further and further from ordinary realities which people can sense for themselves in their interactions. This competition is furthermore one of the different 'wills' to establish the dominance of their particular identity.

The labels and frames of analysis that are used are therefore irrelevant – what is driving the problem is, on the one hand, the need to be benevolent, with the agencies trying to meet that need; and, on the other, the clash of wills between agencies, professionals and intellectuals over the particular labels or frameworks they deem to be 'the underlying factors' or the most likely to achieve 'results'. It seems to matter little whether anyone actually asks for benevolence since such discussion is entirely over their heads and of great irrelevance to them – except insofar as they have to put up with multitudes of different people claiming to represent their causes in different ways. However, because it is clear that, in some instances and for some people, benefit is indeed obtained, then it would be churlish to claim that benevolence is of itself bad.

Taking a step back

Talking of alleviation of poverty or inequality (or whatever the generalized label of the moment) is only done within certain moral contexts (the analyses themselves are products of those moral contexts, or of the 'moral wills' of the professionals), and the morality of the situation is always determined by the donor, not by the person who is labelled or whose situation is so partially described. This is very clearly seen in the examples given above when communities decide to offer or withhold support to particular households. Quite often the aim of an aid programme is 'how to make those people more like the vision we have of ourselves' or how to help those 'who have been like ourselves'.

If this is the case, then talk of 'eradicating poverty', or helping the most marginalized, least powerful, least healthy or weakest is pure cant and hypocrisy unless one adds to this the constant refrain 'as long as those people are doing what we think is right and proper' – in the image of ourselves.

Even if no agency would ever dare do this, its acknowledgement would at least provide some balm for those in the development business who feel so strongly the inadequacies and hypocrisies of what they (and I) do. It might also take us a step closer to seeing a different type of vision for 'development'.

At the moment the development world is very cosy, as much for those who work within it, as for those who sustain it. Little coteries hug themselves in small self-righteous groups, clinging to their particular cause. What is unacknowledged is that such a world is based on the need for a constant supply of beneficiaries, or victims. And this supply is guaranteed because of the diversity of understandings of poverty, or of inequality or of abuses of power. It is not that 'the poor are always with us' in the sense that one type of poverty will always exist, but that whatever the society there will always be some people *categorized* or *labelled* as poorer in the same multiplicity of ways and for the same multiplicity of reasons.

Without thinking about it, without questioning it, people outside the development industry probably recognize this truth. People in the street seem to live quite happily with a whole line of different charity shops each with their own particular niche. They realize that so far no one has found a solution to the problems arising from the differences between people, but they still want to help out. They want to believe in the ability of the organizations to which they give because it makes them feel that in one small way they may be doing somebody some good. The same goes for many of those who contribute their work to aid organizations. This is not necessarily the type of person who will burn themselves alive because of the lack of progress on world poverty or the status of women, and it would be mad to accuse them of the hypocrisies discussed in this paper. We simply are organisms that muddle our ways through life with a multitude of conflicting attitudes, motivations, desires, habits and interactions.

It's like any political game

One way of looking at the situation is to think in terms of the ways in which people believe that political parties represent ideologies. In most modern democracies they don't, and politicians in private acknowledge that they are there to attract the largest number of voters

– which means diminishing the number of contentious issues and establishing broad-based positions with the maximum appeal and the minimum of accountability. Their principal job in reality is the management of conflicting opinions in their constituencies. Yet they also know that it is important to give the impression of having an ideology. There thus results a mismatch when people who wish their political party to pursue a particular ideology see that their expectations are not being fulfilled. Modern development agencies seeking sufficient funding to prop up their vast empires must do the same. The French have a phrase for this process, the 'pensée unique' which signifies the need for the media to pursue as bland a path as possible, thus making all the big media say pretty much the same things, and staying well away from the issues that might drive either advertisers or public away. It is only the small agencies, like the small media, who can pursue their particular ideological paths, and they will attract the small number of donors who share that ideology.

However, as for the people who give in blind faith to the local charity shops, so the majority of people vote for political parties in the blind faith that they might, just might, do some good. Passionate ideologues will always have their place and will always make a lot of noise, but most of the time they are easily sidelined.

The war is with ourselves

The question is not how to keep on bashing at a multiplicity of visions of poverty, power or whatever and pretending they represent one global vision, but to acknowledge the huge diversity of types of poverty, types of inequality, types of injustice; to acknowledge that for the multiplicity of situations there is a multiplicity of approaches, motivations and end points. This may be less sexy, but it is definitely closer to the truth.

The other aspect referred to above, the need to ensure that those on the receiving end are involved in the thinking, planning and assessment of benevolent acts, is something that is promoted endlessly but rarely done in a truthful way. Agencies are simply too frightened of their donors (individuals, agencies, governments or foundations) and of failure to allow this on any scale. It seems to me that the only way out of this is that some kind of understanding is reached – at least between the donor agencies and implementing agencies – that failure is OK, that fuzziness is OK, as long as some kind of honesty can be achieved and as long as the benefits are agreed in some way to outweigh the disadvantages. Unfortunately, honesty rarely, if ever, seems to be repaid.

Another suggestion, which is also unlikely as an achievable goal, is to re-establish the complexity of human interactions, likes and dislikes at the centre of development practice. There is in fact little value in shouting at one another with the various flags we like to use, since there is no common basis for an understanding of the flags or even frameworks. There is no common 'mankind' to whom we should all be addressing ourselves. The war is not with 'those in power' or 'men' or 'the wealthy' or even with the 'ignorant people who fail to see the benefit of our programmes'. The war is with ourselves. The labels and frames we use have no value except, perhaps, as starting points for joint exploration with the groups and societies for which we may feel, in our variety of ways, compassion.[29] Again, very few agencies are likely to want to do this since no end point or objective is defined, and it could lead to the discovery of truths that may be unpalatable to the desire for simple victims – people may in fact prefer to fuel their compassion with lies in order to avoid facing up to the fact that their compassion may be misplaced.

A simple exercise may bring this home. Think for a moment about the variety of neighbours, acquaintances or colleagues you have ever known. Which of them would you help if they looked as if they were in difficulty, and which of them would you be very reluctant to help? What are the criteria for your decision? What emotions or experiences led you to that decision? What purpose lies behind a decision to help or not to help? How do you come to think they might need help in the first place? What makes you interested in their particular problem? How do you verify whether they needed help? What makes you decide to help in a particular way? Everyone's answers to these questions are different. That is exactly what development is about.

Notes

1   Consultant in international health and development. tonyklouda@gmail.com.
2   Rough translation: 'The huge success of television in the 1960s led to considerable centralization and standardization of the way information was provided to the public. The fierce competition engendered by the need for ratings pushed all the television channels to prioritize "info-tainment". In order to keep people's interest, they had to show a constant stream of images of "victims": victims of disasters, of avian flu and, above all, of violence – because there is nothing more spectacular than images of war, of bombings, of burning cars.'
3   'Victim' is a term used here in both senses: (1) a subjective and emotional label implying that the objects are subject to forces supposedly outside their control; (2) objects being worked on for the satisfaction of the person in control without the consent of the 'victim'.
4   'Labelling' in this context refers to the use of categories to define people or situations for the purposes of creating development programmes.
5   Since the use of labels can be patronizing, can reflect power differences, can lead to neglect of those without the label, and because different discourses use different labels and are dependent on the perceptions of those creating the categories.
6   Klouda, A. 'Helping, challenging or using others?' www.tonyklouda.pwp.blueyonder.co.uk/Helping_Challenging_Using.htm, January 2005.
7   Please note that the word 'benevolence' is often scorned as something that might be patronizing or sentimental, perhaps as in 'acts of kindness'. This is not the usage of the word in this paper. It is taken in its more generic sense as 'the will to act for the benefit of someone else'.
8   i.e. social relationships, economic or other environments, class struggle.
9   Selflessness, of course, is not a motivation, but is included here because of its impact on the three motivations.
10   To use the formulation of Ludwig Wittgenstein in his development of Schopenhauer's thinking.
11   Another manifestation of the 'will' referred to by Schopenhauer.
12   This range includes the motivations not only of those who give money, but also the professionals and others who work for agencies.
13   Perhaps a better word would be *e*motivation.
14   There have been many articles on the neo-colonialism of development practice. The point here is merely to place it in the context of motivations.
15   Himmelfarb, G. *Poverty and Compassion: The Moral Imagination of the Late Victorians*, Vintage Books, 1992.

16 I took this delightful phrase ('masquerading as enlightenment and virtue') from an article by Ian Haywood, 'The renovating fury': Southey, Republicanism and Sensationalism, www.erudit.org/revue/ron/2003/v/n32-33/009256ar.html.

17 Library of Congress Prints and Photographs Division, Washington DC, 20540 USA http://lcweb2.loc.gov/cgi-bin/query/I?ils:2:./temp/~pp_rFiN::displayType=1:m856sd=cph:m856sf=3g03141:@@@

18 It also, by the by, shows how times have not really changed at all in the deliberate use of an imaginary sob-story (the story of the poor widow, scorned by rich passers-by, who is inherently a 'good' person but for the neglect of the surrounding world) to engender shallow pity for the implicit state of all people who are classed as 'poor'.

19 And this brings with it, of course, the hint that his understanding of quality of life may be entirely different from that of the Jacobin.

20 The history of the changes in motivation for giving between the Second World War and the present is highly interesting, as it reflects the change of levels of comfort of the general public in European countries, but this cannot be explored here.

21 I remember a conversation with someone from the headquarters of my own agency in 1979. We were looking at a project in a village in Tanzania. I suggested to him that he was unaware of the realities of local life. He chillingly replied 'My reality is the only one that is valid'.

22 Charles Booth, *Life and Labour of the People in London*, vol 1, p26, London, 1892.

23 The concept of 'vulnerability' has been much abused by development agencies. Its use suggests 'risk'. Risk implies that one type of situation carries a greater risk than another. It should be a comparative term, but rarely, if ever, is the situation labelled as 'vulnerable' compared in any measurable way with another possible situation. Again the use is emotive whilst being presented as logical.

24 Rothstein B. and Uslaner E. M. *All for All: Equality and Social Trust*, LSE Health and Social Care Discussion Paper Number 15, first published in April 2005 by LSE Health and Social Care.

25 As has, indeed, been the effect of the policy on the Nordic countries.

26 It should be noted that a desire to reduce inequalities or promote rights is just as value-laden as a desire to help people who are labelled in a particular way.

27 Some killed, of course, as the result of development policies that provide armaments to poor countries, which falls into the category of poverty alleviation.

28 One such author is James Ferguson in his book *The Anti-Politics Machine: 'Development', Depoliticization, and Bureaucratic Power in Lesotho*, Cambridge University Press, 1990.

29 One of the reasons why Arthur Schopenhauer put compassion at the centre of his philosophy – all true morality being founded for him on compassion.

7

'Muslim Women' and 'Moderate Muslims': British Policy and the Strengthening of Religious Absolutist Control over Gender Development

Cassandra Balchin

There is a clear synergy between the British state's foreign and domestic policies relating to the global 'war on terror' on the one hand, and the developmental policies it is pursuing towards Muslim societies on the other. Illustrative of this nexus are policies towards the categories 'Muslim women' and 'moderate Muslims'. Does this signal a fresh direction in British development policy towards women both in Muslim contexts abroad as well as at home, or is this simply a new manifestation of long-standing approaches by European governments (and by extension the policies of both governmental and non-governmental development agencies) towards issues arising from the intersection of gender and identity? Key to answering this question is an examination of who is included and excluded in these categories, as well as the actual outcomes in terms of women's collective struggles for equal rights in Muslim communities.

No matter what the imperatives – developmental or geo-political – it is clear that British policies regarding Muslim communities and countries with a significant Muslim population have largely failed to date. The home-grown repeat of the events of 11 September 2001 in the shape of the London bombings in July 2005 and the continuing rise of fundamentalisms in Muslim contexts abroad where there is significant British development aid, for example Pakistan and Nigeria, are stark evidence that something is not working. The precise nature of any link between disadvantage and extremism – the latter in this instance manifested in the form of religious absolutism – is not clear (Foreign and Commonwealth Office/Home Office (FCO/HO), Summary, 2004, p1). Nevertheless, in the case of the introduction of rigid interpretations of Muslim penal laws in Nigeria, factors related to the religious resurgence have been noted to include the uncertainty and difficulties that have resulted from the poverty and economic and social problems caused and/or exacerbated by World Bank/IMF-type structural adjustment and other economic policies (Imam, 2005). Disadvantage is therefore perhaps best described as a necessary, although not sufficient, condition for absolutism, and thus it is essential to re-examine the labels used in determining policy towards populations experiencing disadvantage and an apparently concomitant rise in religious absolutism.

In discussing these issues, this chapter draws upon my nearly 15 years' experience with the international solidarity network Women Living Under Muslim Laws (WLUML), engagement with women's groups in Britain's Muslim community since early 2002, as well as writings by networkers, and a critical examination of British government policy documents and initiatives both at home and abroad. I build upon analysis developed in an earlier paper critiquing donor practices regarding women in Muslim contexts (Balchin, 2003), updating it to take into account developments since 2002 and focusing more specifically on the British policy context.

This chapter begins with examining how the label 'Muslim women' is at times constructed widely and at other times narrowly, detailing how in both instances this works to women's disadvantage. It then looks at the label 'moderate Muslim' and how its use has impacted upon development policies and strengthened absolutist tendencies. This is followed by an exploration of some of the possible factors underlying such developments, and ends with suggestions as to how theories of intersectionality may be used to overcome the negative impact that this labelling is having upon gender rights and development.

'Muslim Women': Homogenization, submissiveness and collective responsibility

A seminar was held in Britain in July 2006 titled 'Muslim Women and Higher Education: Identities, Experiences and Prospects'. Speakers included political and academic figures as well as institutions, all at the centre of British policy towards 'the Muslim community'. There has, to my knowledge, been no parallel event regarding Hindu or Sikh women – the other two communities that placed religion as their second most important self-defining identity, nor indeed regarding Jewish women and yet this was the community whose individual members cited religious identity as the topmost defining aspect of themselves (Home Office Citizenship Survey, 2001). This was not an isolated event; policy papers and consultations in recent years have included topics such as 'Muslim women and health', 'Muslim women and housing', among others. Yet studies have found that the greatest challenges in terms of higher education and graduate prospects face people much more specifically of a Bangladeshi or Pakistani Muslim background (Halstead, 2005, p135). Even a report funded by the Home Office itself found that 31 out of 61 Muslim respondents felt that ethnic or racial grounds are the main or large part of the reason for unfair treatment on the basis of religion (Weller et al, 2001, p12). The category 'Muslim' can be a signifier of a person's faith or their cultural origins or both. In the British context, this could then include recently arrived Somali asylum seekers, White Scottish converts and third-generation South Asian migrants – who are likely to have more than divergent experiences of education. And this does not even begin to address class experience.

In the aftermath of the July 2005 London bombings, a wide range of women were included in public commentary about the Muslim community's collective responsibility.

At a meeting on 2 August 2005 with Assistant Commissioner Tarrique Ghaffur, the Metropolitan Police Force's highest-ranking Muslim officer, women from the Muslim community shared concerns about the implications of this emphasis on collective responsibility for acts of terrorism with women from the Irish and Black communities who had experienced comparable pressures of collective community responsibility for terrorism, gun crime and drug dealing, as well as with Sikh and Hindu women who had also been victims of increased racist attack since the July Bombings.

A similarly unnecessarily wide or undifferentiated range of people are also included in the 'problem' category of 'Muslim women' in foreign development policy. In 2004/05, DFID and British Council supported the production of a report 'Promoting Women's Rights Through Sharia in Northern Nigeria', as part of its Security, Justice and Growth Programme. The report, which has been heavily criticized by local women's groups and activists, makes innumerable sweeping statements about 'Muslim women'. Some are so broad as to be meaningless: 'Muslim women are generally excluded from decision making at the family and community levels' (Centre for Islamic Legal Studies, Ahmadu Bello University (ABU), 2005, p15). Two pages later, the report notes that 'The independence of Muslim women to do what they want with their income is very much documented', and 'a Muslim woman has power over decisions that affect the children of her brother and over issues that affect the extended family' (ABU, 2005, p17). Does the label 'Muslim' contribute anything to understanding the dynamics taking place here? There is also a worrying conflation of tradition and religious identity: 'The traditional modesty of Muslim women in Nigeria will hardly allow them to participate on the same scale as their male counterparts in political activities' (ABU, 2005, p30).

Such declarations are challenged by historical documentation of women's leadership and political activism in Muslim-dominated areas of Nigeria and ethnicities which include Muslims (Shaheed and Shaheed, 2004, pp52–54, 92–99). Worse, this normalizes a lack of voice for a very wide group of women, especially when accompanied by assertions in the report's 'What Sharia says' section that 'women can vie for any office except that of Head of State' (ABU, 2005, p30), and at the lowest level of decision making that a wife's 'main obligation' includes 'avoiding conduct that may offend [the husband]' (ABU, 2005, p8). These comments contradict the Nigerian constitution's guarantee of non-discrimination on the grounds of sex as well as the British government's obligations under international human rights law. It must also be asked, what is the British government doing by advocating as a means of 'promoting women's rights' in Muslim contexts highly conservative interpretations of Islam? What can possibly be the positive gendered developmental impact when such interpretations are able to claim they reflect 'an authentic understanding of Sharia' (ABU, 2005, p7)? This, despite the fact that such interpretations are highly contested (for example see WLUML, 1997).

'Muslim women': Veiling, authenticity and access to power

Meanwhile, since 9/11 and the immediately subsequent war in Afghanistan, various parts of government have been attempting to reach out to 'the Muslim community', including specifically 'Muslim women'. It is not the place of this chapter to discuss whether this is motivated purely by political expedience or a genuine desire to respond to claims of social disadvantage, or partly both, but instead to discuss the possible consequences of such labelling.

In early 2002, the then Minister for Women Patricia Hewitt began a series of occasional meetings with women from the Muslim community which subsequently coalesced into the Muslim Women's Network (MWN), whose declared aim is 'to mainstream the views of Muslim women to government'. Although the group has gone through some changes in membership composition, emphasis on religious identity has largely excluded the many women and groups with a long history of service provision in the Muslim community who see themselves as secular or who prefer to prioritize other aspects of their identity – and yet who either themselves or whose clients nevertheless experience the kinds of disadvantage raised by the MWN.

A spate of related government-funded initiatives followed in 2005. These included the 'Tackling Extremism Together' process whose seven working groups included one looking at the role of women, and the 'Muslim Women Talk' campaign – both chaired by Labour peer Baroness Pola Uddin and in response to the July bombings; and the previously planned MWN's 'Listening to Muslim Women Exercise'. Irrespective of how far each of these various initiatives actively sought to include secular women from the Muslim community, the actual framing of the issue meant presumptions were made about who was being addressed and thus in practice many were or felt excluded.

This sense of exclusion from the privileged group that apparently[1] had access to the 'ear of government' did not develop in isolation. In the same period, the most visible[2] government participation in issues relating to 'Muslim women' was Home Office Minister for Race Equality Fiona McTaggart's public support for the 'Assembly for the Protection of Hijab ('Pro-Hijab') launched at the House of Commons in London on 14 June 2004. The minister was quoted as stating that the government would do all it could to protect the right of Muslim women to wear hijab.[3] Similarly, the prime minister's high-profile wife, Cherie Blair, appeared as the counsel for Shabina Begum, a girl taking her school to court for refusing to allow her to wear the jilbab [all-covering gown] – even though the school's governors, Muslim parents among them, had allowed shalwar kamiz [baggy pants and long shirt] as appropriate school uniform.[4]

The definition of 'Muslim women' as veiled was reinforced by both the British media and politico-religious groups such as Muslim Council of Britain (MCB) and the Muslim Association of Britain. One of the first statements from such groups widely featured by the BBC the evening after the bombings highlighted the sense of insecurity and need for vigilance against racist attacks among all Muslims, 'especially women in headscarves'.[5] The repeated emphasis on 'women in headscarves' pointed not only to women's bodies and sexuality as being markers of the collectivity (Yuval-Davis, 1997, p38),[6] but also to a very limited definition of women who fall within the category of 'Muslim women'.

Thus the British government and absolutist groups in the Muslim community share an exclusionary definition of 'Muslim women'. Even the equally shared current fashion for condescendingly asserting that 'Muslim women are dynamic', while a welcome change from the previous presumption of overall passivity, is still taking place in a context where there is only one brand visible of 'Muslim woman'. Being a 'dynamic Muslim woman' is thus equated with wearing a headscarf and demanding rights, yet demanding rights per se without the headscarf just is not authentically 'Muslim' enough.[7] At least as far as the

British government is concerned, 'Muslim women' are evidently just a politically expedient category. In 2001, Afghanistan was invaded partly in their name ('Afghan women' being held synonymous with 'Muslim women'). But in July 2006 when news emerged of the threatened reintroduction by the Karzai government in Kabul of the obscurantist and deeply misogynist Ministry of Vice & Virtue, the British government was silent.

Meanwhile, the very narrow construction of 'Muslim women' overlooks the reality that women who may be affected by the discrimination or deprivation experienced by a Muslim community may themselves be from an entirely different faith or cultural background. WLUML pointedly also addresses itself to non-Muslim women married under Muslim laws or living in a context where Muslim laws affect their lives.[8]

Thus policies which address 'Muslim women' either forcibly include women who may not wish to be included or exclude those for whom developmental initiatives and alliances which could address factors behind religious absolutism are relevant.

'Moderate Muslims': The question of immoderation

Around 2003, women's groups in Muslim communities in France, the British-based group Women Against Fundamentalisms, and international networks such as WLUML began to critique what they termed 'the Unholy Alliance' between feminism's traditional presumed allies on the European Left, apparent liberals, and fundamentalist Muslim groups which was allowing the latter's capture of discourse on 'women and culture/religion' (WLUML, 2005). A central feature of this realignment was that certain Muslim groups and figures involved were both being labelled and claiming the label of 'moderates'. There is evidence that fundamentalist infiltration of the anti-globalization movement was a deliberate ploy (Fourest, 2004). Whether or not one accepts this, the Unholy Alliance coincided neatly with the British government's desperate 'war on terror' search for 'good Muslim' allies as distinguishable from 'bad Muslim' terrorists.

On 6 April 2004, a restricted Cabinet Office letter from Cabinet Secretary Sir Andrew Turnbull entitled 'Relations with the Muslim Community' and suggesting a broad inter-departmental initiative, noted that in a recent cabinet meeting ministers 'focused on the need to encourage moderate Muslim opinion to the detriment of extremism, both at home and overseas'.[9] In response, Home Office Permanent Secretary John Grieve shared a joint FCO and HO draft paper titled 'Young Muslims and Extremism'. The draft paper, amongst other suggestions, proposed building capacity amongst information services like the Muslim Council of Britain's website MCB Direct and 'strengthening the hand of moderate student and youth organisations (such as the UMS (Union of Muslim Students) and FOSIS (Federation of Student Islamic Societies)'(FCO/HO, 2004, Summary, p4).

Indeed the word 'moderate' appears on virtually every page without definition at any point, except indirectly in counterpoint: 'By extremism, we mean advocating or supporting views such as support for terrorist attacks against British or western targets, including the 9/11 attacks, or for British Muslims fighting against British or allied forces abroad, arguing that it is not possible to be British and Muslim, calling on Muslims to reject engagement with British society and politics, and advocating the creation of an Islamic state in Britain' (FCO/HO, 2004, p1). Thus any organization that holds misogynist, homophobic or anti-semitic views could, under this categorization, pass for 'moderate'. For example, one recommendation was possible support for the various Radio Ramadan stations that appear locally during the Muslim holy month; that some of these refuse to have women appear on air is ignored.[10]

By mid-2005, the British government's support for certain Muslim groups began to be publicly questioned, with a controversial BBC *Panorama* documentary in the summer[11] coinciding with a report in the mainstream *Observer* (Bright, 2005). In June 2006, a public forum on 'The Challenges of Political Islam' hosted at the School of Oriental and African Studies (SOAS) in London by AWAAZ – South Asia Watch[12] questioned the government's classification of various groups as 'moderate', and a month later Martin Bright, political editor of *The New Statesman*, in collaboration with the Tory think-tank, Policy Exchange, published 'When Progressives Treat With Reactionaries: The British State's flirtation with radical Islamism', based on a damning series of leaked FCO and HO documents. The report argues that 'the Government is engaged in a process of redefining radical Islam as "mainstream"... and the Government's main partners in the Muslim community are drawn from the Islamic religious right' (Bright, 2006, p12).

While progressive forces within Muslim contexts certainly need to examine their own failures, women's rights groups such as those linked through WLUML have recognized the need to initiate a pro-active debate with mainstream human rights groups around understandings of the topic 'religious groups', to expose the practical meaning of 'moderate Muslims', as well as the internal need to grapple with the nuances of the terms they use to define potential allies and enemies. At WLUML's 2006 Plan of Action meeting in Senegal, these issues were discussed and feature in the network's analysis (WLUML, 2006) as well as its planned activities.

Strengthening religious absolutism

Bright's critique of the 'moderates' label and of their claim to being the 'mainstream' middle-of-the-road majority is not new. In 2004, French feminist author Caroline Fourest in a well-sourced book on the high-profile figure Tariq Ramadan had already asked how it was that the views of certain Muslims, which if held by Christian figures would be immediately dismissed as coming from a far-right position, were so willingly accepted as 'moderate' by the European Left. Unfortunately, she asked her questions in French and has yet to find a publisher in Britain for a translation of her work.

As mentioned above, feminists in Muslim countries and communities had raised concerns about the impact that the legitimation of the claim to 'moderation' was having on women's struggles for their rights within Muslim contexts. In a spate of cultural relativism gone mad, discussion of the rights of women from Muslim communities shifted from their right to autonomous choice per se – free from restrictions imposed by state and non-state actors alike – to focusing uniquely on the fundamentalist leitmotif of the 'right to choose hijab'.

Although generalized statements about women's right to work are fashionably touted as proof of a particular group's 'moderate' status, it is ignored that the small print on this right invariably reads 'subject to conditions', which then accord the male presumed head of household the option of withholding the woman's 'right'. It would seem that government policy makers, long blind to the gendered impact of religious absolutism, have changed little.

Although deeper discussion of the link between politico-religious absolutism and socio-economic inequalities would require another chapter altogether, one of our original examples provides some brief clues. The first announcement of Sharianization[13] in Nigeria in November 1999 included a restriction on women's movements in public (Imam, 2005). The grave gendered human rights impact of the provisions have been well documented (Amnesty International, 2004). Despite the passage of some seven years since the introduction of various Sharia penal codes across the northern states, which also envisage heavy penalties for sexual crimes, sexual harassment of young girls while hawking continues, as noted even by the ABU report (2005, p9).

The discriminatory impact is visible beyond gender. The severe punishments provided for theft in these laws have usually not included crimes like embezzlement and the diversion of public resources into private use. Thus, bicycle thieves may run the risk of amputations whilst those in positions of power who steal millions of Naira have been left untouched (Imam, 2005). Equally, religious absolutists have obstructed child immunization in both India and Nigeria, as acknowledged by senior DFID staff and Hilary Benn, the Secretary of State for International Development (House of Commons, 2005, Ev 24 & Ev 52).

The question of who is included and excluded from the label 'moderate' has had a direct impact on humanitarian policy and development funding. Islamic Relief, which widely acknowledges its links with the MCB, has received £3.6 million in humanitarian relief and development aid over the years (DFID, 2005). Equally, had the FCO had a different understanding of what constitutes 'moderate' it might have supported different, more gender equitable, conclusions about the strategies appropriate for promoting women's rights in northern Nigeria. Closer to home, it has since been revealed that the MCB has received at least £150,000 in funding from the HO, a grant whose terms and conditions noted 'MCB will contribute to policy development work by attending meetings, submitting ideas, debating issues, etc, which may need to be on a strictly confidential basis' (Freedom of Information Act Centre (FOIA), 2006). In essence, the British government allowed the MCB's input to be beyond accountability – at least for the community it supposedly 'represented'.

Government support for charities linked with political absolutist organizations is not limited to British support for Muslim charities. In January 2005, Indian anti-communalist activists noted that the Swedish Sida-supported Delhi organization Jan Manch was carrying a press release from a charity with known links with Hindu extremist organizations.[14] Similarly, the legitimation of right-wing religious figures resulting from government policy has not been limited to British policy. Women activists in Muslim communities in the Philippines believe that USAID's efforts in 2003 to secure a joint fatwa promoting reproductive rights from local religious figures was a major factor in enabling the Ulema [religious authorities] to overcome previous differences and work together to form a united political force that subsequently dominated local councils until discredited as having no concrete policies to deal with the area's poverty.[15]

Multiculturalism, racism and global power dynamics

Many within the Muslim community in Britain and abroad have been exasperated by the British state's apparent blindness to the outcomes of its policies towards 'Muslim women' and 'moderate Muslims', many of which are proving to have had an entirely opposite effect from the declared aim. The only explanations for such grave errors seem to lie in analysis of multiculturalism, racism and Orientalist stereotyping of Muslim contexts, modernity and global power imbalances.

In the Philippines example above, local women activists also noted that the area had no prior tradition of securing such fatwas from religious figures. This illustrated the general inability of European and North American governments to be able to relate to Islam except through their experience of Christian traditions. Hence the inclination to create a spokesman-clergy where Islam has none.[16] In the case of Britain, this neatly coincides with multiculturalism's need for 'community representatives'. That such spokespersons are invariably conservative males whose views impact upon women's human rights is generally overlooked.

The British state's policies of exoticizing multiculturalism have further disenfranchised minority communities (Donald and Rattansi, 1992, p2). This is particularly so for minority women, as groups such as Southall Black Sisters and Women Against Fundamentalisms have sought to point out, where 'traditional' has been seen as synonymous with legitimately 'authentic' against the background of flourishing identity politics from the mid-1980s onwards (Sahgal and Yuval-Davis, 1992). Multiculturalism's psychological interpretation of racism as individual prejudice (Donald and Rattansi, 1992, p3) has also eroded the possibilities of engaging with the structural forces that produced social inequities.

The fundamentalism found today across all major religions has been one of the major outcomes of enlightenment modernity (Armstrong, 2000); both politico-religious extremism and modernity share a 'distinctive regime of truths' (Gilroy, 1999), largely centred around notions of 'race' and 'culture'. Hence the British state's sense of comfort in dealing solely with the absolutist groups it defines as 'moderate Muslims'. The fundamentalist leadership has been a prime beneficiary of multiculturalism (Yuval-Davis, 1992).

This need for a single spokesman-voice is apparently at odds with the new emphasis on diversity within Islam. Having ignored decades-long attempts by women activists from Muslim contexts to challenge the myth of one homogeneous Muslim world and ensure recognition of diversities across and within Muslim contexts, British policy both domestic and foreign has more recently found an emphasis on 'Muslim diversity' politically expedient. In Iraq this is manifested as emphasizing the sectarian and tribal distinctions between Iraqi citizens, and at home diversity is used to draw a distinction between 'good' and 'bad' Muslims. This may signal a shift from an earlier categorization. A 1999 study (Silverman and Yuval-Davis) of the British media found a tendency to distinguish between 'our Muslims' – those of a new Commonwealth and Pakistan origin, with their linkages to the British imperial past – and those beyond this pool. But the limitations of any such recognition of diversity need to be explored. One of the few recommendations of the 'Tackling Extremism Together' initiative (see above) that has been implemented is the June 2006 creation of the Mosques & Imams National Advisory Board (MINAB).[17] Quite apart from the foundational question of ideologically divergent interpretations of Islam, it remains to be seen whether 'diversity' extends to the inclusion of women, of lesbian, gay, bisexual and transgender (LGBT) Muslims, and of minority groups such as the Ahmedis and Zikris. If not, a government-funded body could run the risk of violating national equalities legislation.

What appears so far not to have been factored into the British government's understanding of 'diversity' within the Muslim community (and therefore to have coloured understandings of the label 'moderate') are the distinctions between social location, identity and political values: that one is born into a Muslim family does not necessarily mean one identifies as Muslim, and nor does a Muslim identity necessarily mean adherence to a conservative political ideology.[18] Permanent Secretary John Grieve in his 10 May 2004 response to Sir Andrew Turnbull noted that, 'The links between social deprivation among British Muslims and extremism is not simple cause and effect.'[19] Case histories, he points out, indicate that in addition to under-achievers with few or no qualifications, the British Muslims most at risk of being drawn into extremism also include the well educated. If this knowledge had been examined more closely, the conclusion should have been that disadvantage is not synonymous with disaffection, and values – or political ideology – needed to be added as an explanation. Instead, there is a return to the comfortable Orientalist vision of Muslims as bound to be 'Other', which is based on a conflation of identity with values. The FCO/HO report on Young Muslims and Extremism, included in Grieve's response, comments: 'A strong Muslim identity and strict adherence to traditional Muslim teachings are not in themselves problematic or incompatible with Britishness' (FCO/HO, Summary, 2004, p1). This background racism explains how, despite evidence to the contrary, the British state ended up stubbornly refusing to see that they are labelling the wrong end of the spectrum as mainstream (Bright, 2006, p23) and instead legitimizing groups that pursue an absolutist interpretation of religion.

Meanwhile, with the focus so squarely on Muslims, their identity and their politics, wider factors contributing to international instability such as global trade inequalities and militarization are conveniently side-stepped. A critique of the 2005 report prepared for the US Air Force by the influential right-wing American think tank RAND Corporation notes 'all that America needs to do, the report naively suggests, is to devise ways of neutralising the "extremists", with the help of "moderate Muslims", without needing to make any structural changes in its economic, political and strategic policies towards the "Muslim World"' (Sikand, 2005).

But British policy towards 'Muslim women' is not uniformly blind in substance both to gender and to the range of political ideologies held by Muslim groups. For example, in late 2005 the British Council Malaysia sponsored a tour of local women's groups in British Muslim communities by the progressive Malaysian advocacy group Sisters in Islam, which uses both international human rights language and gender-sensitive reinterpretations of Muslim texts to promote women's rights. Similarly, DFID is currently sponsoring a major five-year research consortium on Women's Empowerment in Muslim Contexts, which clarifies that its focus on Muslim contexts is 'because women's empowerment in Muslim contexts is being contested intensely by certain political Islamists'.

But such initiatives do remain isolated examples.

At times a review of British policy discussions becomes immensely frustrating as time and again analysis emerges that ought to lead to more effective policy towards 'Muslim women' both at home and abroad. For example, the FCO/HO report quotes the Prime Minister's Strategy Unit's Strategic Audit as identifying 'three key trends':

1   A small yet vocal minority has become radicalised and has sought to construct a relatively narrow interpretation of Islam, drawn partly from transnational and international sources.

2   A larger group has retained an Islamic identity whilst successfully adapting to and integrating with mainstream British society.

3   A large group no longer identifies positively with their Muslim origins. (FCO/HO, 2004, p8)

Were FCO officials to take any note of the vibrant women's rights movements in most Muslim contexts outside Europe and the Americas, and share this with their HO counterparts, the British government's current 'moderate Muslim' allies might find themselves reallocated to the first group.

But at least for the time being the dots are not being joined up, possibly because of the blindness of the Orientalist vision and possibly also because of the personal influence of some 'Muslim advisors' in the FCO (Bright, 2006, pp24–26).

Alternative approaches: Intersectionality

When gender is factored into a critique of the operation of religious groups, the utility of the British government's current emphasis on 'faith communities' as avenues for addressing disadvantage – to the exclusion of other identities or an intersectional approach – becomes at best unproven. A 2006 research report into how faith communities connect or divide society took as its starting point the government's identification of 'faith communities as important sources of social capital'. Yet the report is throughout characterized by an 'on the one hand' and 'on the other hand' approach. For example: 'Faith buildings are a home where people can share a common life and form bonds with one another' as contrasted with 'But faith association can also produce restricting spaces. Many faith communities fail to listen to women or young people within their number (Joseph Rowntree Foundation (JRF), 2006, pp2–3).

Elsewhere, I have already critiqued the near obsession with religion among European and North American governments and aid agencies, including seeing religion as 'the problem' to the exclusion of all others, and 'the solution' to the exclusion of all others (Balchin, 2003). As I also argued in the same paper, this is not to forget that religion – as faith – may be immensely important to some women and an essential part of women's daily lives, as illustrated in a Pakistan study.[20] But what may well concretely advance policy towards the category 'Muslim women' is a conscious intersectionality approach.

Feminist theorizing, largely but not exclusively outside the hegemonic white 'western' tradition, has established the interconnected nature of social divisions such as gender, ethnicity, 'race' and class (Anthias and Yuval-Davis, 1983; Brah, 1991; Eisenstein, 1994; Harding, 1991; Hill-Collins, 1994; Pettman, 1999). A similar position has been taken by theorists on culture and 'race' (Hall, 1992). An intersectionality approach also rejects attempts to place oppressions in a hierarchy (Adams, 1994; Hill-Collins, 1994) and thus 'Muslim + Women' are no more or less oppressed than 'Women', the latter category simply being so broad as to be unhelpful in understanding the lived experience of oppression. But this is neither the approach of religious absolutists in the Muslim community, who gain political mileage out of the claim of an all-embracing victimhood for all members of the community, nor is it the approach of the British government, whose multicultural multifaith policy precludes the 'joined up' nature of intersectionality.

But while social divisions constitute and are constituted by each other, their discursive nature does not mean they are without material effect (Anthias and Yuval-Davis, 1983), and their interconnectedness can be seen at the experiential and empirical level (Anthias and Yuval-Davis, 1992, p103). It is at this material level that we witness the reproduction of these systems of social classification within relationships of power (Barot et al, 1999, p10). How 'Muslim women' are represented is thus intimately connected with relations of power within Britain.

Some space exists within British policy for an intersectionality approach. The current government at least is attempting to move the entire race and equality juggernaut towards a theoretical acknowledgement of intersectionality with the planned merging of current statutory institutions such as the Commission on Racial Equality and gender-focused Equal Opportunities Commission into the unified Commission on Equalities and Human Rights covering six equalities: race, gender, age, sexual orientation, disability and religion. But whether the existing power brokers within the equalities industry in practice allow intersectionality to take root and whether the government provides the resources required to make this happen remains to be seen.

Conclusion

The above discussion illustrates how the category 'Muslim women' at times includes an indiscriminately wide range of women, undifferentiated by major social classifications such as class and ethnicity, and conflating social location, identity and values. This broadest interpretation of the label is used variously by different forces: by absolutist groups within the Muslim community to set up homogenizing boundaries within which they can assert control over women and on behalf of whom they can claim 'representation' (in contrast to progressive forces who steadfastly refuse to 'speak for'); and by the British state and wider society to hold as wide a group collectively accountable for acts of terrorism – in the case of racist sections of the British public, even including women from other religions (mainly Punjabi Sikhs and Hindus) who are assumed to be Muslim purely on account of their dress.

Yet at other times, when it comes to access to state power and to influencing policy and decision making, the label 'Muslim women' is deployed in its most restricted meaning, actively and by default all but excluding those who do not manifest a visible 'Muslim' identity, stereotypically in the form of veiling. Although veiling is by no means a guarantee of a particular ideology and care must equally be taken not to homogenize women who veil, since veiling is so vocally propounded by absolutist Muslim groups, there is some correlation between identity and values in this particular instance.

Thus these apparently contradictory trends of inclusion and exclusion have coincided to silence women's struggles for gender equality in Muslim contexts, a silencing that has been reinforced by the international legitimation of absolutist groups under the banner of 'moderate Muslims'. The wider result has been to obstruct progressive struggles against absolutism, leaving men and women in Muslim contexts with an unhappy 'choice': either accept a narrowly defined Muslim identity as promoted by right-wing ideology or find themselves largely silenced.

Far from shaking British policy out of the comfort zone of multiculturalism and racist Orientalism that has for decades informed development policy towards women and religious groups in Muslim contexts, the 'war on terror' appears to have exacerbated the deployment of the labels 'Muslim women' and 'moderate Muslim' in ways that will have a long-term negative impact upon gender equality and human development both at home and abroad.

Afterword

In the months following the writing of this chapter in the summer of 2006, the British government's relationship with certain political groups claiming to represent 'the Muslim community', specifically the MCB, has cooled noticeably. It is not clear whether this response has been due to growing protests against the claim to representation from within Muslim communities, or questions raised in the right-wing media (including Bright's report detailed in the chapter), or internal Labour Party leadership dynamics, or any combination of these. What has been noticed, however, is that a previously unheard of Sufi Council of Britain is now becoming more visible. Both media and government seem to have seized upon this new category as the answer to their need for alternative 'spokespersons'. Apparently being interpreted as a Muslim version of New Age religions, the lable 'sufi' is being applied indiscriminately to a range of people and groups with very differing political positions. But while the groups being labelled and the labels used may have shifted somewhat, the gendered impact of inclusion and exclusion sadly appears constant.

Notes

1   The reality of who in practice was able to influence government policy is discussed below in the context of 'moderate Muslims'.
2   Women meeting Patricia Hewitt and subsequently the Muslim Women's Network in its formational days decided it would not be useful to seek media attention, especially since the group itself was debating how far – if at all – it was representative of 'Muslim women'.
3   www.prohijab.net/english/muslimweekly-article.htm.
4   The case was ultimately resolved in the school's favour by the House of Lords. R (on the application of Begum (by her litigation friend, Rahman)) (Respondent) v Headteacher and Governors of Denbigh High School (Appellants) [2006] UKHL 15, on appeal from [2005] EWCA Civ 199. For the full text of the judgement and its discussion of religious freedom and dress codes, see www.publications.parliament.uk/pa/ld200506/ldjudgmt/jd060322/begum-1.htm
5   http://news.bbc.co.uk/go/pr/fr/-/1/hi/uk/4660411.stm.
6   Patel (2005) discusses how clashes between Sikh and Muslim youths in the 1990s were classified as between 'rival religious groups' but were at their root about 'the control of the sexuality of "their" women'.
7   Multiculturalism's need for representatives and homogenized 'authentic voices' is discussed below.
8   www.wluml.org/english/about.shtml.
9   www.stoppoliticalterror.com/media/youngmuslims070805.pdf.

10   This has not gone unchallenged and one Muslim woman in the Midlands successfully complained to Ofcom, the independent media regulator, and had the local station closed down when it refused to air women's voices.

11   John Ware's *Panorama* programme 'A Question of Leadership' was aired on Sunday 21 August 2005. The programme focused in particular on the Muslim Council of Britain and several affiliates, including the Islamic Foundation, the Muslim Association of Britain, the Markazi Jamiat Ahl-i-Hadith and the Leeds Grand Mosque.

12   A UK-based secular network of individuals and organizations committed to monitoring and combating religious hatred in South Asia and in the UK.

13   The Nigerian equivalent of the term 'Islamization' used in South Asia to signify a state project of transforming society through the introduction of laws and other policy measures justified with reference to Islam.

14   www.janmanch.org/press_release/getdetails.asp?id=438.

15   Personal communication with author.

16   The Qur'an does not mandate any clergy and even the founders of the four major Sunni Schools themselves held their interpretations of Muslim laws to be precisely that: interpretations and not rulings binding upon all Muslims. However, for some 600 years the door to fresh interpretation within at least the Sunni Schools was judged to be closed. The entire question of who has authority to interpret is currently one of the greatest ideological controversies among Muslims worldwide.

17   http://news.bbc.co.uk/1/hi/uk/5120338.stm.

18   For a discussion of the distinctions between social location, identity and political values, see Yuval-Davis (2006). WLUML has since its founding in 1984 implicitly rejected the presumption of an automatic correlation between social location, personal identity and political values, and therefore does not define itself as working exclusively with 'Muslim women' (see www.wluml. org/english/about.shtml).

19   www.stoppoliticalterror.com/media/youngmuslims070805.pdf.

20   'Women, Religion and Social Change', a regional study conducted in Sri Lanka, India and Pakistan under the aegis of the International Centre for Ethnic Studies (IECS), Colombo in 1989–1990. The Pakistan study, conducted by Shirkat Gah Women's Resource Centre, Lahore, involved interviews with 407 women from diverse age, class, ethnic and religious backgrounds, in rural and urban locations across the country. A summary of the findings is to be found in Shaheed (1998).

References

ABU (Centre for Islamic Legal Studies, Ahmadu Bello University, Zaria) (2005) *Promoting Women's Rights Through Sharia in Northern Nigeria*, DFID and British Council

Adams, M. L. (1994) 'There's no place like home: On the place of identity in feminist politics', in M. Evans (ed) *The Woman Question*, Thousand Oaks, CA, Sage Publications

Amnesty International (2004), 'Nigeria: The death penalty and women under the Nigeria penal systems', http://web.amnesty.org/library/Index/ENGAFR440012004

Anthias, F. and Yuval-Davis, N. (1983) 'Contextualizing feminism: Gender, ethnic and class divisions', *Feminist Review*, no 15, pp62–74

Anthias, F. and Yuval-Davis, N. (1992) *Racialized Boundaries: Race, Nation, Gender, Colour and Class and the Anti-Racist Struggle*, London, Routledge

Armstrong, K. (2000) *The Battle for God: Fundamentalism in Judaism, Christianity and Islam*, London, HarperCollins

Balchin, C. (2003) 'With her feet on the ground: Women, religion and development in Muslim communities', *Development*, vol 46, no 4, pp39–49

Barot, R., Bradley, H. and Fenton, S. (1999) 'Rethinking ethnicity and gender', in R. Barot, H. Bradley and S. Fenton (eds) *Ethnicity, Gender and Social Change*, London, Macmillan

Brah, A. (1991) 'Difference, diversity and differentiation', *International Review of Sociology*, series 2, no 2, pp53–77

Bright, M. (2005) 'Radical links of UK's "moderate" Muslim group', *Observer*, 14 August, http://observer.guardian.co.uk/uk_news/story/0,6903,1548786,00.html

Bright, M. (2006) 'When progressives treat with reactionaries: The British state's flirtation with radical Islamism', Policy Exchange, www.policyexchange.org.uk/Publications.aspx?id=192

DFID (2005) 'Islamic agencies play vital role in fighting poverty – Thomas', Press Release 14 March, www.dfid.gov.uk/News/files/pressreleases/pr-islamicagencies.asp

Donald, J. and Rattansi, A. (eds) (1992) *'Race', Culture and Difference*, London, Sage Publications

Eisenstein, Z. (1994) 'Imagining feminism: Women of colour specifying democracy', in Z. Eisenstein *The Colour of Gender: Reimagining Democracy*, Berkeley, CA, University of California Press

FCO/HO (Foreign & Commonwealth Office/Home Office) (2004) 'Young Muslims and extremism', April, www.stoppoliticalterror.com/media/youngmuslims070805.pdf

FOIA (Freedom of Information Act Centre)(2006) 'Home office funds Muslim council of Britain', 10 May – updated 5 June, www.foiacentre.com/news-MCB-060510.html

Fourest, C. (2004) *Frère Tariq: Discours, stratégie et méthode de Tariq Ramadan*, Paris, Éditions Grasset & Fasquelle

Gilroy, P. (1999) 'Between camps: race and culture in postmodernity – an inaugural lecture', *Economy and Society*, vol 28, no 2, pp183–197

Hall, S. (1992) 'New ethnicities', in J. Donald and A. Rattansi (eds) *'Race', Culture and Difference*, London, Sage

Halstead, M. (2005) 'British Muslims and education', in the Eumap Project and Tufyal Choudhury, *Muslims in the UK: Policies for Engaged Citizens*, Budapest, Central European University Press

Harding, S. (1991) 'Reinventing ourselves as other: More new agents of history and knowledge', in S. Harding *Whose Science? Whose Knowledge?*, Ithaca, NY, Cornell University Press

Hill-Collins, P. (1994) 'The social construction of feminist thought', in M. Evans (ed) *The Woman Question*, London, Sage Publications

Home Office Citizenship Survey (2001) Home Office, www.data-archive.ac.uk/findingData/snDescription.asp?sn=4754

House of Commons (2005) House of Commons, International Development Committee, DFID's bilateral programme of assistance to India, Third Report of Session 2004–05, 17 March, The Stationery Office Limited, www.dfid.gov.uk/pubs/files/idcreport-india-vol2.pdf

Imam, A. M. (2005) 'Women's reproductive and sexual rights and the offence of zina in Muslim laws in Nigeria', in W. Chavkin and E. Chesler (eds) *Where Human Rights Begin: Health, Sexuality, and Women in the New Millennium*, New Jersey, Rutgers University Press

Joseph Rowntree Foundation (2006) 'Faith as social capital', March, www.jrf.org.uk/knowledge/findings/socialpolicy/pdf/0136.pdf

Patel, P. (2005) Briefing Paper, 'The new offence of incitement to religious hatred', unpublished

Pettman, J. (1999) 'Globalisation and the gendered politics of citizenship', in N. Yuval-Davis and P. Werbner (eds) *Women, Citizenship and Difference*, London, Zed

Sahgal, G. and Yuval-Davis, N. (1992) 'Introducion: Fundamentalism, multiculturalism and women in Britain', in G. Sahgal and N. Yuval-Davis (eds) *Refusing Holy Orders*, London, Virago, (reprinted by WLUML, 2000)

Shaheed, F. (1998) 'The other side of the discourse: Women's experiences of identity, religion and activism in Pakistan,' in F. Shaheed, S. A. Warraich, C. Balchin and A. Gazdar (eds) *Shaping*

Women's Lives: Laws, Practices and Strategies in Pakistan, Lahore, Shirkat Gah Women's Resource Centre

Shaheed, F., and Shaheed, Aisha L. F. (2004) *Great Ancestors: Women Asserting Rights in Muslim Contexts*, Lahore, Shirkat Gah Women's Resource Centre

Sikand, Y. (2005) 'America's policy towards the "Muslim world": A critique of the Rand Report, http://groups.yahoo.com/group/saldwr/message/46

Silverman, M. and Yuval-Davis, N. (1999) 'Jews, Arabs and the theorisation of racism in Britain and France', in A. Brah, M. Hickman and M. Mac an Ghaill (eds) *Thinking Identities: Ethnicity, Racism and Culture*, London, Macmillan

Weller, P., Feldman, A. and Purdam, K. (2001) 'Religious discrimination in England and Wales', Home Office Research Study 220, Home Office Research, Development and Statistics Directorate, February, www.homeoffice.gov.uk/rds/pdfs/hors220.pdf

WLUML (1997) *For Ourselves: Women Reading the Qur'an, Women Living Under Muslim Laws*, Grabels France, WLUML

WLUML (2005) Statement to the World Social Forum, 'Appeal against fundamentalisms', 21 January, www.wluml.org/english/newsfulltxt.shtml?cmd%5B157%5D=x-157-103376

WLUML (2006) 'Plan of action – Senegal', London, WLUML

Yuval-Davis, N. (1992) 'Fundamentalism, multiculturalism and women in Britain', in J. Donald and A. Rattansi (eds) *Race, Culture and Difference*, London, Sage Publications

Yuval-Davis, N. (1997) *Gender and Nation*, London, Sage Publications

Yuval-Davis, N. (2006) 'Belonging and the politics of belonging', *Patterns of Prejudice*, vol 40, no 3, pp197–214

8

Black Umbrellas: Labelling and Articulating Development in the Indonesian Mass Media

Mark Hobart

The relevance of the mass media to development studies is often couched in instrumental terms. For example, how can the media be directed more effectively to explain the purposes and benefits of development to the populaces that are its targets? While this might make sense to those involved in development and its study, it depends on a dated, discredited and indeed incoherent theory of how the mass media works. Granted the prevalence and popularity of the mass media throughout much of the world, some recognition of how it works – as against how government and aid agency officials might like to imagine it works – would seem a fairly pressing priority.

To address these issues, I outline briefly some difficulties with conventional transmission models of the mass media against a background of the role of the media in development in Indonesia, with special reference to television. A comprehensive review of how mass media work is an impossibility. So I confine myself to two themes. The first is how media articulate reality. Out of the myriad differing ways that people can represent what is going on, some groups and representations tend to predominate, or even become hegemonic, the corollary of which is that other groups and other ways of representing events and relationships are disarticulated. And the imperatives of development are widely used as such an articulatory device, through which people are framed and labelled.

The second theme is less obvious, but perhaps even more important. What we take to be the 'meanings' that the mass media disseminate have effectively to be established at the point of production. It is impossible to know what millions of people understand by what they read, hear and watch, or how they engage with the media and relate them to their daily practices. Faced with so complex, contingent and partly unknowable a congeries of issues, politicians, developers and scholars have, perhaps understandably, concentrated on attempts to fix meaning at the moment of production or transmission. So doing avoids awkward questions about how the media are actually used.

Unfortunately the few studies there are suggest that people engage with the mass media in extraordinarily diverse, unexpected and unpredictable ways,[1] which remain unnoticed by various elites attempting to survey, know, regulate and develop mass populations. As a result, development experts and development studies scholars interested in the impact of the mass media find themselves effectively trapped in a closed world of meanings remote from the populations they are concerned to understand. The difficulties of knowing how readers and audiences relate to the mass media underwrite existing hegemonies and further contribute to the disarticulation of the vast majority of the populace. To obviate some of these difficulties, I consider an alternative theoretical account of the media and exemplify what is at issue by considering an Indonesian television film about development and the commentaries of viewers. I write as an anthropologist working in critical media and cultural studies.

The problem

The default position adopted by governments and broadcasters in many developing countries is that the mass media's job is to convey the message and goals of development to their populations as part of the development process.[2] In so doing they commit themselves to a model of the media working by transmitting messages, which, in Gramscian terms, may be commonsense, but is not good sense. Proponents of transmission models also commit themselves to a theory of meaning and communication which rests upon a singular conception – the 'conduit' metaphor, which presupposes words and images to be containers that convey a stable and unchanging essence from senders to receivers (Reddy, 1979). The model also constitutes the recipients as passive subjects. That is they are capable, in principle, of understanding and acting upon messages received, but are not presumed capable of more than that. Were they to be otherwise, a quite different, and more dialogic, model would be required.[3] In other words, an innocent-looking model of the media pre-labels audiences as the subjects of agency, not agents.

Is my dismissal not too hasty? Surely transmission models may have their limitations, but are they not fundamental to social communication? Interestingly, Shannon and Weaver, the founders of the mathematical model of communication, which is the reference for much subsequent usage, are quite explicit that the accounts of communication used for theoretical models in, say, computer design are unsuited to the analysis of human discourse. Writing about the semantic problems of communication (i.e. the relation of how senders interpret messages, as against receivers), Shannon noted that even the simplest acts of communication through speech are 'a very deep and involved situation' (Shannon and Weaver, 1949, p4). Further, they note that social communication assumes pre-understandings between the parties which cannot in principle be achieved through repeated communication. As development studies scholars know, communication also involves complex situational, contextual and cultural considerations. Quite apart from that, most functions of language are non-referential (Jakobson, 1960). Indeed a founding text of media studies, Stuart Hall's 'Encoding/Decoding' (1980), criticizes the transmission model by noting its failure to address the social relations of production and reception.[4]

An example from the mid-1990s in the research village in Bali where I worked makes the point. To disseminate awareness of fast-growing varieties of irrigated rice, which permitted annual triple cropping, the Regency head, a distinguished lawyer, personally headed a team of government agricultural development staff to explain the possibilities. The recommended scheme was two crops of irrigated rice followed by nitrogen-fixing dry crops. Unlike most such addresses, which consist of monologues primarily aimed at fellow officials rather than farmers, the Regent explained clearly and carefully what was involved, then genuinely invited feedback. Apart from a couple of routine polite responses, there was no reaction, despite the Regent's urging open discussion. So what was going on?

The problem was contextual – historical, social and epistemological. After generations of being labelled stupid peasants and being lectured at in Indonesian (a language that, up to the 1980s, many farmers spoke poorly) experience suggested the wisest – indeed only – course was silence. What was to be gained by speaking? Class is relevant too. Whatever their social backgrounds, agricultural development officials are civil servants. A primary purpose of development speeches was the reaffirmation of class superiority by the use of specific language registers,[5] a point of which the farmers were quite aware. It was a rite of labelling. Finally, what the Regent, as a lawyer, did not know and had not been informed of by his subordinates, was that irrigated rice terraces have to be kept continuously moist, otherwise they crumble and the entire infrastructure is destroyed.[6] Were the peasants supposed to lecture the Regent and his officials on hydraulic engineering? That is not to say that shared understanding is always impossible. However, it usually requires a great deal of work and a more dialogic relationship between the participants.

At this point, we need to reconsider ideas of agency. In a critical review, the Oxford philosopher R. G. Collingwood (1942) dismissed the tendency to conflate activity with agency and passivity with patiency. This trend is exemplified in Hollywood films where action men like Schwarzenegger and Stallone are presented as agents instead of instruments, or willing subjects, that is functionaries under orders of some agent. Agents are that which[7] orders or claims responsibility for a course of action to be carried out by instruments upon patients. Agents – be these Balinese kings or boards of multinational corporations – are usually distinguished by being far from where the action is.[8] Precisely because agents tend to keep aloof from action, they need 'willing subjects' to act as their instruments, and 'intellects' to explain the intentions of agents to those affected and to the world at large. This is where the mass media come in – to articulate what is happening and why.[9] Conversely, patients are often active, if unwilling. (Think of peasants being dragooned into being soldiers and cannon fodder.) The Balinese farmers were patients: they were the recipients of decisions and actions over which they had little control. While they were silent, they were not passive in the sense that they simply ignored their lords and masters. They got on with farming as best they could and, behind their backs, roundly criticized the officials as sycophantic, venal and stupid.

The beauty of the transmission model[10] – and so its attractiveness to political elites and planners alike – is that it is neat and locates meaning comfortably within their control. It positions them as agents. In so doing it buries the possibilities of ambiguity, of surplus or vacuity of meaning, and of the contingency and unpredictability of much social life (Laclau, 1990), which would be a devastating challenge to their self-vision of being in charge, and so agents. Last, but not least, transmission models presuppose the populace as recipients of messages to be just that – recipients. To expect them to become agents within a model that has already constituted them as patients is to ask the nigh-impossible.

So what is the answer? Fairly evidently there can be no simple one. If there was one clear outcome to the long-running debate between anthropologists and philosophers about the applicability of human reason to social action,[11] it was the sheer variety and complexity of processes of understanding within, let alone across, cultures. The debate is relevant, because it indicated the extent to which the kind of rational, propositional thinking constitutive of modernity, and so development, comprises one limiting possibility of communication rather than the norm. And even this possibility is shot through with unacknowledged imagery and metaphor (Sachs, 1979; Lakoff and Johnson, 1980).[12] As communication is part of all human relations, a comprehensive theory of communication would require a single total theory of society. If an all-embracing theory of communication is recognized as a pipe dream, an ignored issue in approaches to development communication starts to emerge more clearly: why do the various parties involved in implementing development need such a model so badly? That, however, is another story.

Labelling and articulation

How are such broader considerations relevant to development policy making? Wood has argued that 'labelling is a feature of all social communication', the analysis of which is necessary to 'reveal processes of control, regulation and management which are largely unrecognized even by the actors themselves'. Labelling – or, more accurately 'designation' – involves 'a relationship of power in that the labels of some are more easily imposed on people and situations than those of others' (Wood, 1985, p347). What is at issue is hegemony, which is:

> *the acceptance of selected designations as natural and therefore ubiquitous. These hegemonies are constructed and articulated through unnoticed, common and familiar acts. It is these that structure, determine, foreclose and establish frameworks and boundaries for action … without people even being aware that their behaviour is constrained.* (Wood, 1985, pp351–352)

Does hegemony apply, however, only at the level of designation? What are the presuppositions about what labels are and how they work? Under what conditions do particular clusters of designations become naturalized? How is the power to designate distributed? And how are labels treated by those designated?[13] As the issue of labelling has been addressed by Wood and by others in this collection, I wish to consider some of the presuppositions that inform the frames of reference, including the hegemony of development itself.

'Development' is an overarching articulation. How do we know, in any instance of economic or social change, to what extent the outcome is due to development planning and implementation? The issue is one of both explanation and representation. Fairly uncontroversially, the kinds of change subsumed under development involve a whole host of factors – technical, organizational, political, economic, social and cultural. As economic and social practices, viewed at the local level, are continually changing anyway, precisely what is exclusively or effectively attributable to development planning and implementation is far from self-evident. However commonsensical causal models might seem, theoretically they are antiquated and deeply problematic.[14] For example, what exactly is being asserted? That implementation of development is a sufficient condition of the desired outcome? This is a most improbable claim. That development is a necessary condition? So many factors are necessary in any instance that attributing relative weight is an act of judgement rather than description. However, this has rarely stopped governments and aid agencies *claiming* the efficacy of development projects.

Whatever the actual circumstances, which are often complicated, contested and partly undecidable, we need to consider how development is represented *as* efficacious, successful or whatever, and by whom. And this involves communication and so the mass media, because a central activity in politics is representing desirable change as a result of the agency of those in power. And, precisely because these claims are inherently contestable, such representations have to be repeated, often ad nauseam, in development broadcasting. Put bluntly, it is frequently difficult precisely to determine the success of development independent of claims of what is the case.[15]

What is at issue here is articulation. The critique from cultural and media studies of models of system and structure is that they confuse reality with representations made by different agents or interest groups to different audiences as to how complex events and relationships are articulated under particular circumstances. In place of such attempts at determination, this approach stresses:

> the form of the connection that can make a unity between two different elements, under certain conditions. It is a linkage which is not necessary, determined, absolute and essential for all time... So the so-called 'unity' of a discourse is really the articulation of different, distinct elements which can be rearticulated in different ways because they have no necessary 'belongingness'. The 'unity' which matters is a linkage between that articulated discourse and the social forces with which it can, under certain historical conditions, but need not necessarily, be connected. (Hall, 1996, p141)

Instead of taking development at face value, cultural and media studies aim to examine the conditions under which articulations are made and reiterated. Insofar as the ideals of modernization through development are hegemonic to national political discourse throughout much of the world, the media become central to articulating visions of the desirability and necessity of development to mass populations.[16] The mass media are, therefore, not incidental to development planning and implementation, but partly constitutive of them.

Rethinking reference and representation

The issues adumbrated above are, however, only the tip of the media iceberg in the sea of development. For instance, what is presupposed in how humans are labelled in development? And what is the significance of how development is represented in the mass media?

Granted how widespread the practices of framing and labelling of problems and populations are, and how convenient they are to governments and many aid agencies, they are unlikely to be abandoned in the near future. Their popularity does however illuminate more general problems about how governments, donors and scholars imagine human beings as the subjects of development. Arguably, the broad discourse of development involves two frameworks for representing what development is about, which are incommensurable and mutually contradictory. This is part of a broader disjuncture, which runs between and through academic disciplines, between approaches that work through statistical and informational modelling of populations as against those that privilege 'the philosophy of the subject: will, representation, choice, liberty, deliberation, knowledge, and desire' (Baudrillard, 1988, p214).[17] In an argument that applies equally to debates about the 'effects' of television-viewing and to development policy formulation, Baudrillard pointed out that endless epistemological confusion:

> *results from the fact that there is a compound, a mixture of two heterogeneous systems whose data cannot be transferred from one to the other. An operational system which is statistical, information-based, and simulational is projected onto a traditional values system, onto a system of representation, will, and opinion. This collage, this collusion, between the two, gives rise to an indefinite and useless polemic ... for the simple reason that there is no relationship between a system of meaning and a system of simulation. . . It is this lack of relationship between the two systems which today plunges us into a state of stupor.* (1988, p209)

I suspect that those who have been involved in implementing development projects will recognize the incompatibilities that arise between the demands of the models and attempts to treat people as subjects. Formal models tend to locate agency in the model's original architects but disguise this by imputing agency to its instruments, the development practitioners – a degree of conferred agency which may or may not be realizable in practice. However, as Baudrillard made clear, as with transmission models of communication, claims about the agency of the recipients are incoherent, because they belong to an alien philosophy.

Once again, we are back to the shortcomings of accounts of representation based on referentiality. It was to address these that Baudrillard proposed his much-cited notion of simulacra. Whereas representation 'starts from the principle that the sign and the real are equivalent ... conversely simulation starts from the *utopia* of this principle of equivalence, *from the radical negation of the sign as value*' (Baudrillard, 1983, p11). (Unless indicated otherwise all emphases are in the original.) Elaborating on Foucault's analysis (1970) of how representation has been successively rethought in Europe since the 16th century, Baudrillard (1983, p11) depicted the serial transformations of the relationship of representation as follows:

> *This would be the successive phases of the image:*
>
> – *it is the reflection of a basic reality*
> – *it masks and perverts a basic reality*
> – *it masks the absence of a basic reality*
> – *it bears no relation to any reality*
>
> *whatever it is its own pure simulacrum.*

What exactly did Baudrillard mean by this though?

There is a problem in reading Baudrillard, who was writing in a French academic style, which stresses logical consistency rather than the nuances of applicability. So some cultural translation is required. Was Baudrillard proposing, as is often assumed, that all representation in the late 20th century consists of simulacra? From his other writing, evidently not. Nor does misrepresentation, partial or skewed coverage, or lying imply the existence of simulacra. The lack of simple fit between signs and referents is a common feature of human communication, upon which, positively, the possibility of figurative language and imagery depend.

What Baudrillard was referring to is a singular condition, made possibly by the global development of mass media, by which the relationship of signs to their referents becomes attenuated to the point of virtuality. In a world with such a super-abundant proliferation of images and words, previous signs come to provide proximate references for subsequent representations. An example is television advertisements, which work by 'sounding' off previous advertisements and established stereotypes. (And with stereotypes, we are back to how humans are labelled in the mass media.) Evidently different phases of the image coincide and overlap. Only in some instances is reference to the world so minimal as to comprise full-blown simulacra. Baudrillard's point, however, was to show just how pervasive and inextricable from the workings of the electronic mass media these are.

What is the relevance of Baudrillard to development studies? The various worlds of development implementation, aid agencies, international organizations and scholarly commentary work have distinctive histories of portraying relevant issues. Subsequent discussion therefore is not just about representing current actualities in order to meet the interests and goals of the organizations, but it is also to articulate these concerns within a pre-existing discourse, which is itself a site of contestation. Insofar as donor governments and funding agencies (and indeed the recipients) need to justify the rationale for development aid to other constituencies and engage broader publics, the mass media become vital, because they articulate knowledge and understanding of the world for most people, according to a logic of representation that has precious little to do with the intricacies of development economics and technology. As the media studies scholar, John Fiske, commented appositely on television news:

> *Third World countries are, for example, conventionally represented in western news as places of famines and natural disaster, of social revolution, and of political corruption. These events are not seen as disrupting their social norms, but as confirming ours, confirming our dominant sense that western democracies provide the basics of life for everyone, are stable, and fairly and honestly governed. When deviations from these norms occur in our own countries they are represented as precisely that, deviations from the norm: in Third World countries, however, such occurrences are represented as their norms which differ markedly from ours. For the western news media, the Third World is a place of natural and political disasters and not much else.* (Fiske, 1989, p285)

Such hegemonic articulations are built up from previous representations from a hodgepodge of eclectic sources circulating in the mass media. In other words, the hegemonic account of the under-developed world by the West to a significant degree constitutes an elaborate simulation.

Two aspects of these processes are immediately relevant. The first is the recognition of the sheer complexity of representation and communication in the modern world. Utterances and depictions that aim to describe events and prescribe courses of action arguably work best within what Wittgenstein (1958) once designated 'language games': that is within closed worlds within which the participants share mutual knowledge and agreement over goals. As we saw, when Balinese local officials meet local farmers, complications are already rife. Even such attempts at communication, if these they be, take place within a framework of articulatory practices over which the participants have scant control. And such articulations work according to processes of representation in which the referents are at best only in part about what they seem.

A second point is that development is not simply the practical business of helping other, less fortunate people. It is implicated in how one of the world's largest industries routinely represents others in a complex process of global cultural translation to readers and television viewers in rich countries. A primary function of these media is at once to engender and channel fear, and to assuage it by presenting viewers' circumstances as comparatively safe and favourable. In an important sense, underdevelopment is not about the under-developed, but about who 'we', and 'the West' are.[18] Images of underdevelopment serve to create the illusory impression of coherence, even 'identity', to what more commonly resemble fragmentary, conflicting and non-unitary processes.

Black umbrellas

The New Order regime, between 1966 and 1998, defined itself around development, with President Suharto designating himself *Bapak Pembangunan*, the Father of Development. Although at the time widely regarded as a grandiose gesture, the launching of a television satellite, Palapa, in 1976 and placing a television set in every village in the archipelago[19] was in fact a brilliant appreciation of the centrality of the mass media to development. A vast audience of Indonesians was created who could be addressed no longer as Sukarno's revolutionary masses, but as subjects to be developed. Television was so central to the New Order's self-articulation as the agent of development that it is hard to imagine the regime's survival without it.

Before commercial television channels were licensed and began broadcasting in 1989, state television, TVRI, had a monopoly. Programmes explicitly about development projects and planning usually took up at least two hours a day. And much other broadcasting was inflected towards naturalizing development – through soaps, cartoons, religious programmes, talking heads or whatever – as the self-evident goal and justification of government. Further, regular news broadcasts were overwhelmingly slanted towards to two themes: the ubiquity and success of development and the luminous presence of the President as the agent behind it all.

By the 1990s, despite draconian censorship and intimidation of journalists, critics began openly to describe TVRI as the 'propaganda arm of government.'[20] As the role of television under the New Order has already been documented (Kitley, 2000), I wish to consider not how 'messages' about development were articulated by the producers, but how they were understood by viewers, the people that this hegemony was supposed to embrace. Because space is limited, the issues can most effectively be highlighted through viewers' reactions to a feature-length television film, *Payung Hitam* (Black Umbrella broadcast by TVRI Bali on 18 July 1993), which was critical of certain aspects of development.[21] The results are surprising.

The plot consisted of two interwoven stories.

The minor plot (with which the film starts) is about an expedition to the region by research students from the state university in Bali. They have seen an ancient man, but when they took photographs, there was nothing on the developed film. They report back to a sceptical Dean who, after persuasion, agrees to two staff members accompanying a second expedition to discover the truth. (The protagonists in the two stories meet coincidentally, but the plots remain separate until near the end.)

The main story concerns the plan for a development project to attract tourists to the mountainous part of Bali in an area devoted to horticulture for the lowland market. The story starts with a small boy, Wayan Dod, aged about 13, being told he must leave school unless his father pays the fees. (His father is a gambler who later descends to raiding Dod's piggy-bank to fund his forays.) The father refuses. When Dod's mother urges his father to pay, he says he has no money.

> Mother: *And what's the reason! Sell one of your fighting cocks.*
> Father: *What? Sell a cock? I've told you, we're not wealthy folk. The kids don't need to carry on in school anyway. What's the point of all that education, when they're just going to be unemployed after? You'd do better to get them work in the fields, tending strawberries like Pak Ariadi. You can earn that way.*[22]

However, Dod labours away in the marketplace, as one of several boys who provide an escort service with black umbrellas for visitors in this notoriously rainy part of Bali. There follow scenes of two officials from an unnamed, and rather mysterious, Indonesian development agency, who meet the village head to negotiate the planned arrival of coachloads of tourists to see authentic tropical horticulture (coffee and strawberries!) and animal husbandry. The village head and the 'peasants' whom the developers meet are rapturous at the prospect of tourists (i.e. income).One official however is concerned that when their boss comes from Jakarta, it might be raining, so he would not see the project in a good light. The other replies that the village head will see to that.

The headman calls on Dod's father, Rugeg, to find the best rainmaker on the island and explains how much money is in it for them all. Rugeg duly obeys. The rain clouds clear. The boss from Jakarta is impressed and the project receives his blessing. Tourists turn up and express delight at everything. Everyone is quietly talking about how much money they are going to make. The rainmaker is called in so frequently to stop it raining that the village head offers to make a house available for him. (These scenes are cross-cut by shots of the expedition searching the same area for the ancient man. They encounter a figure dressed like a hermit in a loincloth, who brings a storm down on them before vanishing.)

Meanwhile the umbrella trade has dropped off completely because it rarely rains. The little boys discover who is responsible and confront the rainmaker with the problem. He says it is too late, he has signed a contract. If they have any complaints, they had better go to the village head. Shortly afterwards the rainmaker meets Rugeg, whom he advises to look after his children properly, otherwise they will take to looking after themselves and will then be naughty and disobedient.

Meanwhile, the boys are in despair. One of them suggests they go and see his grandfather (who it transpires is in fact the hermit) who lives in a cave. However the boys are followed at a distance by two members of the expedition. The boys explain the development project. The project and the tourists are a good thing, the hermit says. Dod explains that the rainmaker is destroying their business and asks the hermit's help in thwarting him. The hermit replies: 'As a matter of fact hindering other people in the course of their work is forbidden in my view. We are not permitted to make things difficult for others.'

When the rainmaker next attempts to stop the rain, the hermit engages him in a spectacular battle of *sakti* (supernatural power). The rainmaker loses and falls into a coma. The boys return to the hermit's cave, but they are followed by the police, where they find the two academics in conversation with the hermit. At first the police try to arrest the boys, 'so that their parents shall know that their children have engaged in criminal activities. They have dared to interfere with the village development project'. The police then add that the rainmaker is ill. The hermit tells them it is the rainmaker's own fault for being arrogant and claiming to be the most *sakti* person in Bali. The village head then turns up and orders the hermit's arrest for not living in a house like other people. The hermit retorts that the cave is beyond village jurisdiction and he can do as he wishes there. He has intervened on the boys' behalf because their parents have failed to do so.

> Hermit: *And what's more you, as Village Head, have failed in your responsibility to your subjects. Without paying attention, you have violated these children's rights to earn a livelihood in this village.*
> Head: *These are only children's concerns, only a few people. But the development of agrotourism (wisata agro) is in the interests of the many.*
> Hermit: *That does not mean that the weak must be crushed, does it? Even though they are children, they still have the right to make a livelihood in their village.*[23]

At this point the male lecturer introduces himself and intervenes. Everyone immediately defers to him. He suggests they return to the village to discuss how to balance the rival interests and advises them to leave the hermit in peace. He was only protecting the children's interests. On the return journey, the lecturer reminds the officials that the children are their heirs and whatever is done must bear them in mind. He points out that the farmers will be in trouble if they change the rainfall (the hermit had pointed to the arrogance of his rival trying to change nature) and resolves the problem of rainfall by noting that it is 'authentic', that they can build regular shelters for tourists along the way and sell goods there, and the boys can make money from tourists for their umbrella services.

Almost everyone is now happy except the rainmaker who is still unconscious. The hermit goes to heal him and discovers it is his long-lost brother[24] whom he feared dead when his family were killed by a volcanic eruption. They are reconciled; the rain pours down; and the film ends with Dod happily running through it in search of customers with his black umbrella.

Commenting, labelling and articulating

How the film reiterates the conventional labels of Indonesian development projects at the time is fairly clear. Several features may be worth noting however. Agency is remote. Even the project boss from Jakarta is presented as effectively part of a chain of instrumentality, which reach down to the rainmaker and the gambler. Ordinary Balinese are depicted as willing patients, who gratefully and uncritically accept the benefits of the project. The academic and the hermit are organic and traditional intellectuals respectively who, in seeing eye-to-eye, articulate seamlessly the desirability of modern development with traditional values. As the intellect representing the ultimate agency behind the project (something like 'government', certainly not the project boss, who failed to appreciate the damage caused), the academic is empowered to enunciate on what is right and is accepted by everyone unquestioningly. The film therefore not only labels[25] but reiterates a host of presuppositions which make the labelling possible, apposite and acceptable to the participants, and presumably audiences.

The disruption, the crisis which leads to the critical re-evaluation of what such development projects should be about, is attributed to a small boy, who is given two separate labels. First he is a child, therefore subject to others who may reasonably determine his fate without consultation. Second, however, he stands for the future – an appeal to Balinese ideas about descendants, who are vital to the continuity of the patriline. It is in this latter capacity, not the former, that his interests are deemed relevant. However, it is two categories of people who are *not* labelled, but are backgrounded as if this were their natural place, who are significant. These are the 'ordinary' villagers and women. The film's thesis – that development should benefit everyone – does not extend to women, who are virtually absent from the film. When they do appear, they are confined to the classic New Order role of mothers and wives.[26] They are more infantilized than their own male offspring. While the film suggests the efficacy of labels in development, it also shows how large sections of society are made invisible and disarticulated. So the film indirectly highlights how the presuppositions behind labelling are themselves normalized through the mass media.

What did my fellow viewers make of the film though? Three were particularly vocal: an old actor in his 80s, an ex-village headman and a landless labourer (that evening all present were males). I asked if they had enjoyed it. The labourer was enthusiastic. It was very good, most appropriate. It was just like that in life: small people are ignored in development and lose out badly. The old actor broadly concurred. The ex-headman was less impressed. 'What was the *panglèmèk*?' he asked. (*Panglèmèk*, the moral point, is considered a crucial part of a performance, without which it becomes pointless entertainment.) As the others argued it through, they became more confused as to the point. Where the film was useful, the ex-headman said, was in its aim to reach development officials, to impress on them the need to think about the poor, not just the rich. If the rich get a thousand Rupiah (then about £0.30), the poor should get one hundred. So everyone benefits.[27]

The old actor returned to the moral point. Was it somehow in the implications of stopping the rain? The moral part was poorly done, the ex-headman retorted. Look at how they showed the father stealing from the son's saving box. The film was all over the place. I returned to the actor's question. Was stopping the rain arrogant? Yes, it showed a grave lack of *panglokika* (appreciation of the diverse needs of those under your authority). You should not meddle unthinkingly with the environment. Consider what happened with the water flow when the government dammed rivers for new irrigated rice land.[28]

Throughout these exchanges I was slightly surprised that my fellow viewers were more muted than on other occasions, when they tended to dissect the apparatuses of power, wealth and development with forensic panache. It soon became clear why. The acting was bad. The characters were badly delineated, the speech was stiff and unnatural; no one looked the part. The film was in Indonesian – the language of development. But plays based on Balinese village life do not work in Indonesian. The result was ridiculous. Yes, the producers of the film had been sufficiently clever (literally 'slippery') in castigating the failings of government officials that it would be hard to bring legal charges against them. But most viewers would not get the point. Unless the acting is convincing and the point well made, who is going to notice? They should have used one of several Balinese theatre genres that audiences could relate to. It takes really first-class and courageous performers (they named two famous figures) to bring off a piece like that.[29] The film's actors were frightened. If no one realized the point, it was a waste of time. That, as far as they were concerned, was that.

The commentaries on the film make several important points. Attributions of hegemony by scholars may themselves become hegemonic insofar as these do not reflect how people actually engage with the development going on around them. The recognition from critical media studies that knowing the conditions of production tells us little about the conditions of reception, use and commentary applies with equal force to development studies. On what grounds are we justified in labelling the peasant farmers who chose to remain silent after the Regent's peroration the subjects of hegemony? Here the researcher's relationship with her or his subjects of study is crucial. Only by appreciating what went on after the officials had left and knowing how farmers related the speechifying and (largely inadequate) technical support to their daily practice would it be possible to question the vision of the compliant subjects of hegemony. Models of how the masses are interpellated remain ideal and top-down. How people actually engage with being labelled and addressed requires critical ethnographic studies of how – indeed whether – interpellation works in practice.

That is not to say that Balinese villagers always heroically resist hegemony. Rather, the clumsy attempts of officials and television producers alike to implicate them in the national discourse of development at best might convince the perpetrators. Under such circumstances, how effective is labelling in development policy making? Evidently Balinese are implicated in development, but not under conditions of their own choosing. Not least, they are affected by the distribution of resources that flow from development aid. However, as these are largely organized along pre-existing lines of patronage, most people's implication into development is tangential or even antagonistic. Labelling takes place in a context of unstated presuppositions and a history of past practices of articulation.

This brings us to what is silenced, the absence of labels and processes of disarticulation. As the village commentators percipiently noted, discussion of development was taking place in the wrong language and so, to most of the supposed addressees, was articulating vacuities. To me however, the most salutary point the commentators made was their recognition that the capacity to engage people is not simply a function of narrative, ideology or structure, but depends intrinsically on the quality of the performance (cf. Richards, 1993). The next stage of critical inquiry would seem to require recognition of articulation, disarticulation and interpellation as practices, and the increasingly central role of the mass media. Until then, development studies scholars are likely to find themselves reclining in the shade of some very black umbrellas.

Notes

1   Among the few studies are Caldarola (1990); Hobart (e.g. 2000, 2001); Spitulnik (1993); and the collections by Ginsburg et al (2002) and Rothenbuhler and Coman (2005).

2   The media in many developing countries emphasize the following goals: the primacy of the national development task (economic, social, cultural and political); the pursuit of cultural and informational autonomy; support for democracy; and solidarity with other developing countries (McQuail, 1994, p131).

3   On dialogic models, see Morson and Emerson (1990).

4   Unfortunately Hall, however, merely supplements, not replaces, transmission models. For a fuller discussion, see Hobart (2005).

5   In Jakobson's terms (1960), the function of such speeches is 'conative' – that is the effect of the message on the receivers. They are also 'emotional', in that they refer to how senders relate to their own messages. Jakobson distinguishes six functions of language, appreciation of which would help refine critical analysis of development discourse.

6   In the flat plains of Bali, where the administration resides, this is a minor issue compared to the highlands, where investment in terracing and hydraulics is enormous – and, of course, greatly admired by tourists who can see 'authentic' rice fields.

7   I use the impersonal form, as agents are usually 'complex' (that is, they comprise groups or sets of people with complex internal power relations). Only in the limiting case are they individuals, a point obscured by the American cultural imperatives of individualism, which require, however implausibly, that individuals always be identified as agents.

8   For an extended use of Collingwood's approach applied to India, see Inden (1990).

9   Evidently, such explanations are contestable and arguably never neutral. The appearance of objectivity is created by 'exnominating' (i.e. leaving unnamed, see Barthes (1973, pp137–142)) the 'normal' subject position. In developed countries, this is conventionally the bourgeoisie.

10   Transmission models do not formally preclude receivers of messages subsequently becoming senders. However this possibility is contingent upon circumstances, history and social practice, not a feature of the model. Moreover any such reply is conceived as a mechanical supplement to the originating act.

11   For example: Wilson (1970); Hollis and Lukes (1982); Overing (1985).

12   In Indonesia, the common term was *pembangunan* which had connotations of 'building' or creating from raw materials, which required careful control, so defining the nature of appropriate agency. On different Indonesian words for 'development', see Hobart (1993, p7).

13   That is: how are people interpellated (Althusser, 1984), and do they recognize themselves, as subjects?

14   Causal models have been recognized since Hume as primitive and explanatorily largely vacuous. Their enduring popularity is precisely because they enable complex relationships to be articulated in simple terms for particular audiences and purposes.

15   Obviously one overriding need is to represent the state – or government of the day – as the agent of development and successfully in charge. Problems arise when things go wrong, as they invariably do. The job of development broadcasting and the news is to attribute beneficial change to government policies and programmes and to finesse away the failures. How this was achieved by Indonesian state television is well described by Kitley (2000).

16   Hegemony, according to the theorist behind much cultural studies, Ernesto Laclau, consists of those articulations which have been accepted in society as natural and self-evident at any moment. Rather than hegemony being fixed and immutable, it depends on changing practices of articulation (Laclau and Mouffe, 1985).

17 Although he was writing originally about 'the uncertainty which surrounds the social and political effects of opinion polls (do they or do they not manipulate opinion?)', Baudrillard was making a general point about theoretical models.

18 My point is that 'the West' and 'the masses' cannot be studied independently of their representations, including notably the mass media. The process is also gerundive: the masses exist *to be developed, to be regulated, to be educated.*

19 These comprised black and white sets, powered in remoter regions by rechargeable car batteries.

20 'Stories behind the news: When will the rights come?', *Vista-TV*, no 023, 17 August 1996, pp24–25.

21 I watched a video of the programme, which has been recorded as part of a long-running project to monitor Balinese television, with several Balinese, introduced below. Unfortunately the recording was cut before the final credits, so details of its provenance are unknown. The film was in Indonesian with occasional Balinese words.

22 Dod's father was alluding to the fact that education, without contacts and money to buy position, does not ensure employment, a point the viewers agreed with.

23 Interestingly this argument reiterates the classic distinction between utilitarian and Kantian approaches to morality. The village head argues for the greatest good of the greatest number, while the hermit defends the rights of all humans, no matter how they are categorized.

24 This is a familiar narrative device and, once again, contains potentially irresolvable conflict between competing interests by providing an overarching frame of reference to which all should submit.

25 The absurdity of labels is delightfully (but I think unintentionally) illustrated by the threat of arresting the hermit for not living in a house like everyone else!

26 The polite designation of *Bapak*, Father, for men and *Ibu*, Mother, for women, which has survived the New Order, is not symmetrical, because Mother designates a purely domestic and supportive role, whereas Father articulates the family to the polity and the public sphere.

27 As the viewers made clear, if the rich do not benefit substantially, they will not be interested.

28 This was a sore topic throughout much of Bali, because it reduced the supply to existing fields. In fact, as part of Bali's 'development', the Suharto government planned to authorize permits for so many golf courses that they would, in effect, have absorbed almost the entire water requirements of the island, in which irrigated rice was the main crop.

29 These two often featured in short, masked theatre pieces, *Bondrès*, usually sponsored by government development agencies. However, the actors were so skilled that they could elegantly satisfy their sponsors and excoriate them for corruption and the failed implementation of projects at the same time.

References

Althusser, L. (1984) 'Ideology and ideological state apparatuses', *Essays on Ideology*, London, Verso

Barthes, R. (1973) *Mythologies* (trans A. Lavers), London, Paladin

Baudrillard, J. (1983) *Simulations* (trans P. Foss, P. Patton and P. Beitchman), New York, Semiotext(e)

Baudrillard, J. (1988) 'The masses: The implosion of the social in the media' (trans M. Maclean), in M. Poster (ed) *Jean Baudrillard: Selected Writings*, Oxford, Polity

Caldarola, V. J. (1990) 'Reception as cultural experience: Visual mass media and reception practices in Outer Indonesia', unpublished PhD dissertation, University of Pennsylvania

Collingwood, R. G. (1942) *The New Leviathan: Or Man, Society, Civilization and Barbarism*, Oxford, Clarendon Press

Fiske, J. (1989) *Television Culture*, London, Routledge

Foucault, M. (1970) *The Order of Things: An Archaeology of the Human Sciences*, London, Tavistock.

Ginsburg, F., Abu-Lughod, L. and Larkin, B. (eds) (2002) *Media Worlds: Anthropology on New Terrain*, Berkeley and Los Angeles, University of California Press

Hall, S. (1980) 'Encoding/decoding', in S. Hall (ed) *Culture, Media, Language: Working Papers in Cultural Studies, 1972–79*, London, Unwin Hyman

Hall, S. (1996) 'On postmodernism and articulation: An interview with Stuart Hall', in D. Morley and K.-H. Chen (eds) *Stuart Hall: Critical Dialogues in Cultural Studies*, London, Routledge,

Hobart, M. (1993) 'Introduction: The growth of ignorance?', in M. Hobart (ed) *An Anthropological Critique of Development: The Growth of Ignorance?*, London, Routledge

Hobart, M. (2000) 'The end of the world news: Television and a problem of articulation in Bali', *International Journal of Cultural Studies I*, vol 3, no 1, pp79–102

Hobart, M. (2001) 'Drunk on the screen: Balinese conversations about television and advertising', in B. Moeran (ed) *Asian Media Productions*, London, Routledge Curzon

Hobart, M. (2005) 'The profanity of the media', in E. Rothenbuhler and M. Coman (eds) *Media Anthropology*, London, Sage Publications

Hollis, M. and Lukes, S. (eds) (1982) *Rationality and Relativism*, Oxford, Blackwell

Inden, R. (1990) *Imagining India*, Oxford, Blackwell

Jakobson, R. (1960) 'Concluding statement: Linguistics and poetics', in T. Sebeok (ed) *Style in Language*, Cambridge, MA, MIT Press

Kitley, P. (2000) *Television, Nation, and Culture in Indonesia*, Athens, OH, Ohio University Press

Laclau, E. (1990) *New Reflections on the Revolution of Our Time*, London, Verso

Laclau, E. and Mouffe, C. (1985) *Hegemony and Socialist Strategy: Towards a Radical Democratic Politics*, London, Verso

Lakoff, G. and Johnson, M. (1980) *Metaphors We Live By*, London, University of Chicago Press

McQuail, D. (1994) *Mass Communication Theory: An Introduction*, London, Sage Publications

Morson, G. S. and Emerson, C. (1990) *Mikhail Bakhtin: Creation of a Prosaics*, Stanford, CA, Stanford University Press

Overing, J. (ed) (1985) 'Reason and morality', *ASA Monographs in Social Anthropology* 24, London, Tavistock

Reddy, M. (1979) 'The conduit metaphor: A case of frame conflict in our language about language', in A. Ortony (ed) *Metaphor and Thought*, Cambridge, MA, Cambridge University Press

Richards, P. (1993) 'Cultivation: Knowledge or performance?', in M. Hobart (ed) *An Anthropological Critique of Development: The Growth of Ignorance?*, London, Routledge

Rothenbuhler, E. and Coman, M. (eds) (2005) *Media Anthropology*, London, Sage Publications

Sachs, S. (ed) (1979) *On Metaphor*, London, Chicago University Press

Shannon, C. and Weaver, W. (eds) (1949) *The Mathematical Theory of Communication*, Urbana, IL, University of Illinois Press

Spitulnik, D. (1993) 'Anthropology and mass media', *Annual Review of Anthropology*, vol 22, pp293–315

Wilson, B. (ed) (1970) *Rationality*, Oxford, Blackwell

Wittgenstein. L. (1958) *Philosophical Investigations* (trans G. E. M. Anscombe), 2nd edn, Oxford, Blackwell

Wood, G. (1985) 'The politics of development policy labelling', *Development and Change*, vol 16, no 3, pp347–373

9

Labelling 'Works': The Language and Politics of Caste and Tribe in India

Arjan de Haan[1]

The title of this chapter emphasizes implications of labelling in terms of policy and political practices, in the case of India, and primarily in relation to historically deprived groups of 'scheduled caste' and 'scheduled tribe' – though discussion of the evolvement of labels for other groups is essential to comprehend the dynamics. I focus on how labels have changed actual and perceived realities, looking at how policy responses, including affirmative action, build on these labels, in turn altering their use and greatly impacting on social and political relations.

Part 1 of the chapter sets out some of the 'basics' of the Indian social structure as represented by the core labels of 'caste' and 'tribe', and considers how labels and social structures have evolved historically, with particular reference to India's most deprived groups, the *Dalits* – 'scheduled castes' in the official language – and *Adivasis*, or 'scheduled tribes'. A remarkable feature of the nomenclature is the continuity – though always contested – of labelling and accompanying political dynamics since the colonial period, probably contributing to the surprisingly unquestioning way in which the 'SC/ST' terminology is used, for example by officials and activist researchers. Against this unifying framework, the chapter emphasizes the large diversity of SC/STs across India, the main changes in society's structure during and since the colonial period, and different experiences cutting across the caste structure, particularly those based on gender.

Part 2 describes administrative and policy practices vis-à-vis deprived groups: protection against violence and abuse, the promotion of economic interest and empowerment, and the affirmative action including reservation in government jobs and educational institutions. This focuses on the ways in which labels are employed within these practices, and how the labels have helped to create an administrative industry of its own.

Part 3 very briefly discusses the limited evidence available on the impact of state programmes for deprived groups. The fact that little independent evidence exists, and that most evaluations are official, itself suggests that the administrative machinery has not built up or is accompanied by channels of accountability.

Part 4 reflects on the way donors have contributed to the use of labels: in general, donors have reflected little on dominant political and administrative procedures, and possibly reinforced them by emphasizing targeting.

Part 5 looks at how, although relatively little reduction has been made in material disparities, India has made great progress in the area of representative democratization with historically marginalized groups finding entry into the political power structures. Access to such structures has occurred at different points in time in different parts of the country. The labels have formed important instruments in the struggles for power, and official categories that for decades were instruments of control at some point were turned against the rulers.

The Conclusion looks at the manifold ways in which labels can operate, how they 'work', particularly over longer periods of time. Starting from the colonial origins of the caste and tribe labels, these have been used as repressive instruments (notably regarding 'criminal tribes'). But they were also used in much more progressive ways, for example in the Constitution and the optimism of leaders immediately after Independence. Finally, the labels took on a life of their own through administrative practice and political contestation.

The caste structure evolves (as does the interpretation)

This part of the chapter highlights some of the 'basics' of the Indian social structure, particularly the labels of 'caste' and 'tribe', and how these have evolved historically. The histories of the 'caste structure' and of labelling or categorization are inextricably intertwined for a number of reasons: for describing the history of a caste structure we are dependent on colonial documentation; this partly drew on representations by sections of the Indian population, which in turn were responses to colonial projects and interests; and finally the historiography on which this chapter draws provide yet another filter of the 'real' history. The description below, too, essentializes or simplifies a complex reality.[2]

India possibly has the world's most elaborate official framework for designation of different social groups. Hindus have formed by far the largest religion, followed by Muslims (13 per cent of the population), Christians, Sikhs, Buddhist and Jains. Dalits, or 'scheduled castes', form 15 per cent of the population. Adivasis, or 'scheduled tribes', form about 8 per cent of the population, mostly outside the main religious groupings. The clarity with which these categories are regularly employed may be misleading against the diversity that these categories represent. The term Adivasis comprises a large group of almost 90 million people, in 300 officially recognized communities, and 461 in the Anthropological Survey of India. Some of these groups consist of more than 1 million people; some as few as 500. They live across the entire country, often in relative geographical isolation, but in the north-east tribals constitute the majority. Levels of development across the groups are widely different. Though scheduled tribes exist outside the caste system, their existence is by and large defined through their interaction with mainstream (Hindu) society.

The term caste summarizes an equally complex reality, one that has attracted much scholarly attention during the last two centuries. In daily interaction, it is often used with a generic meaning as 'group', possibly referring to religion, regional affiliation, nationality etc. In a more restricted sense, caste can refer to both the *varna* system – which divides the population initially into four (later five) mutually exclusive, endogamous, hereditary and occupation-specific groups of Brahmins, Kshatriyas, Vaisyas, Sudras and Ati-Sudras ('untouchables', 'Dalits'); and the *jati* system which divides the population into 3000 regionally specific groups, and which are used for the official affirmative action policies.

Bayly's detailed study of the phenomenon, as part of the New Cambridge History of India, analyses caste as 'a contingent and variable response to the enormous changes that occurred in the subcontinent's political landscape both before and after colonial conquest ... caste as we now recognise it has been engendered, shaped and perpetuated by comparatively recent political and social developments.' Practices of representative government initiated in British-ruled India 'served further to enhance the importance of caste affinities in the political arena' (Bayly, 1999, preface, p4). For example, the 17th century witnessed the spread of lordly or Kshatriya-centred manifestations of caste values, illustrated through the rise of the Maratha kingship of Shivaji Bhonsle. This period saw the affiliation of new post-Moghul rulers with Brahmans, diffusion of these values to the upper peasantry, and continued power of martial groups and so-called tribals. The social status of Brahmans continued to rise under colonial rule, as they achieved quasi-legal status in administrative practices, and approval of colonial officers. 'Pollution' became a defining feature of everyday caste experience, and company officers and Indian clients began to articulate the (Brahman) logic of caste, which greatly influenced later Orientalists (Bayly, 1999, p89). Surveys and laws in the early 19th century emphasized caste (and religion) as a crucial unit of Indian life.

With respect to the intermediate and lower castes too, Bayly emphasizes the historical processes that shaped caste dynamics. Under influences of economic changes, insecurity of the landed elite and urban growth, and processes of state formation with increasingly explicit social stratification, the population came to be classified under a complex caste differentiation. The peasant movements of the early 20th century showed growing awareness of caste, being opposed to the 'twice-born' landlords. Emerging trading groups like the Marwaris also increasingly adopted Brahman forms of lifestyles, and their practices were emulated by many landed groups. Finally, 'untouchability', in its most well-known form of 'scavenging', was shaped by the rise of new employment in cantonments and industrial areas. The relatively new bonds based on varna and jati may have been reinforced during the periods of insecurity of the 1920s and 1930s.

Most of the histories of the caste structure are presented without much reference to gender. The inclusion of women as members of a certain caste in the 1871/72 Census appears fairly novel. Practices of hypergamous and 'upward' marriage caste status may have been a more permanent feature for men than for women. Women were doubly repressed by norms of untouchability, as the dependent status of the lowest castes may have been defined by the sexual availability of women, an issue that still emerges in recent 'caste wars' and peasant movements such as that in Bihar, in which higher castes portray a picture of lower castes lacking the moral and physical resources to protect women from other people's lust (Bayly, 1999, p357). In many cases new occupations have been taken up by men, hence relegating the maintenance of old traditional ones to women (Deshpande, 2003, p113).

British rule had the effect of intensifying trends towards ritualization in social life that had started before the colonial period. British officials became intensively engaged in acquiring detailed social knowledge, culminating for example in the 1871/72 Census. These exercises have been interpreted as hegemonic exercises, of divide and rule, while Bayly emphasizes the wide diversity and contradictions of accounts of travellers, missionaries and scholar-officials. Caste was not always the all-pervasive and timeless phenomenon of later Orientalist accounts, or equally fundamental to the lives of most Indians in the all-India Census.

A key factor influencing debates on caste in the second half of the 19th century was the science of race, during the 'age of high imperialism'. The 1901 Census promoted an understanding of caste in terms of biologically determined race characteristics, or to 'prove' the racial theory of Indian (Aryan) civilization (Darity and Deshpande, 2003, p8), which led to the still existing practice of investigations into the distinctions in skin shade and phenotypical features.[3] Though the racialization of the debate has been important, and has influenced anthropological practices,[4] it appears to me that with respect to the understanding of caste and tribe, its consequences have remained limited. At least, as highlighted by Bayly, during this period the work of Ibbetson in Punjab, and others emphasized the fluidity of the caste structure, and promoted an occupational understanding of caste.

The science and debates about tribal or indigenous groups obtained a more clearly categorical or racist character – reflecting a different nature of exclusion. The Indian Civil Service emphasized the distinct identity of tribals from mainstream Hindu society. The extreme example of the use of labels for exerting power was through the categorization 'Criminal Tribes'. The Criminal Tribes Act was initiated in 1871 in northern India, and in 1911 became applicable across India. Its origins can be traced in the evolving debate around criminality, and arose out of policies of political control (Radhakrishna, 2001). The mainly itinerant communities were officially transfixed within the existing Hindu hierarchy, with the label linked to a profession (rather than hereditary). In 1948 this was amended into the Habitual Offenders Act, but this retained features of community-based legislation, and even the term criminal tribe has remained in common use (Bayly, 1999, p273).

The evolution of the understanding of caste – and how this foreshadowed late- and post-colonial policies – cannot be seen in isolation of the colonial interaction with social reform and nationalist movements, with all its diversity. The official emphasis of tribes' identity, as different from Hindu society, was contested in reform movements, and nationalist anthropologists maintained they were part and parcel of Hindu society. Moreover, views of Indian scholars and practitioners on caste were as diverse as those of colonial officers. For example, in 1863 the Aryan race theory appeared in the writings of G. M. Tagore, professor at University College, London. Many pandits applied the techniques of classic Sanskrit debate to counter western accounts of caste. By the end of the 19th century three main views on caste had emerged (Bayly, 1999, p154): a reformist view that saw caste as a negation of nationhood (e.g. M. G. Ranade, a Bombay High Court Judge); those who emphasized the spiritual order of caste, as a potential basis for regeneration (e.g. J. B. N. Bhattacharya, Swami Vivekananda); and a view that emphasized jati as ethnographic fact and a potential source of self-improvement (e.g. S. V. Ketkar).

By the end of the colonial period, hundreds of caste associations and caste conferences had emerged. By the time political representation was introduced in the 1930s, association on the basis of caste had become commonplace. Pressure for positive discrimination had emerged, and translated into policies to expand access of non-Brahmins in education and public services (Weisskopf, 2004, p10). Early discussions about provisions for uplifting the backward and collectively deprived – and processes of sanskritization, including in the context of peasant protests – played an important role in perpetuating rather than eliminating claims of caste.

Views on caste and its importance varied greatly within the Nationalist movement. Nehru saw the emerging nation in casteless terms, and opposed group-based reservations. Differences between Gandhi and Amebdkar, the untouchables' leader, pervaded and have continued to influence the political sphere. While Gandhi showed sympathy for the condition of the lower castes, he perceived social change to occur within norms of Hindu society and stratification (that is, the original fourfold varna system, which excluded untouchability) (Gandhi, 1933). Gandhi argued for removing injustices faced by 'untouchables' as part of attempts to unify against the British, a 'course of reform without challenging the social fabric of Indian society'. Gandhi thought that the heart of the caste Hindu could be changed, and he called upon the individual responsibilities of caste Hindus towards lower caste groups. Social work among deprived groups – including the Bhil community in Gujarat, where the term Adivasi appears to have been invented (Bayly, 1999, p248) – promoted the norms of pure caste Hindu life. Gandhi's coining of the term 'Harijan' – child of God, a term rejected and replaced by the term Dalit by campaigners in the 1970s – and emphasis on 'uplift' and 'civilization' illustrate his emphasis on moral reform within the existing social-religious structure.

Ambedkar deemed all social inequalities unnecessary and unjustifiable. He rejected the graded inequality of the four varnas, and the segregation within the Hindu community. He opposed ideas for separate schools – arguing 'the untouchables do not want water. What he wants is the right to draw water from a common well' (Verma, 1999). Ambedkar considered Gandhi the enemy of the depressed, and advocated group-based politics to achieve the objective of equality. Crucial was the debate on separate electorates for untouchables, parallel to the special electoral representation created for religious minorities under the 1935 Government of India Act. The Communal Award of 1932 gave the depressed classes a double vote, one in the general electorate and one in a special constituency. But Gandhi strongly resisted, entered fast unto death, and the compromise Poona Act provided reservation of seats in central and state legislatures. The 'reservation' that resulted has been seen by some Dalit advocates as a defeat, but the debate did lead to the 'Scheduling' of thousands of untouchable and tribal groups.

While it may be disputed how 'new' caste is as an overarching framework, and the stability of the basic caste division,[5] the framework has undergone enormous historical changes, including during the colonial state with its 'modernizing' role of civilization and categorization.[6] How the labels emerged at the time of Indian Independence was the result of a complex interplay of colonial official forces, and countervailing Indian forces that were split between, say, Nehruvian views of the need to create a secular state, a Gandhian view that looked for reform within the caste structure, and radical views like Ambedkar's that looked for special political representation. The outcome of this set the scene for further reaffirmation of the labels. But this too was not an inevitable outcome – as discussed in the rest of this chapter, which considers the specific circumstances in which official state policies reaffirmed the usage of caste categories, and how subaltern responses reinforced these.

Caste and tribe in modern state policy

The promotion of deprived groups is enshrined in the Indian Constitution, and is delivered through elaborate administrative and financial mechanisms. This part of the chapter describes the administrative and policy practices through which the labels of caste and tribe have been employed, and how the existence of labels has helped to create an administrative industry of its own.

While the origins of affirmative action or reservation policies are to be found in late-colonial organized movements, the Government of India's approach to historically marginalized groups draws on provisions made in the Indian Constitution, which contains explicit state obligation towards protecting and promoting social, economic, political and cultural rights. The Directive Principles of State Policy commits the state to 'promote with special care the educational and economic interests of the weaker sections of the people and, in particular, of the Scheduled Castes and the Scheduled Tribes, and ... protect them from social injustice and all forms of exploitation.' The Constitution officially abolished untouchability, and the disadvantages arising out of enforcement of untouchability. It mandates positive discrimination in government services, state-run and sponsored educational institutions and legislative bodies. Amendments to the Constitution enabled representation of SC and ST men and women in local governance structures.

In defining who to include in the Schedules, the government used the 1931 Census, containing information at the level of jati, and a list created in 1936: for SCs this focused on backward communities in terms of untouchability or 'polluting' status, mixed with economic, educational and local political criteria; and for STs spatial and cultural isolation, closely correlated with socio-economic deprivation. Currently, the National Commissions for SC and ST are responsible for considering castes for inclusion or exclusion from the Schedule, which needs to be ratified in Parliament.

The group classifications have continued to go through various stages of attempts of reformulation, of scheduling and de-scheduling. For example, in the mid 1960s a committee recommended the de-scheduling of various communities, but this was successfully resisted. Politically, probably the most significant and long-lasting impact came from the 1980 Mandal Commission Report, which introduced into the administrative and political arena the category 'Other Backward Classes' (more on this in the next section). Finally, the fairly recent People of India project identified no less that 4635 caste and tribal communities.

Both the process of scheduling and the principle of reservation have been heavily debated. Classifications of communities, and creation and dismantling of castes have been criticized.[7] Inconsistencies in comparisons across states, sometimes even regarding classification as 'caste' or 'tribe', are almost inevitable.[8] Critics of reservation have argued that this is based on too broad categories indicating collective deprivation of communities. Some have argued that the classifications create incentives for reaffirmation of caste identity (which we come back to below), and others have emphasized that the numerically limited policies of affirmative action create a 'creamy layer' among deprived communities.[9]

At present, policies exist in three areas. The first includes legal safeguards against discrimination. This includes enactment of the 'Anti-Untouchability Act' of 1955, which was renamed the Protection of Civil Rights Act in 1979, and the Scheduled Caste/Tribe

Prevention of Atrocities Act of 1989. Under the first Act practices of untouchability and discrimination in public places and services became treated as offence, while the second provides legal protection against violence and atrocities by high castes. These policy measures are monitored annually, with consistent high levels of violence directed against deprived groups.

The second policy area focuses on the economic interest and empowerment of deprived groups, through education and anti-poverty programmes. States can make special provision for the advancement of deprived groups, through reserved seats for SC and ST students, supported by number of financial schemes, scholarships, special hostels, concessions in fees, grants for books, remedial coaching etc. There are income generation programmes for poverty reduction, and apex financial organizations exist to develop entrepreneurial skills and provide credits for deprived groups.

The third and most controversial area consists of reservation, operating in three spheres: government services, admission in public educational institutions, and seats in central, state and local legislature and bodies. Over time the scope of reservations has expanded to include government housing, government spaces for shops and commercial activities etc. Reservation quotas are formulated on the basis of shares of total population. Some services are excluded from reservation, particularly the judiciary and defence. The reservation is accompanied by special provisions to enhance the ability of these groups to compete for government jobs, including relaxation of minimum age and of standards of suitability, relaxation in fees, provisions for pre-examination training, separate interviews, and provision of experts from SC/ST backgrounds on selection committees.

The Constitution provides for reservation of seats for SCs and STs in the central and state legislatures, and in local bodies at district, *taluk* and village level. The constitutional provision of reservation is complemented by statutory provisions for enhanced political participation, like smaller election deposits for members of these groups. Unlike the reservation in government service, there is a time limit for political reservation, extended every ten years.

A fairly recent innovation in the policy framework has been the Special Component Plan (SCP), which provides financial allocation from the general sectors in state and central plans, equivalent to the percentage of deprived groups to the population. It is an umbrella programme, intending to dovetail all public schemes to the different needs. In addition, the Special Central Assistance fills critical gaps in the state SCP.

The monitoring of these programmes is carried out by a number of official bodies (Thorat, 2005). At the Government of India level the Ministry of Social Justice and Empowerment for Scheduled Castes, Other Backward Castes (OBCs) and Minorities is responsible for monitoring – with corresponding departments at state level. In the 1990s National Commissions were set up to facilitate SCs, STs, OBCs, Minorities and the Safai Karamcharis (Scavengers) in claiming their rights – again with corresponding state commissions. The monitoring tends to have a strong quantitative focus (like numbers of students from deprived groups), and is input-oriented.

Affirmative action is confined to government and government-aided sectors of services and educational institutions. Private enterprises and educational institutions have been excluded from the purview of the policy. However, under the coalition government formed in 2004 a debate about reservation in the public sector has been initiated. This has been informed, partly, by activists' concern over the decline in employment in public services since the 1990s, under economic policies of liberalization. Opinions about the desirability of such an extension are predictably diverse, and the government has put much emphasis on a process of consultation before proceeding with legislation.

Successive Five Year Plans, the government's overarching development policy framework, show gradual public policy changes. Initially, the focus was on the enforcement of legislation to prevent atrocities (which seems to have remained unchanged), and on focused and additive programmes to the general development schemes. The assumption was that overall development programmes would be tailored at the field level to suit the needs of these groups. But during the 5th Plan Period it was concluded that development expenditure was not sufficiently focused on these groups, and a new mechanism for fund allocation from the general budget was introduced. During the 1990s, a 'rights and empowerment' discourse found currency, and the Plan committed itself to a three-pronged strategy of social empowerment, economic empowerment and social justice. However, these changes have not been accompanied by substantial changes in programme content or monitoring frameworks.

Successive government plans have envisaged a key role for civil society in the implementation of government programmes, and in the consultation leading up to those plans. An important section of civil society has indeed become part of the apparatus that implements targeted programmes in rural and education sectors, and some of these efforts are likely to have reinforced the dominant paradigm, particularly of targeted approaches.

This clearly articulated policy framework has been the outcome of different interpretations of the nature of, and policies to address, deprivation of marginalized groups. The 1950 Constitution contains many of the contradictions that were highlighted in the late colonial debates – and many of the present-day politics still carry these marks, while some of the language continues to reflect old Orientalist stereotypes (Bayly, 1999, p275). The Constitution is explicitly 'secular', without reference to religious symbols, emphasizing equality of all citizens. Caste was not only seen as a barrier to progress, and as incompatible with democracy, but there was general optimism that the system would soon dissolve. Yet, the Constitution prescribed for state agencies to recognize caste and tribe, through the provisions for advancement of scheduled castes and tribes – later extended to 'other backward castes' – based on the group taxonomies rather than, say, forms of individual means testing or universalism.

The impact of state policies

A full-scale assessment of impact of the policies described above is well beyond the scope of this chapter, but a few observations are relevant. First, it is remarkable how little academic or independent analysis exists regarding the impact of reservation policies – certainly compared to the rich body of literature in the US or UK. Analyses show strongly contrasting pictures, maybe particularly around reservation where the 'vulgar vote bank politics' in which these policies are embedded is contrasted with positive assessment of perhaps slow and intangible but very important symbolic changes brought by these public policies. Regular official monitoring reports and reviews exist of course, but monitoring has a strong focus on inputs, without for example assessing impact on poverty or human development indicators.

Against the well-known evidence of continued disparities across social groups (see below), very little knowledge exists about the impact that policies have had on reducing these disparities. Arguably, the silence is due to a weakness in systems of accountability, of organized demands to know about how public policy is performing. The evidence on Orissa I am familiar with points to poor performance even at the level of utilization of funds – with the special programme for southern Orissa a prime example (see further, de Haan (2004)). One cannot generalize the picture of Orissa to India as a whole, most importantly, perhaps, because Dalit and Adivasi identity have been very weakly articulated in Orissa. But it does show that the programmes, per se, and constitutionally enshrined as they are, are unlikely to make a big impact on deeply entrenched social differences. What they have done, however, is reinforce the categories as such. They have labelled blocks (territorial divisions) as 'tribal' (almost half of Orissa's block have majority tribal population). And the focus on social groups in development programmes has led to tribal identity being associated with poverty in the official jargon.

While we cannot generalize from these findings, some of the features are common across India, and indeed some of the shortcomings in policies in Orissa are attributable to the fact these are centrally formulated. A bureaucratic approach to issues of deprivation has predominated, without contributing much to challenging power relations within the bureaucracy or political system. This is illustrated, for example, by obvious 'casteist' or racist (vis-à-vis tribal groups) behaviour and language by senior officials, by a visible (even to an outsider) social discrimination of senior officials from deprived groups, and by the lack of positive impact of senior politicians like chief ministers and members of parliament from tribal backgrounds. The point is not that that power has not been challenged in India – it has, as described below – but that in the absence of systems of accountability or challenges the administrative system can continue to contain discriminatory attitudes, while the official categories function to fixate the groups in an official hierarchy.

Donors in India: Categories reaffirmed – if unintentionally

From my experience of working for DFID in its Orissa programme, I conclude that there has been next to no questioning of existing categories. Whereas in the academic community the usage of categories has been contested, the development community has followed the dominant national paradigm – as I illustrate with a number of examples I am familiar with.

Much of the policy dialogue is, probably inevitably, marked by silence on categories. Budget support discussions have not done much in terms of interrogating sector-level policy instruments. Welfare ministries have generally not received much donor attention. Initiatives by civil society to carry out tribal budget exercises have been limited, and generally have not been part of the donor dialogue. In the case of Orissa, the lack of organized voice among deprived groups (and adverse government–civil society relations) has resulted in limited dialogue between civil society and donors. Affirmative action has generally remained off the radar screen of donors.

Other parts of the donor programmes have a strong emphasis on targeting. For example, part of the argument around the pro-poorness of the provision of electricity revolves around numbers and proportions of SC/ST users. Targeted livelihood projects like watershed development similarly include social categories besides indicators of land possession and water access: of course, in many cases economic and social indicators of deprivation overlap. Forestry work is almost automatically targeted to tribal groups.

An advanced form of a targeting approach is found in the primary education sector. Building on NGO-led experiences of reaching to – in particular – remote tribal groups in Rajasthan and the right to education, the centrally sponsored scheme Sarva Shikhsa Abhiyan (SSA) has a primary focus on bringing primary education to the last remaining deciles of the population, often implying Adivasi communities. Clear output targets are set, and elaborate delivery and monitoring mechanisms – subject to implementation strengths and weaknesses at state level – ensure strong central control over the delivery of services. Local participation is a key element of the programmes, seen both as an essential element for delivery, particularly in remote areas, and as a way of adapting the programme to locally specific needs (e.g. the possibility and funding for translations in local languages). This approach has found much support from the international community, starting with funding for NGO initiatives in Rajasthan, and now by the World Bank, European Commission and DFID for the national programme.

The targeted approach indicates that the sword of labelling has two edges. On the one hand, in the circumstances of, for example, education in India, the targeted approach for remote rural communities may well be the only or best way to deliver on the constitutional commitments to education. Designed as it is with strong progressive inputs, providing in principle space for diversity, it has enormous emancipatory potentials, and certainly in education forms a sine qua non for broader empowerment. The key question here, however, is whether the categories employed risk reinforcing the stigma and discrimination of the targeted groups. Certainly the donor debate has a strong focus on quantitative outputs, with much less attention – in my experience – to quality and, in particular, content of education and attitudes of teachers – which has been a key element of strategies to address discrimination and stereotyping elsewhere.

Political without substantive democratization: What role social categories ?

Debates around policy practices to address deprivation of marginalized groups have been overshadowed by the emergence of 'caste politics' and 'vote banks', or what Shah (2002, p28) calls the 'democratic incarnation of caste'. This has had contradictory and unexpected effects. Historically marginalized groups have found significant entry into the political power structures without an equal measure of material progress, particularly in terms of reduction of disparities.

Indian data provide detailed pictures of the well-being of social groups, at national and state level, and for some indicators even district level. Both Census and National Statistic Office data allow for a description of trends in disparities over time, and data are publicly available to researchers. Much debate has been generated, for example, around the poverty trends during the 1990s, but by comparison little on the disparities across social group. In terms of income poverty, as measured through national statistics despite declining poverty, analysis suggests that the social group disparities have *not* been reduced, and if one compare the trends for deprived groups in lagging areas with the overall trend one observes a very rapid increase in disparities.[10] Though conclusions are sensitive to measures used and the trends are far from uniform in India, and different for different groups, it remains striking that in the presence of the extensive policy framework as described above disparities continue to be large. Moreover, quantitative analysis suggests that the existing group disparities are not due to differences in, for example, education, suggesting deprived social groups suffer from differences in returns to assets, or discrimination.

Other indicators show similar pictures. Overall, progress in primary education has been steady. Some states, like Kerala, have historically good records of providing public services, some states have more recently made big jumps forwards, and other states continue to lag behind. Social group disparities continue to exist at levels of primary education, perhaps particularly in the states generally performing badly, and mechanisms operate to continue to exclude social groups from the benefits of public services. In the health sector too, where India's performance of providing public services is poor by international standards, significant social group disparities remain. A final indicator and key for well-being relates to ownership of land, particularly because of the close association in many cases between land ownership, or access to resources more broadly, and identity formation. Dalits have far less access to land, work more often as agricultural labourers, have somewhat higher rates of unemployment, and may be less mobile in terms of finding job opportunities elsewhere. Adivasis tend to have on average somewhat more land, but this is very likely land of poor quality, without access to irrigation and essential inputs. Moreover, Adivasis are disproportionally affected by forced displacement, often without adequate compensation.

This picture of continued disparities in the socio-economic sphere is in contrast with the radical changes in the political sphere. One of the most surprising developments since Independence – intensified from the 1970s onwards – has been that the democratic system and electoral politics have adopted the language of caste. As described by Alam (1999a, 1999b) for example, the 'extension of democracy' has given agency to the categories of SC and OBC, and often to specific castes (e.g. Yadavs, Kurmis). Entry of Adivasi communities into the political field has remained more limited, while religious categories of course came to the centre of attention during the 1990s.

Different stages of politics of scheduled castes can be discerned. First, groups of castes obtained political agency – usually implying the separation of the political from the social sphere, as ritual status does not necessarily change simultaneously. In most states, landowning castes had taken control over state politics by the mid-1950s, and in many states this was subsequently challenged by other castes. The rise of politicians like Kanshi Ram in Uttar Pradesh and Laloo Prasad Yadav in Bihar illustrate a much greater equality in the political sphere than was possible even in the 1970s. Claims to equality are based explicitly on caste, and often refer to past deprivation and injustice to justify their own behaviour, including corruption. And at the other end of the spectrum, higher castes too have increasingly tended to articulate their interest *as castes* (Alam, 1999a, 1999b).

The decline of the power of the Congress party – still in parts of India regarded as the party of the poor – is generally seen as being associated with the rise of caste politics. With the installation of the first non-Congress government in the 1970s, arguments were formulated that caste needed to be given a place in public life on grounds of social justice (Beteille, 1996). The attempt by V. P. Singh's government in 1990 to implement the Mandal Commission report – primarily, the extension of reservations to OBCs – at least in north India added a new, stronger and much more disputed dimension to the role of caste in politics. Many observers agree that the extension of democracy has been a 'messy' process. Participation has increased substantially, but it has often been interpreted as leading to a disregard of procedure, and as contributory factor to a crisis of governability (Kohli, 1990).

At the panchayat level of the electoral system quotas introduced through the 73rd Constitutional Amendment have had enormous impacts. Conflicts between democratic structure and traditional power structures based on caste and landownership have emerged, sometimes violent. People with lower caste backgrounds – and women – often find it difficult to assert themselves, and often withdraw. Yet, gradually a greater acceptance of non-traditional leadership seems to have developed, there are enough individual stories of leadership that emerged to remain optimistic, and the success of representation at decentralized levels cannot be seen in isolation from broader social inequalities.

The Hindutva movement that dominated the political scene for much of the 1990s has had a big impact outside the main Hindu–Muslim dichotomy, and in the context of the discussion here on labelling the question of the interaction of different forms of social differentiation appears important. At the period of heightened 'communal' tensions, the question of Indian identity, of who is an Indian, has been central to public debate and contestation. The Hindutva movement was an attempt to unite, against Muslims, and in the process other forms of differentiation were under-emphasized. A renewed project of Sanskritization was initiated, highlighted for example in the debates around history curricula and textbooks, which was explicitly anti-Muslim, but also with potential implications for how the histories of deprived groups are narrated. As Shah (2002) in the context of communal riots in Surat and elsewhere notes, the 'Hindutva movement has made serious attempts to forge a unity among Hindus, without disturbing the relative power relations among the castes', and aimed to unite all as one varna and jati. The Hindutva movement had implications for what may be a long-term trend towards cultural assimilation of Adivasis, by incorporating their youth in anti-Muslim movements, but perhaps even more significantly by long-term and well-designed activities in deprived areas.

This attempt to forge a new identity has the potential for further differentiation of categories. While the Bharatiya Janata Party and allied organizations have made an attempt to include all non-Muslim groups in the Hindutva fold, their position vis-à-vis, for example, reservation and attempts to raise the profile of Dalit and Adivasi issues around the Durban international conference on race was opposed by many activist groups. For Kancha Ilaiah (1996), born in a shepherd caste family, the Hindutva ideology sharply raised the awareness of distinctiveness:

> *Suddenly, since about 1990 the word 'Hindutva' has begun to echo in our ears... Suddenly I am being told that I am a Hindu. Otherwise I am socially castigated ... I [and] all of us, the Dalitbahujans of India, have never heard the word 'Hindu' – not as a word, nor as the name of a culture, nor as the name of a religion in our early childhood days... But today we are suddenly being told that we have a common religious and cultural relationship with the [Brahmins] and the [Baniyas]. This is not merely surprising; it is shocking.*

The 2004 general elections in India have been a momentous shift back to a secular trend. It is partly in the nature of coalition governments that the interests of different groups can be articulated strongly. The debate on reservation within the private sector initiated under the current government indicates a strong commitment to addressing issues of relevance to deprived groups. At present, this seems to imply a continuation of the long-term trend towards reinforcing existing labels, in a dominant paradigm of quantification of benefits and access rather than cultural contestation, but it suggests expanding space for reclaiming the labels in the way Ilaiah uses and reaffirms the term Dalitbahujan – of using these for emancipatory purposes.

Thus, while socio-economic disparities continue to exist, the rise of 'casteism' has been unmistakable. Social identities, particularly caste related, have come to the forefront of India's political agenda, and have given a new and largely unexpected dimension to the way categories and labels have evolved, entirely opposite to the expectations of many progressive observers after Independence who believed that 'caste' would soon be a thing of the past. The rise of identities and of deprived groups has manifested itself much less in struggles for 'substantive equality', like land reform, than in contestation about the participation in the politics of the formerly dominating groups, and some have (Shah, 2002) argued that the way political leaders have focused on political mobilization may have contributed to an impasse in solving economic and social problems.

Conclusion

Labels 'work' in complex but unmistakable ways. 'Caste' is still very much prevalent in the lives and experience of many Indians. The autobiographical materials of authors like Valmiki and Ilaiah, and the large number of annually recorded atrocities against Dalits and Adivasis, show that discrimination is very common, even if not unchanging. Historical studies show both long-term and relatively rapid 'adaptations' of the caste system, including urbanization for example. However, conclusions and hopes regarding crumbling of the system have tended to be belied by subsequent historical experience, and Dalit and Adivasi identities tend to reconfigure themselves.

This chapter has focused on the role that categories play in these complex historical changes. This started from the idea that categories are part of 'hegemonic tendencies', and the historical description showed how state formation was indeed responsible for the fixation of categories of caste and tribe, though this happened in very contradictory and historically contingent ways, and was given a strong push by the emphasis on group-based politics of Ambedkar and other Dalit leaders. The post-colonial state, in equally complex trajectories, has tended to reinforce the categories created under colonial rule, though of course with a much stronger emancipatory (and nation-building) objective, and with the advocacy of an increasingly large group of deprived groups, ending up in programmes for affirmative action or reservation for almost 50 per cent of the population. Finally, vote bank politics have increasingly brought caste and other social identities to the foreground of Indian politics.

The key question, theoretical as well as practical, that follows from this is: How are we to interpret the fact that labels, originally created to exert power (even though these processes were always contradictory), have subsequently become an instrument of a struggle, by deprived groups, over political and economic resources? And are terms like SC, ST and OBC, as Guru (2001) posits, still a deliberate and artificial construction of the state, trapping deprived groups into perpetual passivity and subordination? It may be useful to highlight that though the complexity surrounding discussions of caste may be unique to India, the question of such a 'turnaround' is relevant in other contexts too, for example in the US where labels around race have been continuously reformed, and are increasingly interpreted as social and not racial categories, with much inconsistency and contradictions, reconfigurations etc.[11] This question takes us well beyond a discussion of labels – highlighting their importance in broader political processes – and into discussion of the role of ethnicity and diversity in the context of state formation and national identities.

There is a very strong critique of affirmative action, and reservation in India in particular (which as the second section argued has played an enormous role in the institutionalization of older labels), that argues that this contributes to divisive identity group politics, including for example within the working class movement (Bambhiri, 2005). The opposition to the Mandal Commission report showed the potential divisiveness, as do the complicated processes of claims for and subdivision by groups, to be included or excluded from lists and reservations.

However, the outcomes of such processes are contingent, and the contexts in which such policies and the labels operate are of primary importance. Labels have played a key role in the process of state formation over the last centuries, in ever-changing ways. They were a way to gather knowledge and establish control in the colonial period, and subsequently became the subject of heated debates on representation in the post-colonial political set-up. The initial optimism of progressive governments has given way to more pessimistic assessments of how 'vulgar naked election politics' came to shape the use of labels and manipulation of identities, and more recently the machinations of the right-wing movement. But in the post-2004 history – again – there is increased space for the progressive use of labels, which possibly – and hopefully – will be an instrument of emancipation rather than control.

Notes

1   This paper is partly based on experience of working for DFID in India, during 2001–2004, particularly in Orissa (documented more extensively in de Haan (2004)). It benefited much from interaction with and comment from colleagues, including Shalini Bahuguna and Sushila Zeitlyn. Thanks also go to Rosalind Eyben and Joy Moncrieffe for encouragement to explore this theme, and to Harsh Mander and Ben Rogaly for comments. Errors remain my own.

2   A case in point is the way different terms are used interchangeably: Scheduled Caste, Untouchable, Dalit, Dalitsbahujans; and Adivasi and Tribal Caste or community (e.g. Deshpande, 2003, p124). The context usually justifies the use of a term, but the freedom with which different terms are employed may be an important and under-emphasized aspect of the discussion presented here; indeed, Gopal Guru criticizes the multiplicity of (construction of) terms, implying the possibility of privileging one category over the other (see Guru (2001) on the Dalit and 'Bahujan' categories). Simultaneous discussion of 'caste' and 'tribe' has the potential to homogenize the experiences of a wide range of groups, and the different process of discrimination they are subjected too. In this context, it is essential to recognize the diversity and agency of groups and individuals, and lack of representation (Valmiki, 2003).

3   Around the Durban conference on discrimination, the debate on caste and race came back; the continued importance of the issues is shown in the edited volume by Thorat and Umakant (2004).

4   The work of Berreman has been interpreted as a defence of the 'caste school of race' in American sociology of the 1930s, which developed an analogy between racism in the south of the US and the Indian caste system (Michael, 1999, pp24–27).

5   Deshpande highlights that while the occupational structure has over time undergone a profound change, the caste divisions have remained more or less the same (Deshpande, 2003, p113).

6   An extreme example elsewhere of the impact of the colonial state on articulation of categories is of course the Rwanda case, where Hutu and Tutsi were constructed as political identities, often overcoming practical problems in creating mutually exclusive categories. After Independence and certainly in the 1990s there was little doubt over the categories in Rwanda, and the racialization of the differences reinforced the colonial legacy of categorization (Mamdani, 2001). I would suggest that more (comparative) research would be helpful to explore the impact of late-colonial processes on social contracts as established after Independence.

7   'For example, the Kolis of Gujarat are the creation of a census category which clubs together castes such as the Patanvadia, Bareeya, Khant and Thakor. Initially, these separately followed the rituals of Rajputs and struggled for three decades to be acknowledged as Kshatriyas, so as to get high social status. They felt insulted if they were called Kolis, which indicated a group with low social status. But now they have started calling themselves Kolis so that they can garner material benefits, which is the surest way to improve social status. Social status based on the observance of rituals has become increasingly redundant' (Shah, 2002, p11).

8   For example, the Banjara nomadic community is listed as ST in four states, SC in five states, and OBC in another four, while 'none of these classifications speak to the specificities of the nomadic way of life' (Pant, 2005).

9   Already in 1959, Ram Manohar Lohia, who did believe that the left had to address class, gender and caste domination, argued that the 'policy of uplift of downgraded castes and groups is capable of yielding much poison', as more influential groups may monopolize benefits and protect their position, and elections might become acrimonious. 'Perhaps the most disastrous feature of the whole situation is the uplift of a limited section of backward and low castes into the ruling classes of the country' (Shah, 2002).

10 De Haan and Dubey (2003). For the purpose of this paper, it is important to highlight that the official categories used – e.g. SC, ST, OBC, Other – hide an enormous amount of diversity and underestimate disparities between top and bottom of the social ladder (Deshpande, 2003).

11 Hirschman (2004, p403), who argues that a key objective is to replace current concepts with notions of ethnicity, which is explicitly subjective, and recognizes multiple ancestry and heterogeneity.

References

Alam, J. (1999a) 'Is caste appeal casteism? Oppressed castes in politics', *Economic and Political Weekly*, 27 March

Alam, J. (1999b) 'What is happening inside Indian democracy?', *Economic and Political Weekly*, 11 September

Bambhiri, C. P. (2005) 'Reservation and casteism', *Economic and Political Weekly*, 26 February

Bayly, S. (1999) *Caste, Society and Politics in India from the Eighteenth Century to the Modern Age*, The New Cambridge History of India, IV.3, Cambridge, Cambridge University Press

Beteille, A. (1996) 'Caste in contemporary India', in C. Fuller (ed) *Caste Today*, Delhi, Oxford University Press

Darity, W. and Deshpande, A. (eds) (2003) *Boundaries of Clan and Color: Transnational Comparisons of Inter-Group Disparity*, London, Routledge

De Haan, A. (2004) 'Disparities within India's poorest region: Why do the same institutions work differently in different places?', Background Chapter for *World Development Report 2006*, www. worldbank.org/socialpolicy

De Haan, A. and Dubey, A. (2003) 'Extreme deprivation in remote areas in India: Social exclusion as explanatory concept', Chapter for Manchester Conference on Chronic Poverty

Deshpande, A. (2003) 'Recasting economic inequality', in W. Darity and A. Deshpande (eds) *Boundaries of Clan and Color: Transnational Comparisons of Inter-Group Disparity*, London, Routledge

Gandhi, M. K. (1933) 'Caste must go', in G. Shah (ed) *Caste and Democratic Politics in India*, Delhi, Permanent Black, pp80–82

Guru, G. (2001) 'The language of Dalitbahujan political discourse', in M. Mohanty (ed) *Class, Caste, Gender: Readings in Indian Government and Politics*, vol 5, New Delhi, Sage, pp256–267

Hirschman, C. (2004) 'The origins and demise of the concept of race', *Population and Development Review*, vol 30, no 3, September, pp385–416

Ilaiah, K. (1996) *Why I Am Not a Hindu: A Sudra Critique of Hindutva Philosophy, Culture and Political Economy*, 2nd edn, Kolkata, Samya

Islam, S. (2003) 'Labelling tribals: Forming and transforming bureaucratic identity in Thailand and Indonesia in a historical setting', *Gateway – An Academic Journal on the Web*, Spring

Jadhav, N. (2003) *Outcaste: A Memoir*, New Delhi, Viking

Kohli, A. (1990) *Democracy and Discontent. India's Growing Crisis of Governability*, Cambridge, Cambridge University Press.

Mamdani, M. (2001) *When Victims Become Killers. Colonialism, Nativism, and the Genocide in Rwanda*, Princeton, NJ, Princeton University Press

Mayer, A. (1996) 'Caste in an Indian village: Change and continuity 1954–1992', in C. Fuller (ed) *Caste Today*, Delhi, Oxford University Press

Michael, S. M. (1999) 'Introduction', in S. M. Michael (ed) *Dalits in Modern India: Vision and Values*, New Delhi, Vistaar Publications, pp1–35

Pant, M. (2005) 'The quest for inclusion: Nomadic communities and citizenship questions in Rajasthan', in N. Kabeer (ed) *Inclusive Citizenship: Meanings and Expressions*, London, Zed Books, pp85–98

Radhakrishna, M. (2001) *Dishonoured by History: 'Criminal Tribes' and British Colonial Policy*, New Delhi, Orient Longman

Shah, G. (2002) 'Introduction: Caste and democratic politics', in G. Shah (ed) *Caste and Democratic Politics in India*, Delhi, Permanent Black

Srinivas, M. N. (1962) 'Caste in modern India', in M. Mohanty (ed) *Class, Caste, Gender: Readings in Indian Government and Politics*, New Delhi, Sage, pp154–182

Thorat, S. K. (2005) 'Affirmative action policy in India: Dimensions, progress, and issues', chapter presented at workshop at Economic Commission for Africa, Addis Ababa, 11–12 July

Thorat, S. K. and Umakant (2004) *Caste, Race and Discrimination: Discourses in International Context*, Indian Institute of Dalit Studies, Jaipur and Delhi, Rawat Publications

Valmiki, O. (2003) *Joothan: A Dalit's Life* (trans A. P. Mukherjee), Kolkata, Samya

Verma, V. (1999) 'Colonialism and liberation: Amebdkar's quest for distributive justice', *Economic and Political Weekly*, 25 September, www.epw.org.in

Webster, J. C. B. (1999) 'Who is a Dalit?', in S. M. Michael (ed) *Dalits in Modern India: Vision and Values*, New Delhi, Vistaar Publications, pp68–79

Weisskopf, T. E. (2004) *Affirmative Action in the United States and India: A Comparative Perspective*, London and New York, Routledge

Wood, G. (1985) 'The politics of development policy labelling', *Development and Change*, vol 16, no 3, pp347–373

10

Exploring the Intersection of Racial Labels, Rainbow Citizenship and Citizens' Rights in Post-Apartheid South Africa

Linda Waldman

Before the 1990s no South African claimed to be either Khoisan or, as a matter of fact, Khoekhoe or San. There were however those who admitted in varying degrees of self-identity to be coloured, Griqua, Nama, Korana, Karretjie people, Bushmen, Khomani etc. But by the mid-nineties a significant number of people formerly known as coloured claimed to belong to one or other category of indigenous Khoisan. (Bredenkamp, 2001, p196)

South Africa has a unique history in the use of race and language as tools for controlling citizenship and rights... (United Nations Commission on Human Rights (UNCHR), 2005, p6)

In South Africa, the end of the first decade of democratic governance has led to a reflexive mood as citizens, NGOs, bureaucrats and government officials consider South Africa's economic growth, lessons learnt, progress made and development policies since the end of apartheid rule. For anthropologists, one process that stands out and has caused considerable reflection on apartheid and its associated identity labels has been the resurgence of identity politics (Sharp and Boonzaier, 1994; Robins, 1997, 2000; Seideman, 1999). Termed 'Khoisan[1] revivalism' (Bredenkamp, 2001) or 'neo-Khoe-San resurgence' (Besten, 2006), this process has involved a 'significant number of people generally classified as coloured in South Africa [who] began to appropriate the convenient composite term Khoisan for the purpose of their self identity and as way of reconstituting a claim to indigenous culture' (Bredenkamp, 2001, p191). This chapter examines this process of Khoisan revivalism, from the perspective of the Griqua people in South Africa, in relation to processes of governance. It deals with the power of labelling to define identities, through an examination of how identity and governance were rigidly controlled during the apartheid years and apartheid racial policy dictated people's identity. In examining how the state legally enforced racial labels, the chapter also considers the processes of counter-labelling and people's own adaptation of ethnic labels to refute racial state categories. Since the end of apartheid, the widescale 'claiming' of alternative identities has occurred and the democratic government has adopted a rights-based constitution. This leads, in the chapter, to an assessment of how diverse ways of framing issues produce labels of identification which, in turn, results in different policy choices and outcomes.

With its democratic and pro-poor constitution, which guarantees its citizens' rights to housing, health care, food, water, social security and a healthy environment, the South African government has made considerable advances in reducing poverty. Nonetheless, during this past decade government policy has been heavily influenced by donor-advocated preferences, pro-poor growth through private-sector investment, markets and decentralization receiving more emphasis than rights-based approaches (Jung, 1999; Scoones and Wolmer, 2003; Sustainable Livelihoods in Southern Africa (SLSA) Team, 2003). The contradictions between the Reconstruction and Development (RDP) and Growth, Employment and Redistribution (GEAR) programmes reflect the state's attempt to reconcile social justice with economic growth. Its dominant policy narrative in recent years has therefore been to facilitate poor and marginal people's economic enhancement through private investment and economic participation (SLSA Team, 2003). The post-1994 constitution indicates that people's rights are important and that political and legal processes should protect their entitlement to organize and claim constitutional rights through mobilization. The constitution thus recognizes the so-called 'first generation' and 'second generation' of human rights, which are concerned with people's liberty, political involvement, social and economic rights. One area in which increasing mobilization has happened is in terms of claims to indigenous rights, first-nation status and self-determination. This campaign, by Griqua and other Khoisan peoples, challenges the South African government to recognize the so-called 'third generation' of human rights or collective rights as integral to the South African constitution and to fully integrate Khoisan people into its processes of governance.

Identity politics in South Africa

In May 1994, South Africa underwent a 'truly remarkable' transition from an apartheid and racist-dominated government to a government of national unity. South Africa appeared to the rest of the world as a 'textbook case of democratization' (Adler and Webster, 1995, p76). In addition to electing a democratic government, South Africa partook in the 'international game' of states; it began to develop a nation – the now famous 'rainbow nation' – which legitimated it in the eyes of the international 'community' (Simpson, 1994, pp464, 472). For most South Africans this process was a positive development, which would lead to a new collective society not dominated by ethnic and racial classifications.[2] However, as illustrated in the opening quote, democracy brought with it a resurgence of identity politics as coloured people throughout South Africa reclaimed former Khoi (nomadic pastoralists) and San (nomadic hunter-gatherers) identities. Some academics recognized the significance of this process. Giliomee (1991) argued that ethnic categories should not be omitted from the new constitution and that the new dispensation had to allow for power-sharing between ethnic and minority groups; others warned against disregarding ethnicity because of the weight of meaning associated with it for many South Africans (Dubow, 1994; Grundlingh, 1991; Muller, 1991; Pakendorf, 1991). While the African National Congress (ANC) experienced great difficulty in dealing with the multiple expressions of ethnic sentiments and claims that arose in the early 1990s (Dubow, 1994, p356), those people who had been categorized 'coloured' under the apartheid government took advantage of the new political dispensation to promote an indigenous and 'first nation' identity. In so doing, they were 'manifesting a process of psychological, cultural and socio-political repositioning within the national and international order' (Besten, 2006, p1). The historical process of labelling associated with this new 'claiming' of identity meant that, for the Griqua people of South Africa, inherent in this transition to democratic governance was both an increased threat to their identity and the promise of new possibilities. Understanding this dichotomy requires an exploration of their historical circumstances prior to the dawning of South Africa's democracy.

Griqua identity

The significance attached to labels has long been a feature of Griqua identity. The name Griqua was adopted in 1813 when representatives from the London Missionary Society persuaded a heterogeneous collectivity at Klaarwater (Griquatown) – then called *Bastaard* or *Basters*[3] – to change their pejorative name (Halford, 1949; Nurse, 1975; Ross, 1976). This diverse category of 'mixed-race' descendants of indigenous Khoi (nomadic pastoralists), autochthonous San (nomadic hunter-gatherers), escaped slaves, *Boer* (Afrikaner) frontiersmen, Africans (predominantly Tswana) and European settlers had formed a frontier society on the borders of the Cape Colony (Ross, 1976, p1). At the time, their pejorative name contrasted with their collective ambition to establish themselves as independent, 'civilized' and equal to white colonial society (van Vreeden, 1957, p30). Although people had sought to remove the pejorative connotations of the name 'Baster' through a process of counter-labelling and strong identification as Griqua, the negative connotations of primitiveness were not easily dismantled. In the late 1980s and early 1990s, 180 years after this attempt at counter-labelling, there were still widespread stereotypes of Griqua people as backward, primitive and uncivilized. As this chapter will later show, leaders have constantly sought to improve the status of the Griqua through campaigning for political recognition; many of their followers and broader society have, however, believed these negative associations to be true.

The search for social standing among the Khoi during the 18th century had led them to be among the first missionary converts to Christianity (Gerstner, 1997, p29; Elbourne and Ross, 1997). Christianity was to 'become a core component of Griqua identity' and 'adherence to the church became a marker for allegiance to one or other of the political factions in various Griqua captaincies' (Elbourne and Ross, 1997, p40). Situated on the border of colonial society, Griqua leaders or *Kapteins*[4] initially controlled large tracts of frontier land through the powerful combination of weapons, missionary support and Christianity. This, however, was not to last.

Powerful Griqua polities, established at Griquatown, Campbell, Philipolis and Griqualand East during the colonial period, were based on four principles, all of which contributed both to the establishment and consolidation of the polities and, ironically, to their downfall. First, Christianity was used to assert independence. This induced leaders to cooperate with missionaries and to facilitate the outward spread of the Christian message from their stations. With time, however, it also led to the development of trained Griqua crusaders who rebelled against missionary authority and asserted their ability to evangelize and rule the neighbouring people. Second, there was a need to accumulate a comprehensive following in order that the missionaries and colonial authorities would recognize the might of the Griqua. Griqua society thus developed an inclusory nature whereby any person could attach him- or herself to the Kapteins as a dependent follower and hence to adopt the label 'Griqua'. Although this had the advantage of bolstering the numbers of people settled at Griqua stations, it also led to severe internal divisions and conflicts that undermined the strength and authority of the Kapteins. This internal conflict was seldom dealt with directly, since leaders and their followers simply left whenever conflict arose. This tendency to *trek* away from trouble in search of autonomy, land and independence represents the third principle. Although, on the whole the Griqua adopted the missionaries' demands of a settled existence, each Kaptein sought to secure freedom, independence and agricultural wealth through access to land. Thus, when conditions were such that autonomy, independence and land were under threat, the Kapteins responded by trekking to new, unexplored territory. The Griqua search for territory in which they could live out their ambitions of economic prowess, political autonomy and social acclaim has certainly fostered and helped to retain a Griqua identity. But the tendency to trek fundamentally undermined Griqua attempts to present themselves as a unified force and to stand undivided in the face of the broader forces that challenged their identity. The fourth tendency, perhaps most detrimental to the Griqua Kapteins, was their reliance on the colonial authorities for the protection of Griqua independence and sovereignty. Not only did this lead to infighting between the various Kapteins as they jockeyed with each other to secure treaties, it also meant that they were left with few means with which to defend themselves when the colonial authorities, no longer seeing any need for the Griqua, disregarded the clauses in their treaties and the recognition of Griqua independence in order to claim ownership of Griqua land. As a result of these combined processes, the history of the Griqua can be seen as one in which they 'lost out in the struggle for land, capital and resources in industrializing South Africa' (Beinart, 1986, p260).

The Griqua also lost out in terms of being able to determine who they are, to claim an identity and a label for themselves. The heterogeneous and autonomous Griqua societies described here did not last beyond the turn of the century – a time when ideas about coloured identity were forged and racial segregation was becoming widespread (McEachern, 1998, p501). As illustrated in the following section, people retained a Griqua and Christian identity throughout the 19th and 20th centuries despite being officially labelled coloured; they constantly sought wider recognition, with associated formal status and respect, for themselves.

The year 1948 heralded the beginning of National Party rule in South Africa and, more importantly, the start of apartheid's rigid racial classification system that relegated Griqua to a subsidiary of the category 'coloured'. Academics, concerned with issues of identity and labelling, tended to restrict themselves to the study of local dynamics in relation to, and shaped by, apartheid (see Eriksen, 1993; Dubow, 1994). This resulted partly from the use of participant observation, which tends to force a narrow focus on research topics, and partly from anthropologists' relationship with the apartheid state (Gordon and Spiegal, 1993; Sharp, 1997). Many studies explained the emergence of ethnic identities by showing how these facilitated access to resources within the context of localized and apartheid-structured political economies (see, for example, James, 1990; Sharp and Boonzaier, 1994; Webster, 1991). Prior to the 1994 elections and the development of a democratic government, anthropologists tended to reject ethnic particularism primarily because of the manner in which ethnicity was mobilized by the apartheid government as a means of enforcing political division and economic exploitation (Dubow, 1994; Sharp, 1996). Ethnic identity was therefore seen from two perspectives during the apartheid era, which have been summarized as 'naming' and 'claiming' by Comaroff (1996). 'Naming' referred to the primordial and essentialist approach adopted by the apartheid state to delimit other weaker collectivities. For this reason any acknowledgement of the primordial elements of ethnic identity resonated strongly with the imposition of racial categorization by apartheid engineers. 'Claiming', however, referred to the understanding of ethnic identity in a 'situational, contextual, and subjective sense.' According to this usage, ethnicity is understood as a form of social identity that acquires content and meaning through a process of conscious assertion and imaging' (Dubow, 1994, p368). It was this social constructivist approach that anthropologists and historians adopted, insisting that South African ethnic identities were historically constructed. The deconstruction of primordial discourses of identity during the 1980s thus acted as a critique of apartheid domination and came to be termed 'exposé analysis' (Gordon and Spiegel, 1993).

During the apartheid years, the government approach to identity was one of 'naming'. As early as 1953 it was recognized by government officials that this labelling process would pose many problems and that it would be difficult to prove people's 'race'. The main challenge officials experienced was how to distinguish coloured people from African people. Officials may have felt that they had some idea of what coloured and African people looked like and that their classification was therefore relatively sound, but Griqua people posed a particular problem because of their heterogeneous origins. The 1957/58 Race Relations Act reported:

> *Another group of people who are encountering great difficulties are the Griquas of the Northern Cape, who have mixed White, Hottentot, Bush and a little African blood, but who over the years became a distinctive group with a distinctive appearance, speaking the Griqua Hottentot language ... In recent years some of the younger ones have inter-married with Africans, and have adopted Afrikaans as their home language. They have, however, been regarded as Coloured: those who draw pensions are paid at Coloured rates, and most of the men hold certificates of non-liability for Native taxation.*
> *... At the time of writing, their position was extra-ordinarily confused. They were not Africans for the purposes of the Representation of Natives Act, yet could not qualify for the Coloured voters' roll. Some of them, while holding certificates of non-liability for Native taxation, had been issued with reference books making them liable to pay poll tax.* (South African Institute of Race Relations (SAIRR), 1957–1958, p32)

Since Griqua society had been an open society which welcomed others, this made it particularly difficult to apply apartheid labels. Those individuals who verbalized their Griqua identity to government officials were classified African and were then subject to the relevant legislature and repressive conditions. Under different circumstances, these same people qualified for coloured registration; and they thus often carried documentation requiring them to pay poll tax and documentation exempting them from paying it.

What is especially evident here is how different ways of framing questions about race and ethnicity, coupled with different processes, produce labels which, in turn, lead to policy decisions and outcomes. Many Griqua received papers labelling them as African and/or as coloured and had to comply accordingly to both restrictive legislation and associated benefits; whereas they themselves, as individuals, believed in their Griqua identity.

With time, Griqua came to be seen as a sub-category of 'coloured', a label which Muller describes as having 'never represented any kind of homogenous group in South Africa, except in the eyes of the apartheid regime' (Muller, 2002, p15). They felt their loss of Griqua identity acutely and campaigned throughout the apartheid years for recognition of Griqua as an identity (and label) in its own right, rather than a sub-category of coloured in the Population Registration Act. Officials of the apartheid government, however, argued otherwise:

> *The object of the Griquas' dogged struggle has always been the right to register as Griquas without intimidation, but the officials claim that there is no reason to be a Griqua since a Griqua is a coloured and a coloured is a Griqua on the grounds of the definition that 'a coloured is neither white nor Black nor Asiatic', and thus all the other coloureds must be classified in this class.* (President's Commission, 1983, p76)

Griqua people embraced 'colouredness', but also drew on their Khoi heritage and stressed similarities with other African tribes. To be Griqua was, according to them, distinct from other coloured people and from South Africa's black tribes. As such, they claimed, special dispensations should be considered for the Griqua people. Echoing this view, local government officials – who were personally acquainted with Griqua people – described them as a category of 'mixed descent with ethnic blood'.[5] However, centralized government authorities relied on the official classification of 'coloured' and on the implications inherent in that label, to inform their handling of 'the Griqua'.

Campaigning for Griqua ethnic identity

In accordance with the idea that Griqua identity was an identity more 'ethnic' than was encapsulated in the label 'coloured', Griqua people campaigned for a homeland[6] similar to that 'occupied' by other black South Africans. In the 1970s, Kaptein Adam Kok IV called on the government to establish a homeland for the Griqua and their children. This demand for land formed a common thread in Griqua negotiations with the apartheid government, as Saks comments:

> *(t)hroughout the apartheid era, virtually unnoticed by most South Africans, a small Griqua lobby on the political fringes was pressing for the realisation of a receding dream, the statutory recognition of a distinct Griqua National entity and the establishment of a Griqua homeland under the policy of Separate Development.* (Saks, 1997, p109)

Many Northern Cape Griqua people believed that they might have gained land in this form, especially as the Griqua people of Kranshoek (in the Western Cape province) had acquired access to government land.[7] But the apartheid government steered clear of such investment in the Griqua. Instead, Griqua claims for land were, in the 1980s, re-directed back to the Griqua, who were to prove that they were a unified group rather than a diverse collection of heterogeneous people – as defined by the label 'coloured' – before the government would respond (Waldman, 1989). In part, this may have been because Griqua people were scattered throughout South Africa with no firm geographical boundaries.[8]

The constant demands for land and the persistent mobilization of Griqua leaders – such as Andrew Abraham Stockenstrom le Fleur, Adam Kok IV, Daniel James Kanyiles – resulted in many government reports commissioned to research various Griqua issues. The President's Commission, undertaken in the 1980s, recognized that the 'majority of the Griquas believe that they have an identity of their own and that they are consequently a separate people by descent' (President's Commission, 1983, p73). The recommendations, however, made no mention of territory or a homeland, emphasizing instead the 'preservation and promotion of culture' (President's Commission, 1983, p1). The Commission further reinforced the application of the 'coloured' label, arguing that '(t)he committee therefore does not foresee a constitutional dispensation for this population group separate from the dispensation for the Coloured group' (President's Commission, 1983, p10).

It is clear that the Commission considered the Griqua as part of the broader category 'coloured', and hence as different from African people and not in need of a homeland. It is also probable that by 1983 the government was aware of the political sensitivity and international criticism associated with its homeland policies. Moreover, the attitudes of the Griqua leaders and organizations were ambiguous and while campaigning for Griqua recognition and a homeland similar to those occupied by black people, they also supported segregation, as these policies had the side effect of preserving coloured privilege (see, for example, Edgar and Saunders, 1982; Besten, 2006; Waldman, 1989). Apartheid authorities were generally, although not always, unopposed by the Griqua in matters such as race legislation and even in the enforcing of white privilege.

Post-apartheid and the abolition of labels

Although, as suggested above, 1994 saw the end of official racial classification, these divisions could not be so easily eradicated in civil society. Ironically, the abolition of racial classification also resulted in a resurgence of demands for ethnic recognition. These ethnic demands focused on national and international arrangements. Highly prominent in indigenous Khoisan revivalism were various Griqua leaders who firmly insisted on their identification as Griqua. During the apartheid years, they argued, Griqua people were placed in the category 'coloured' and their own identity was ignored. Post-1994, Griqua leaders complained that they were essentially being told that 'they must get out of the coloured bus and into the rainbow bus. It's all the same, there's no difference between the buses, one is called coloured, the other is called rainbow'. As suggested in this statement, being acknowledged as South African or as members of the rainbow nation was not enough for the leaders of the Griqua people. They felt that this, like the apartheid classification of them as coloured, failed to acknowledge their specific ethnic identity. Their insistence on recognition of Griquaness can be seen, not only as a mobilizing strategy, but also as a means of securing their pride and dignity within South African political circles. It was at this historical juncture that many of the negative labels initially associated with 'Baster' – and later with Griqua – identity (discussed above) were shed. Instead of being associated with primitiveness and backwardness, Griqua identity was now reframed as a positive experience of indigeneity and of ethnic pride. In addition, the reclaiming of Khoisan identities is intricately interwoven with concerns over the 'restitution of traditional land, historical continuity, distinctive cultural characteristics, group consciousness and unity' (Le Fleur, 2006, p3). Claims to Griqua identity are thus interlinked with Khoisan demands to review the 1913 cut-off point for land claims as they lost their land prior this date.[9] The relationship between identity, dignity and land was poignantly summarized for me by one Griqua person who said, 'A Griqua without land is like a man without trousers'.

In engaging in these mobilization processes, Khoisan people often articulated synchronic and primordial versions of their identity in which they stressed that their identity and descent were interlinked and stemmed from time immemorial. These processes meant that academics were faced with new theoretical and conceptual issues. When previously marginalized categories of people – such as the Griqua – began articulating claims to an indigenous and primordial identity, these claims were not the same as apartheid's imposition of labels and did not deserve similar robust, deconstructive analysis (Sharp, 1996). Instead, anthropologists were faced with difficult moral decisions:

> *Striking those discourses [imposed by the apartheid government] down was an easy intellectual task, in that it did not call for any difficult moral choices. But now we are faced not only with the imposition of 'otherness' by the powerful on the powerless, and with the inscription of this 'otherness' in the cultural rhetoric – the texts – of those who have power. We are also faced with the claiming of 'otherness' as a weapon in the hands of those who see themselves as weak, and as a means of articulating their demands for recognition, dignity and resources. Now we have some difficult distinctions to make.* (Sharp, 1996, pp102–103)

Academics felt they were caught between deconstructing these discourses, as indeed they had done in the past, or accepting essentialist notions of ethnic identity for political reasons. As Sharp points out, there were problems with both these approaches. On the one hand, it was difficult to accept these discourses wholly and uncritically and, on the other, it was impossible to distinguish between deconstruction for academic purposes and the political undermining of people's claims. Thus both these approaches came to be seen as equally limiting for academics, as expressed by Sharp who indicated the need for new theoretical perspectives.

Sharp and Boonzaier's analysis of Nama claims to an authochonous and primordial identity (1994) can be seen as a response to these conceptual challenges. Their solution was to see the ritual enactment of these discourses as a performance: in which Nama people were 'able to approach these discourses as good actors in a play' (Sharp, 1996, p94). Their argument was that indigenous people articulated primordial discourses of identity when necessary, but that they did not wholly believe their own performances. Rather, these actors were able to analyse, critically and reflexively, their own discourses of primordialism.

This approach was soon criticized by Robins for its failure to recognize that 'cultural hybridity, fragmentation and inconsistency' are fundamental components of Nama existence. Sharp and Boonzaier's analysis of Nama identity drew on a political economy model of reality which they saw as contradicting the ideological position emphasized by the Nama themselves. In seeing Nama articulations of their primordial links with their ancestors and the land they occupied as a performance, Sharp and Boonzaier created a distinction between one reality (the one the Nama could be seen to engage in daily) and their articulation of that reality (Robins, 1997; also see Sharp, 1997). Their articulation of an autochthonous identity, Robins argued, has to be seen as more than an instrumental act guaranteed to secure certain economic gains. 'It is precisely because of their shattering encounters with Western domination and ethnocide that the cultural world of Namaqualanders is comprised of fragments, reinventions, incoherence, disjunctures, silences and hybridity' (Robins, 1997, p26).

Thus the study of 'difference' in post-apartheid South Africa provided academics with new challenges and the need to seriously rethink their anthropological approach. Part of this reworking involved the recognition of ambiguity and hybridity as a fundamental condition of many minority peoples and also of the paradox inherent in all nation-building projects (Sharp, 1997). It also entailed a recognition that all discourses of ethnic difference were relational and that indigenous peoples were 'entering into a dialogue with wider society' both within – and beyond – the borders of South Africa (Sharp, 1996, p92).

Within South Africa, after 1994, Griqua leaders demanded that they be accommodated in the House of Traditional Leaders. Anthropologists at the Department of Constitutional Development (DCD), who had been responsible for the selection of traditional leaders of South African homelands during the apartheid era, addressed these demands. They based their investigation on the apartheid understanding that ethnic identity was clear-cut, with established 'traditional' leadership, comprising of homogeneous cultural communities. In so doing, they failed to recognize the role of apartheid governance in creating these ethnic categories and the homogeneous communities that fitted their labels. Not surprisingly, it was impossible to find these ethnic criteria in the case of the Griqua. Traditional rules of succession had not been adhered to and had, instead, proved to be exceptionally adaptable (see Edgar and Saunders, 1982, p207; Comaroff, 1974; Costa, 1997). There was no homogeneous population living in a defined geographical territory and no obvious paramount ruler. Even attempts to use more 'modern' criteria such as membership of Griqua cultural organizations proved impossible as many organizations did not keep formal records.

The process of creating a South African nation-state thus entailed processes of homogenization (the calls for a rainbow identity) and, simultaneously, of 'othering' (the insistence on the part of Griqua leaders that they are not merely South Africans) in which identity labels came to assume new significance. These simultaneous processes of nation-building and ethnic safeguarding, taking place shortly after the birth of a new South Africa, meant, however, that it was difficult to determine where the Griqua stood in relation to other South Africans and what measures should be prescribed by way of redistribution or compensation for apartheid discrimination. The application of indigenous rights to Khoisan people within South Africa provides a new level of differentiation and labelling. As Lehmann has recently argued, 'if all members of a national society are indigenous, there is obviously no special significance to *being* indigenous. Indigenous then is merely a fact that describes all members of the population, but cannot serve to vest particular members with rights that other members do not enjoy' (Lehmann, 2004, p97, original emphasis). Indigenous rights, Lehmann suggests, are crucial because they are an indication of power relations: 'because indigenous communities are not able to realise their aspirations through the ordinary democratic processes in the ways in which majorities are in theory able to do...' (2004, p99). The labelling of people as indigenous will therefore help them to live their lives in the manner of their choosing, while still being integrated into the modern South African state. Nonetheless, the implications of self-determination and of constitutional accommodation are difficult issues for the state to grapple with and will have significant legal implications. Thus, as Lehmann documents in her paper, there has been considerable debate over precisely which South Africans should be considered indigenous and who should not.[10]

Griqua people also aligned themselves with organizations that operated beyond South Africa's borders, such as the United Nations Indigenous People's Forum – from which it drew inspiration for land claims, recognition, restitution, autochthony and first-nation status – and African organizations such as the African Commission on Human and People's Rights and the establishment of the Indigenous Peoples of Africa Co-ordinating Committee. This engagement with international figures, with other minority peoples about human and indigenous rights, provided South Africans with new ways of defining problems and seeing solutions (Merry, 2001). Around the world, marginalized 'Fourth World Nation' groups have used international forums to press for recognition and claims. This has resulted in greater recognition and legitimacy for marginalized people, but this has also forced them to conform to fixed notions of tradition (see Robins, 2000). As is the case with domestic debates about who should be considered indigenous, these processes have led to transformations in terms of what it means to be indigenous. As Cowan et al (2001) note, there is a 'paradox' in that rights can be both constraining and enabling.

Pressure from Griqua organizations, which had powerful international backing from the United Nations Indigenous People's Forum, has forced the Department of Constitutional Development to seek some form of resolution. The first step towards a resolution occurred in 1996 when the government publicly acknowledged that the Griqua were officially recognized as an important component of South African society. This was followed by the formation of a new alliance, the National Griqua Forum, in 1998. In May 1998 this was complemented by an announcement by the Minister of Constitutional Development that it would, in conjunction with the Geneva-based International Labour Office, examine the question of constitutional rights for vulnerable minorities. By 1999, the Department of Constitutional Development initiated a wider-based National Khoisan Forum (later to become the National Khoisan Council) 'to promote dialogue with the government in regards to the constitutional accommodation of Khoe-San traditional leaders' (Besten, 2006, p294). As had been the case with the Griqua National Forum, this organization served to legitimate some leaders and exclude others. The state has taken a number of actions designed to meet the demands of the Khoisan leaders, including: establishing the Commission on the Protection of the Cultural, Religious and Linguistic Minorities and creating the Pan South African Language Board; the recognition of indigenous language and the need to actively develop these languages in the 1996 Constitution; the exploration of indigenous people's rights by the South African Human Rights Commission in 2000; the Department of Provincial and Local Government's recognition of historic injustices against Khoisan people in 2004; and, in that same year, Cabinet's adoption of a memorandum leading to official recognition of indigenous communities. Although these measures have been profoundly significant in terms of affirming Griqua (and other Khoisan) indigeneity, helping to establish a sense of belonging and contributing towards a sense of selfhood or identity, the question of constitutional accommodation remains unanswered despite pressure from international forums such as the United Nations and from indigenous people.

As evidenced in the complex and unresolved negotiations, the demands for the constitutional accommodation of the Khoisan and, more recently, for the 'responsible application of the notion of self-determination'[11] (le Fleur, 2006, p6), are particularly challenging for the South African government to address, particularly in the light of South Africa's experience of apartheid, in which labels of identification forced people to act and live in prescribed ways. In contrast, the current South African rights-based constitution acknowledges that all people have the right to 'participate in the cultural life of their choice'. It recognizes that:

> *Persons belonging to a cultural, religious or linguistic community may not be denied the right, with other members of that community:*
>
> *a) to enjoy their culture, practise their religion and use their language; and*
> *b) to form, join and maintain cultural, religious and linguistic associations and other organs of civil society. (South African Constitution, 1996)*

South Africa acknowledges that 'all rights are fundamental, universal, equally important for all human beings and cannot be separated from each other' (South Africa Human Rights Commission (SAHRC), n.d.). Nonetheless, South Africa's focus has been on civil and political rights, social and economic rights, 'or 'first generation' rights, and second generation' rights.[12] These second-generation rights have been summarized as: the right to housing, education, food, health, land, water, social security and environmental rights (SAHRC, n.d.). In contrast with civil and political rights, which are absolute, immediate, justiciable and negative in the sense that the state should avoid taking action in relation to these rights, these rights are pragmatic, to be realized gradually, they are aspirational and positive in the sense that the state needs proactively to seek to provide them. But, despite being one of the world's most progressive constitutions, indigenous mobilization is pushing the South African government to do more. The demands of the Khoisan are demands for the integration of a 'third generation' of rights – the contentious collective rights associated with group identity, self-determination, culture and indigenous minorities. Integrating these rights into the constitution will 'send a clear message to Africa and the world that indigenous rights are a necessary component of human and civil rights in modern democracies' (Le Fleur, 2006, p7).

Mobilization by the Griqua and other Khoisan collectivities, and their support from national, African and international forums, has put collective and continuous pressure on the government. The SAHRC reported that the 'situation of indigenous people in South Africa is critical' and that this motivated the Special Rapporteur of the United Nations on the Human Rights and Fundamental Freedoms of Indigenous People, Mr Stavenhagen, to visit South Africa at the invitation of the South African government (SAHRC, 2006, p19). During this time, he consulted widely with indigenous people, government representatives, civil society organizations, donor organizations and so forth. While recognizing the government's 'tremendous efforts' (UNCHR, 2005, p16) and commitment to the 'protection and promotion of human rights' (UNCHR, 2005, p6), his report argued that 'national framework legislation ... should be promptly enacted with the full participation of indigenous communities' (UNCHR, 2005, p17). Such an approach, however, raises new questions about South African citizenship, identity and the importance of labelling.

Conclusion

South Africa's leading discourses of national identity, the rainbow nation and African essentialism have, like previous apartheid discourses, excluded the possibility of valuing coloured identity in positive terms (Erasmus, 2001). This has resulted in a resurgence of indigenous Khoisan identities, widespread national mobilization for Griqua recognition and, finally, attempts at constitutional accommodation as they seek for greater legitimacy in political and legal spheres. Thus the claiming of Griqua identity has had a significant effect at national level politics in terms of emphasizing people's rootedness within South Africa.

The South African account illustrates a nuanced and complex system of identity politics. Coloured, Griqua, Khoisan, indigenous, first-nation status, South African: these are all labels and all of them can be applied – and indeed have been applied – to the people discussed in this paper. Each label, each category, each name implies a different relationship with the South African state, with other South Africans and with dominant power relations. Each name also has different implications for how the Griqua are to be integrated into democratic South Africa. Different forms of integration, in turn, have widely varying socio-economic implications. The battle for recognition, for constitutional accommodation, is primarily about identity and pride, but it is also about how people live their lives on an everyday basis. Identity, the claiming of labels, and the identifying of others through labels, have implications about the land on which one lives, the education one's children can benefit from, the places where employment might be sought and a myriad of other factors.

As academics seeking to explain the resurgence of Khoisan identities in South Africa have learnt, one cannot draw a clear-cut distinction between daily life, behaviour and identification. The blurred lines remain, even when the existing (and previous) governing system's framework does not allow for such ambiguity. As academics, they are faced with new challenges. How will legal frameworks accommodate labels – such as indigenous – and what kinds of actions are possible on the basis of identification? Lehmann has recently argued that '(g)iven South Africa's racially polarised history, a history that favoured minorities at the expense of the majority, introducing legal concepts that rest on accepting a claimant-group's indigenous status, and therefore, the majority's non-indigenous status, is arguably inappropriate' (Lehmann, 2004, p109). How can identity be reaffirmed without resorting to applying and using labels? Furthermore, in what ways are exercises of deconstruction possible or do they always undermine people's values and meanings? What new ways are there for understanding debates about the politics of identity? Cowan et al (2001) examine 'culture' as an object of rights discourse and aim to see the pursuit of human rights as a cultural process in its own right, but how might this translate into issues of policy and governance?

In seeking to adopt an indigenous identity, the Griqua and other Khoisan movements are challenging all South Africans to engage in a process of exploration: What does it mean to be South African? How similar, and how different, are we from each other? What does living in the 'rainbow nation' imply? Which differences can we recognize – and legislate for – in ways that do not reproduce the racial discrimination of the apartheid era?

Notes

1   The term 'Khoisan' has generally been taken to refer to the indigenous San hunter-gatherers and Khoikhoi pastoralists. It is nonetheless highly contested, with many San people refusing to accept the term because it is originally a Khoi name and with many Khoi people preferring the spelling Khoe or Khoe-San as a means of asserting their historical connections and right to claim the language and label of their identity. Academics have also discussed the difficulty of distinguishing historically between these peoples. Nonetheless, as the term Khoisan continues to be used as a collective term for both the Khoi and the San within academia, I have followed this usage here for purposes of consistency.

2   The use of the terms 'racial' and 'ethnic' identity have both political and historical significance in South Africa. Although interwoven and often used interchangeably, the apartheid government conceptualized difference in terms of race and primordial biological characteristics. Thus politically conservative supporters of apartheid policy often spoke about South Africa's black population in terms of clear-cut racial differences. In response to this, and in order to challenge these apartheid constructions of race, social anthropologists with more liberal political views emphasized the social construction of ethnic identity to refer to the same people. With time, the term 'ethnic identity' became incorporated into the apartheid government's discourse, enabling the government to draw on international processes for justification of its action, but without any shift in the manner in which identities were conceptualized or policy implemented (see Boonzaier, 1988; Sharp, 1988; Skalnik, 1988; West, 1988).

3   The word '*Baster*' or '*Baastard*' translates to mean bastard or child of illegitimate birth. However, the word gained additional social and economic meanings in the context of the Cape Colony. Socially, *Baster* came to indicate children of mixed parentage, especially children born to white and Khoi parents, but it also referred to children of Khoi and slave unions. Economically, the term *Baster* referred to people of a slightly better class who were transport riders, craftsmen or small farmers and did not perform menial work such as farm or domestic labour (Legassick, 1979; Nurse et al, 1985).

4   In English: Captain. I use the Afrikaans term here, which is the same term used when people in the Northern Cape talk about the historical Griqua leaders. Other academics have chosen to use the Dutch spellings of the word – *Kaptyn* (Edgar and Saunders, 1982) or *Kapteyn* (Kinsman, 1989).

5   Undated Memorandum submitted to the President's Commission by the Municipality of Griquatown, c. 12 April 1983.

6   The homelands, or Bantustans, were tracts of land set aside by the apartheid government for occupation by black people. These homelands were purportedly independent, but individuals still had to migrate to urban areas in order to earn a living and to fulfil the labour requirements of a capitalist and divided society. Increasingly, they became dumping grounds for elderly, sickly or unemployed people, who struggled to survive in these overpopulated areas (Posel, 1991).

7   Rented from white owners, a Griqua collectivity occupied this farm from the late 1920s until 1957 when the apartheid government purchased the farm 'for the benefit of the Griqua' (Besten, 2006, p150) in recognition of their loyalty and support of the apartheid vision.

8   This geographical spread results partly from historical events that shaped the South African political landscape. It also stems from Griqua responses to these events, which were characterized by leaders' almost endemic tendency to *trek* (journey) with their followers, to new areas.

9   South Africans who were forcibly removed from their land during the years 1913–1994 can claim compensation through the government's programme of land restitution.

10   In South Africa, as in many other African countries, the definition is complicated by the argument that all Africans are indigenous in the sense that they are original inhabitants, 'non-dominant' and are culturally separated from white colonists (Saugestad, 2000, pp5–6). An attempt to move beyond this definition has led some to use a post-colonial definition that stresses internal differentiation. In this definition, indigenous people are, according to Eriksen (1993, p126), 'non-state people' who are well positioned to spur controversy against the state (also see Suzman, 2000; Nthomang, 2000; Thornberry, 2000). The United Nations Working Group on Indigenous Populations, which considers indigenous to refer to 'non-dominant groups of aboriginal or prior descent with distinct territorial and cultural identities' (UNCHR, 2005, p8-9), is the definition being adopted by Khoisan and Griqua people who emphasize their 'first nation' and authochonous status within South Africa.

11   Self-determination is explained by Le Fleur (2006, p6) to mean 'an embodiment of the need of indigenous people to determine their own future and their own destiny, in so far as it has relevance in terms of local powers over schooling, decisions on curriculum content in schools, control or even joint control over natural resources, such as national parks, mining industries and tourism in traditional areas, etc.'

12   These first- and second-generation rights result from the Universal Declaration of Human Rights in 1948, the International Covenant on Civil and Political Rights in 1966 and the International Covenant on Economic, Social and Cultural Rights in 1976, which collectively form the International Bill of Human Rights.

References

Adler, G. and Webster, E. (1995) 'Challenging transition theory: The labour movement, radical reform, and transition to democracy in South Africa', *Politics and Society*, vol 23, no 1, pp75–106

Beinart, W. (1986) 'Settler accumulation in East Griqualand from the demise of the Griqua to the Natives Land Act', in W. Beinart, P. Delius and S. Trapido (eds) *Putting a Plough to the Ground: Accumulation and Dispossession in Rural South Africa 1850–1930*, Johannesburg, Ravan Press

Besten, M. P. (2006) 'Transformation and reconstitution of Khoe-San identities: A. A. S. le Fleur I, Griqua identities and post-apartheid Khoe-San revivalism', Unpublished PhD thesis, University of Leiden

Boonzaier, E. (1988) 'Race and the race paradigm', in J. Sharp and E. Boonzaier (eds) *South African Keywords: The Uses and Abuses of Political Concepts*, Cape Town, David Phillip

Bredenkamp, H. C. J. (2001) 'Khoisan Revivalism and the Indigenous Peoples issue in post-apartheid South Africa: a question of self-identity?', in A. Barnard and J. Kenrick (eds) *Africa's Indigenous Peoples: 'First Peoples' or 'Marginalized Minorities'?* Edinburgh, Centre of African Studies, University of Edinburgh

Comaroff, J. L. (1974) 'Chiefship in a South African homeland', *Journal of Southern African Studies*, vol 1, no 1, pp36–57

Comaroff, J. L. (1996) 'Ethnicity, nationalism and the politics of difference in an age of revolution', in E. N. Wilmsen and P. McAllister (eds) *The Politics of Difference: Ethnic Premises in a World of Power*, Chicago, University of Chicago Press

Constitution of the Republic of South Africa (1996) www.polity.org.za/html/govdocs/constitution/saconst.html?rebookmark=1

Costa, A. (1997) 'Custom and common sense: The Zulu royal succession dispute of the 1940s', *African Studies*, vol 56, no 1, pp19–42

Cowan, J., Dembour, M.-B. and Wilson, R. A (eds) (2001) 'Introduction', in *Culture and Rights: Anthropological Perspectives*, Cambridge, Cambridge University Press, pp1–26

Dubow, S. (1994) 'Ethnic euphemisms and racial echoes', *Journal of Southern African Studies*, vol 20, no 3, pp355–370

Edgar, R. and Saunders, C. (1982) 'A. A. S. le Fleur and the Griqua Trek of 1917: Segregation, self-help, and ethnic identity', *The International Journal of African Historical Studies*, vol 15, no 2, pp201–220

Elbourne, E. and Ross, R. (1997) 'Combating spiritual and social bondage: Early missions in the Cape Colony', in R. Elphick and R. Davenport (eds) *Christianity in South Africa: A Political, Social and Cultural History*, Cape Town, David Philip

Erasmus, Z. (2001) *Coloured by History, Shaped by Place*, Cape Town, Kwela Books

Eriksen, T. H. (1993) *Ethnicity and Nationalism: Anthropological Perspectives*, London, Pluto Press

Gerstner, J. N. (1997) 'A Christian monopoly: The reformed church and colonial society under Dutch rule', in R. Elphick and R. Davenport (eds) *Christianity in South Africa: A Political, Social and Cultural History*, Cape Town, David Philip

Giliomee, H. (1991) 'Nation-building in a post-apartheid society', in W. S. Vorster (ed) *Building a New Nation: The Quest for a New South Africa*, Pretoria, University of South Africa Press

Gordon, R. and Spiegel, A. (1993) 'Southern Africa revisited', *Annual Review of Anthropology*, vol 22, pp83–105

Grundlingh, A. M. (1991) 'Nation-building and history in South Africa: Probing the pitfalls and prospects', in W. S. Vorster (ed) *Building a New Nation: The Quest for a New South Africa*, Pretoria, University of South Africa Press

Halford, S. J. (1949) *The Griquas of Griqualand: A Historical Narrative of the Griqua People: Their Rise, Progress, and Decline*, Cape Town, Juta & Company

James, D. (1990) 'A question of ethnicity: Ndzundza Ndelebele in a Lebowa village', *Journal of Southern African Studies*, vol 16, no 1, pp33–54

Jung, C. (1999) 'Race matters', *African Studies Review*, vol 42, no 3, pp56–62

Kinsman, M. (1989) 'Populists and patriarchs: The transformation of the captaincy at Griqua Town, 1804–1822', in A. Mabin (ed) *Organisation and Change: South African Studies*, vol 5, Johannesburg, Ravan Press

Le Fleur, C. (2006) 'Khoe and San call for government to speed up policy dialogue with indigenous communities', C. R. Swart Memorial Lecture: University of the Free State, Bloemfontein, www.uovs.ac.za/news/newsarticle.php?NewsID=466

Legassick, M. (1979) 'The northern frontier to 1820: The emergence of the Griqua people', in R. Elphick and H. Giliomee (eds) *The Shaping of South African Society 1652–1820*, Cape Town, Maskew Miller Longman

Lehmann, K. (2004) 'Aboriginal title, indigenous rights and the right to culture', *South African Journal of Human Rights*, vol 20, pp86–117

McEachern, C. (1998) 'Mapping the memories: Politics, place and identity in the district six museum, Cape Town', *Social Identities*, vol 4, no 3, pp499–521

Merry, S. A. (2001) 'Changing rights, changing culture', in J. K. Cowan, M.-B. Dembour and R. A. Wilson (eds) *Culture and Rights: Anthropological Perspectives*, Cambridge, Cambridge University Press

Muller, C. A. (2002) 'Covers, copies, and "colo[u]redness" in postwar Cape Town', *Cultural Analysis*, vol 3, pp19–46

Muller, P. J. (1991) 'Nation-building and political pluralism', in W. S. Vorster (ed) *Building a New Nation: The Quest for a New South Africa*, Pretoria, University of South Africa Press

Nthomang, K. (2000) 'Exploring the "indigenous/autochthonous" minefield: Social policy and the marginalisation of indigenous people in Africa', Paper presented at the Africa's Indigenous Peoples: 'First Peoples' or 'Marginalised Minorities' Annual International Conference, Centre of African Studies, University of Edinburgh, 24–25 May

Nurse, G. T. (1975) 'The origins of the northern Cape Griqua', *Institute for the Study of Man*, Paper no 34, pp2–21

Nurse, G. T., Weiner, J. S. and Jenkins, T. (1985) *The Peoples of Southern Africa and their Affinities*, Oxford, Oxford University Press

Pakendorf, H. (1991) 'Space to build a nation', in W. S. Vorster (ed) *Building a New Nation: The Quest for a New South Africa*, Pretoria, University of South Africa Press

Posel, D. (1991) 'Curbing African urbanization in the 1950s and 1960s', in M. Swilling, R. Humphries and K. Shubane (eds) *Apartheid City in Transition*, Cape Town, Oxford University Press

President's Commission (1983) *Report of the Constitutional Committee of the President's Council on the Needs and Demands of the Griqua*, Cape Town, The Government Printer

Robins, S. (1997) 'Transgressing the borderlands of tradition and modernity: Identity, cultural hybridity and land struggles in Namaqualand (1980–1994)', *Journal of Contemporary South African Studies,* vol 15, no 1, pp23–44

Robins, S. (2000) 'The Khomani San and the politics of land, "community" and "development" in the Kalahari', presented at the Africa's Indigenous Peoples: 'First Peoples' or 'Marginalised Minorities' Annual International Conference, Centre of African Studies, University of Edinburgh, 24–25 May

Ross, R. (1976) *Adam Kok's Griqua*, Cambridge, Cambridge University Press

Saks, D. Y. (1997) 'Remembering Adam Kok: Griqua nationalism in the apartheid era', *Quarterly Bulletin of the South African Library*, vol 53, no 3, pp109–115

Saugestad, S. (2000) 'Contested images: "First peoples" or "marginalized minorities" in Africa?', Royal African Society Scotland Lecture, presented at the Africa's Indigenous Peoples: 'First Peoples' or 'Marginalised Minorities' Annual International Conference, Centre of African Studies, University of Edinburgh, 24–25 May

Scoones, I. and Wolmer, W. (2003) 'Introduction: Livelihoods in crisis: Challenges for rural development in southern Africa', *IDS Bulletin*, vol 34, no 3, pp1–14

Seideman, G. (1999) 'Is South Africa different? Sociological comparisons and theoretical contributions from the land of apartheid', *Annual Review of Sociology*, vol 25, pp419–440

Sharp, J. (1988) 'Two worlds in one country: "First world" and "third world" in South Africa', in J. Sharp and E. Boonzaier (eds) *South African Keywords: The Uses and Abuses of Political Concepts*, Cape Town, David Phillip

Sharp, J. (1996) 'Ethnogenesis and ethnic mobilization: A comparative perspective on a South African dilemma', in E. N. Wilmsen and P. McAllister (eds) *The Politics of Difference: Ethnic Premises in a World of Power*, Chicago, University of Chicago Press

Sharp, J. (1997) 'Beyond exposé analysis: Hybridity, social memory and identity politics', *Journal of Contemporary African Studies*, vol 15, no 1, pp7–21

Sharp, J. and Boonzaier E. (1994) 'Ethnic identity as performance: Lessons from Namaqualand', *Journal of Southern African Studies*, vol 20, no 3, pp405–415

Simpson, M. (1994) 'The experience of nation-building: Some lessons for South Africa', *Journal of Southern African Studies*, vol 20, no 3, pp463–474

Skalnik, P. (1988) 'Tribe as a colonial category', in J. Sharp and E. Boonzaier (eds) *South African Keywords: The Uses and Abuses of Political Concepts*, Cape Town, David Phillip

South African Human Rights Commission (SAHRC) (n.d.) 'Socio-economic rights: Know your rights', Johannesburg, South Africa, www.sahrc.org.za/know_your_rights.pdf, accessed 18 September 2006

South African Human Rights Commission (SAHRC) (2006) Shadow report on South Africa's Compliance with the provisions of the International Convention Against all Forms of Racial Discrimination', June, www.sahrc.org.za/sahrc_cms/downloads/CERD_Shadow%20 Report.pdf

South African Institute of Race Relations, *Race Relations Survey, 1957–1958*, M. Horrell (ed), Johannesburg, SAIRR

Sustainable Livelihoods in Southern Africa Team (2003) 'Livelihood dynamics: Rural Mozambique, South Africa and Zimbabwe', *IDS Bulletin*, vol 34, no 3, pp15–30

Suzman, J. (2000) 'Indigenous wrongs and human rights: National policy, international resolutions and the status of southern Africa's San people', Paper presented at the Africa's Indigenous Peoples: 'First Peoples' or 'Marginalised Minorities' Annual International Conference, Centre of African Studies, University of Edinburgh, 24–25 May

Thornburry, P. (2000) 'Africa's indigenous peoples: "First peoples" or "marginalised minorities"', Paper presented at the Africa's Indigenous Peoples: 'First Peoples' or 'Marginalised Minorities' Annual International Conference, Centre of African Studies, University of Edinburgh, 24–25 May

United Nations Commission on Human Rights (UNCHR) (2005) 'Indigenous issues: Human rights and indigenous issues: Report of the Special Rapporteur on the situation of human rights and fundamental freedoms of indigenous people, Rodolfo Stavenhagen (28 July to 8 August 2005)', 15 December, www.universalhumanrightsindex.org/documents/853/827/document/ fr/text.html#_edn6

Van Vreeden, B. F. (1957) 'Die Wedersydse Beïnvloeding van die Blanke, Bantoe en Kleurlingkultuur in Noord-Kaapland', Unpublished MA thesis, University of the Witwatersrand

Waldman, P. L. (1989) 'Watersnakes and women: A study of ritual and ethnicity in Griquatown', Unpublished BA(Hons) dissertation, University of the Witwatersrand

Webster, D. (1991) 'Abafazi bathonga bafihlakala: Ethnicity and gender in a Kwazulu border community', in A. D. Spiegel and P. McAllister (eds) *Tradition and Transition in Southern Africa*, Johannesburg, Wits University Press

West, M. (1988) 'Confusing categories: Population groups, national states and citizenship', in J. Sharp and E. Boonzaier (eds) *South African Keywords: The Uses and Abuses of Political Concepts*, Cape Town, David Phillip

Afterword: Changing Practice

Rosalind Eyben

This book's origins: The World Development Report on inequality

We all label ourselves and others to signal different aspects of our identities. Labels are a means to construct our social world: they define norms in relation to others who bear similar or different labels. Similarly, labelling is commonplace within the world of international development. Officials, politicians, journalists, activists and researchers, we all use 'frames' and 'labels' to help our analyses and to describe to others what we do. We quantify and measure categories of people to define needs, justify interventions and to formulate and channel solutions to perceived problems. While they may be efficient, such labelling processes are also dynamic and political. Therefore, they can produce unintended, and sometimes unwelcome, consequences. For example, labelling may shift – or sustain – power relations in ways that trigger social dislocation and prejudice efforts to achieve greater equity. Thus the purpose of this book has been to highlight key dimensions of the power of labelling and, importantly, to encourage greater self-awareness and more sensitive and nuanced responses to local political contexts. This is the particular focus of this Afterword.

The idea for this book originated when the editors learnt that the World Bank was planning to make inequality the subject of its World Development Report (WDR) for 2005/06. Like many others, we welcomed this readiness to engage on an issue of fundamental importance which the Bank had for a long time avoided. We wondered whether there was a real opportunity to engage in a dialogue with the report's authors and the wider development research constituency on the links between concepts of inequality and how people are labelled and label themselves.

We asked ourselves:

- Why do labels such as 'the poor' matter so much in development practice?
- Is categorization and labelling integral, or necessary, to the allocation of scarce resources?

- How do externally imposed categories trigger unintended changes in social relations?
- Do policy makers sustain the relations and structures that underpin inequalities when they adopt or work within pre-existing categories?
- How would rethinking the labels we use contribute towards shifting power relations in favour of people living in poverty?

We soon discovered that these questions were of little interest to those who were drafting the report, commissioning background papers and organising worldwide consultations on the subject. Because of the Bank's lack of interest in reflecting on its own power in constructing knowledge of inequality, we were worried that the WDR might actually reinforce the prevailing tendencies of top-down labelling by governments, the media and international development organizations.

The WDR is conceptually informed by an understanding of society in terms of categories of things that can be counted, leading to an understanding of inequality as about measurable differences between categories of individuals as defined by the 'objective' observer. Conceiving inequality in this way suits the conventional bureaucratic development planning approach to poverty reduction. It also handles inequality in terms of abstraction and statistical variable analyses rather than through an engagement with the experience of discrimination and subordination.

While the WDR *did* go so far as to enquire *who* decides what categories to create, it failed to pursue this when deciding 'to let data availability dictate the group definitions' (WDR, p28) – ignoring that what gets collected as data is decided on the basis of prior framing of the problem in terms of what knowledge is required and why. As Cornwall and Fujita comment in relation to an earlier World Bank report – the Voices of the Poor – one of the power effects of what I describe as the categorical approach is to domesticate a diversity of people into a category that holds within it a normative appeal for intervention on their behalf.

Through its authoritative voice and enormous influence on the construction of knowledge in the practice and representation of development, reports such as this WDR assume a hegemonic status, making it difficult or perhaps pointless to challenge. From the evidence of what has and has not been posted on the Web, this appears to have been the case (brought together and summarized on 'Facing North and South'). Twenty-year-old concerns about the power of labelling continue largely to be ignored in the world of policy practice.

Nevertheless, the contributors to this book are largely optimists, prepared to believe that the global political crisis may be a window of opportunity to reveal the power of labelling. Hence, as Moncrieffe discusses in the Introduction, one aim of this book has been to re-invigorate and update the critical thinking on this issue. But a second aim has been to point to some possibilities for changing the practice of government bureaucracies, international development organizations, the media and academic researchers. To this second objective I devote the remainder of this Afterword.

Recognizing and responding to the politics and power of labelling

That the 'what', 'why', and 'how' of labelling is still so rarely examined raises important issues concerning processes of policy and practice and the perspectives of those who influence the theory and knowledge that drive it. What follows are some practical steps that every reader of this book is encouraged to take – and to encourage others to take.

Reflecting on the political impact of the labels we use

My political understanding of social reality sees labels and identities as created through diverse historical processes that are shaped by power relations. Thus because observable disparities between classes of individuals are often signs of these operations of power at work public policy actors will find it difficult to achieve the goals they have set themselves if they seek to do something about measurable observable differences – for example in educational achievement between the two sexes – without addressing the power relationships of which these disparities are symptoms. We need to understand the politics and power of the categorization processes we employ because otherwise our own labelling can unintentionally thwart intended goals and result in undesirable consequences.

People may use labels to gain political capital. De Haan (Chapter 9) discusses how labels of 'caste' and 'tribe' are deeply ingrained in public policy responses in India, and are closely associated with privileged access to resources. These labels have not been static; they evolved during the colonial period and with the build-up of the Indian administration after Independence. Policies of targeting groups using these labels – through programmes of socio-economic development, and affirmative action ('reservation') – have reinforced the way people label themselves and how they are labelled by their community, and have contributed to the reaffirmation of caste identities in the political sphere. This, in turn, has led to further development and refinement of the labels, in particular through extension of programmes to other groups, and the creation of sub-divisions within labels. De Haan observes that while he was working for DFID in India, the country office team unconsciously assumed a certain political stance because of their unquestioning application of labels transmitted to them by the Indian state apparatus.

Similarly, Balchin (Chapter 7) problematizes the British government's labelling of 'Muslim women' and its political effects. The current emphasis on framing religion as a central development issue may help to narrow the spaces for secular alternatives, which is preferred even by many believers. While religion is undoubtedly important for many women and is certainly part of public political discourse in Muslim countries and communities, it may not be the most significant factor determining the parameters of women's everyday existence. Through the use of its single category of 'Moslem women' in a report commissioned by its office, Nigeria DFID ran the risk of reinforcing the perspective that women's place was in the home and that they had no public voice. Balchin also notes the unintended consequences of a USAID initiative in the Philippines that labelled women as 'Muslim': it led to a political engagement with traditional religious leaders that reinforced their power and undermined wider efforts to reduce poverty.

These examples from donor practice could doubtless be replicated many times over. Enquiring how the labels we use might support or undermine the politics of social justice is not an easy task. It means first of all recognizing that labelling is always a political act, a difficult thing to appreciate for those accustomed to thinking of themselves as either objective observers or impartial bureaucrats. Taking this step of understanding themselves as political actors is already an important move towards critical reflection on their discourse and practice and one that may reduce the risk of unsought consequences of the kind that Balchin discusses.

Acknowledging the significance of labelling for resource allocation

The labelling of people by public institutions in Europe and North America has been part of a wider intellectual paradigm, which considers categorization, measurement and quantification integral to rational and objective decision making. The bureaucratic forms of government that developed alongside the scientific revolution used social statistics to provide the evidence necessary for rational choices in the allocation of resources.

These 'official' labels were generally portrayed and accepted as objective facts, though many were rooted in intensely political processes. For example, bureaucracies frequently used racial and other group classifications that were created in the imperial and colonial periods, when authorities counted, categorized, taxed and deployed slave, servile and forced labour, often over vast geographical areas. By adopting these very labels, bureaucracies have – both deliberately and inadvertently – supported social hierarchies. Thus, for some, such as the Brahmins in India or the Tutsi in the Great Lakes region of East Africa, social privilege was reinforced, while for most others, such as those given the blanket colonial label of 'Indian' in the Americas, servile or subordinate status was emphasized. Bureaucratic labelling instigated other political processes as well: in some places, people used labels to gain and manipulate political capital; in others, they contested labels and set about counter-labelling.

How government officials, political parties and aid agencies can respond to the claims of politically marginalized groups without creating perverse outcomes is discussed by de Haan and Moncrieffe in relation to perpetuating discrimination and stigmatization. From another angle, Gupte and Mehta (Chapter 4) note how labels can be used to define people as problem and thus deny them adequate resources to compensate for suffering that was none of their making. Describing those displaced because of dams and other big development projects, the authors consciously opt to use the label 'oustee' rather than the more common 'development-induced displaced person' because 'oustee' is more political, emphasizing the forced removal of people from their homes for an allegedly greater common good.

Thus, once we recognize that labelling and counter-labelling play an important role in resource allocation, readers concerned for greater global equity can make more informed choices as to how their own self-labelling and their labelling of others will help them pursue this aim.

Identifying practical strategies to tackle labels that stigmatize

Development agencies can reproduce labels that stigmatize. Moncrieffe (Chapter 5) argues that many, including some development practitioners, regard Haiti as a beggarly society, afflicted by voodoo and well nigh impossible to transform. These perceptions may partially explain the dictatorial rather than participatory approach to policy making that is evident in some development agencies; the discrimination against Haitians that is prevalent in a number of countries within the region; and the frequent expressions of futility, particularly from members of the Haitian public. Her case study of labelling and child poverty in Haiti emphasizes these points. Children, on the whole, have little priority in the government's agenda and some are labelled in ways that prejudice their life chances. Aid agencies, she argues, must be aware of the 'meanings' of the societal labels they adopt by stimulating changes to the (negative) meanings of labels and promoting the use of constructive symbols. In order to facilitate these, agencies could encourage self-labelling, facilitate community-based dialogue between differently labelled people, encourage educational initiatives and prioritize support to those working with children and young people.

Labels can stigmatize as a means of creating dependency and, as Gupte and Mehta discuss, a certain way of looking at people as helpless and dependent. They quote a Liberian refugee in Ghana: 'Don't give me material assistance. Give me economic opportunity so that I can help myself ...' (p74)

Creating spaces for deliberation and encouraging diversity of ways to frame problems

The media and government agencies are actors that could if so motivated consciously choose to use their power for enabling multiple voices to debate how problems are framed and to support challenges to the labelling of people associated with that framing. This requires acknowledging and responding to the labels that people give themselves, as Waldman discusses with reference to the Griqua of South Africa (Chapter 10). In post-apartheid South Africa academics have had to learn to question the relevance and morality of their practice of rejecting essentialist labelling strategies – a stance developed during the time of apartheid, while the Griqua are themselves demanding that their self-labelling be recognized by the state.

Recognizing the complexity and politics of self-labelling and counter-labelling means encouraging citizens' participation, guided by a deeper understanding of how power influences group dynamics. Such a shift in approach has to be substantive – there is no easy quick fix, as Hobart makes clear in his story of the peasants of Bali staying silent when given space and permission to dialogue with the local administration (Chapter 8). What might look like a participatory process could make it appear that those at the receiving end have the possibility for alternative framing and self-labelling but, as Hobart points out, this degree of conferred agency may not be realizable in practice because of the 'incompatibilities that arise between the demands of the models and attempts to treat people as subjects'. Following this line of thought, the current emphasis in international development arenas of recipient 'country ownership' that I discuss as a positive trend

(Chapter 2), may prove to be unfeasible in any meaningful sense unless and until those shaping the model – OECD politicians, citizens, government officials and the media – recognize and address their own past behaviour: 'After generations of being labelled stupid peasants and being lectured at in Indonesian (a language that, up to the 1980s, many farmers spoke poorly) experience suggested the wisest – indeed only – course was silence.' (p130)

Accepting other people's framing and labelling and thus simultaneously bearing in mind two or more different ways of viewing the world is far from easy. I have never seen a civil servant's submission to a minister with the comment that there are two or even three ways of approaching a problem, all equally valid. People working in bureaucratic organizations are trained to think of there being a correct solution to a problem, based on untheorized 'objective' evidence. To shift to an acceptance of multiple frames means asking questions about who we are and why we understand the world in a certain way because of who we are. However, this is what is required to reduce top-down labelling of 'others' and to engage in a dialogic relationship with people as to how they label themselves.

Moncrieffe identifies some critical questions that might help politicians, researchers and others recognize multiple framings and better contribute to more dialogic relationships. Her questions include asking:

- How do our socially constructed dispositions influence how we frame issues and conceptualize categories of people?
- Do we have deep knowledge of how social relations on the ground contribute to differing poverty experiences?
- How do we as development actors intervene in social contexts, such as Haiti, and with what consequences?
- What is required to improve social conditions so that people can develop the capacity to contest, resist and transform the dispositions that block their own empowerment?

Facilitating policy responses that reflect people's own stories

A number of contributors to this volume emphasize that the labelling of others is a kind of representation (Cornwall and Fujita in Chapter 3), a 'spectator sport' (Klouda in Chapter 6) and when, for example, turned into a report, such as 'Voices of the Poor' or into a film such as 'Black Umbrellas', the labelling makes sections of society seriously traduced. 'It is a theatrical event in the sense that a series of artfully contrived pictures or presentations are provided to a public that demands a certain type of show' (Chapter 6, p5)

In some cases, people's whole life-stories, their multiple identities, are reduced to specific cases/problems. Mehta and Gupte's research on forced migration shows that the almost arbitrary categorization of who constitutes a 'refugee' or an 'oustee' can lead to systematic exclusion of large groups of people who may be in an equally precarious situation.

Ironically, the 'Voices of the Poor' exercise was at the time an innovative and ambitious attempt to bring people's own stories into the policy domain. Yet, argue Cornwall and Fujita, the way the exercise was designed and managed, as well as how the findings were distilled is a travesty of the original intention. When the policy response is already decided, the stories must be adapted to fit it.

Responding to the shifting complexity of identities and resisting the temptation for neat categories and easy quantification

As this book makes clear, labels are not fixed; they change in relation to context and over time. For those using labels in relation to making resource allocation and other policy decisions, recognizing this entails tracking societal dynamics, the challenge that Waldman describes as facing the academics in South Africa. It meant their having to recognize greater ambiguity and diversity than had previously been necessary for them to do under the apartheid regime.

Neat categories are easier to manufacture the more distant one is from the experience of those one is labelling. I have suggested this is a particular problem of international aid agencies, but Klouda sees it as a challenge to the citizens of rich countries who try to act charitably towards 'the poor' in their own country and elsewhere. Hobart takes the argument further and suggests that for political elites everywhere it is important to be distant from where the action is, burying 'the possibilities of ambiguity, of surplus or vacuity of meaning, and of the contingency and unpredictability of much social life which would be a devastating challenge to their self-vision of being in charge' (Chapter 8, p130) Balchin makes the same point in relation to how the UK Government understands what is a 'dynamic Muslim woman': 'Yet demanding rights per se without the headscarf just is not authentically "Muslim" enough' (Chapter 7, p183). Meanwhile, it is hard to insist on ambiguity and shifting identities when senior politicians and bureaucrats insist on clear categories of people with numbers attached to them (Chapter 2).

Two steps to helping reduce the distance between the labellers and those they are labelling would be first to expand time frames for decision making to accommodate people's own efforts to define and explain their situation, identifying for themselves the labels that best suit them as part of a wider political process of building social solidarity. The second would be to make a conscious effort to embrace ambiguity and complexity. This is something that all the book's contributors recognize is difficult, although some are more optimistic than others. One way of making such an effort is to not rely on the reporting of others, often massaged to fit with their own preconceptions, but to develop a habit of finding out for oneself in a reflectively critical frame of mind (Irvine et al, 2006).

Conclusion

Changing our practice *is* possible and this book provides some examples. Balchin notes that British policy towards 'Muslim women' is not 'uniformly blind in substance both to gender and to the range of political ideologies held by Muslim groups', providing examples of good practice. Likewise, Moncrieffe notes that PLAN International in Haiti has begun to reflect on how it uses power in its programming, working to transform the ways in which it perceives children and how children perceive themselves. In my own chapter I identify some other policy processes occurring in today's political and aid environment that those seeking to reduce the power of labelling as 'othering' could seek to support and strengthen. Both de Haan and Waldman describe the historical dynamics of nation-building, with the processes of labelling and counter-labelling sometimes having negative and sometimes positive effects, allowing us the possibility to see how most usefully we could support the positive and reduce the negative.

In his original work on this subject, Wood commented: 'The issue is not *whether* we label, but *which* labels are created, and *whose* labels prevail to define a whole situation or policy area, under what conditions, with what effects' (1985, p349).

Twenty years later the issue stays the same. However, the time may now be ripe to interrogate the power of labelling and to start a public debate on how we categorize and why it matters.

References

Facing North and South – Blogger (2005) 'World Development Report 2005/06', World Bank carbon finance, http://redemo.seodata.com/World-Bank/re-10204_World-Development-Report-2005-06.aspx, accessed 23 October 2006

Irvine, R., Chambers, R. and Eyben, R. (2006) 'Relations with people living in poverty: learning from immersions', in R. Eyben (ed) *Relationships for Aid*, London, Earthscan

Wood, G. (1985) 'The politics of development policy labelling', *Development and Change*, vol 16, no 3, pp347–373

Index